Advance Praise

James Crenshaw is the preeminent interpreter of biblical wisdom in this generation. His work is distinguished by his deep existential concern, especially on the subject of theodicy, which is at the heart of the book of Job. This is a work not only of exegesis, but of biblical theology in the best sense.

—John J. Collins
Holmes Professor of Old Testament
Yale University

Like Matthew Arnold in "Dover Beach," Bertrand Russell in "A Free Man's Worship," and Archibald MacLeish's *J.B.*, James Crenshaw's Job finds solace for his integrity, not in a god who answers to human trust, but in human solidarity in the face of a cruel world. This book about Job is itself a Joban cry.

—J. Gerald Janzen,
Author of At the Scent of Water:
The Ground of Hope in the Book of Job

Excellent commentaries on Job abound; Jim Crenshaw's "reading" of Job adds to the list and raises the bar. If contemporary readers wish to enter fully into Job's world—his irreparable losses, his relentless questions about the moral order of the universe God has created—they can find no better guide for the journey than a commentator whose expertise, artfulness, and eloquence are acutely attuned to the admonitions of Shakespeare's King Lear: "If thou wilt weep my fortunes, take my eyes." Crenshaw has read, felt, and immersed himself in Job's fortunes with eyes and heart chastened by a world overfull with inexplicable suffering that continues to claw at the heavens—Joban-like—for justice.

—*Samuel E. Balentine*
Professor of Old Testament
Union Presbyterian Seminary, Richmond, Virginia

James Crenshaw, one of the foremost scholars of wisdom literature, brings more than forty years of scholarship and teaching to bear on his reading of the book of Job. Respected for not only the breadth of his knowledge but also the passion with which he explores difficult theological questions of human suffering and divine justice, Crenshaw has written a commentary marked by careful exegesis and deep insight into the many perennial issues raised by the book of Job.

—*Carol A. Newsom*
Charles Howard Candler Professor of Old Testament
Candler School of Theology, Emory University

READING JOB

Smyth & Helwys Publishing, Inc.
6316 Peake Road
Macon, Georgia 31210-3960
1-800-747-3016
© 2011 by Smyth & Helwys Publishing
All rights reserved.
Printed in the United States of America.

The paper used in this publication meets the minimum
requirements of American National Standard for Information
Sciences—Permanence of Paper for Printed Library Materials.
ANSI Z39.48–1984   (alk. paper)

Library of Congress Cataloging-in-Publication Data

Crenshaw, James L.

   Reading Job / By James Crenshaw.
   p. cm.
   Includes bibliographical references and index.
   ISBN 978-1-57312-574-1 (pbk. : alk. paper)
   1. Bible. O.T. Job--Commentaries. I. Title.
   BS1415.53.C74 2011
   223'.107—dc22
   2011002331

Reading Job

A Literary and Theological Commentary

James L. Crenshaw

SMYTH&HELWYS

PUBLISHING, INCORPORATED · MACON, GEORGIA

Also by James L. Crenshaw

Prophetic Conflict (de Gruyter, 1971)

Hymnic Affirmation of Divine Justice (SBL, 1975)

Samson (John Knox, 1978)

Gerhard von Rad (Kaiser, 1979)

A Whirlpool of Torment (Fortress, 1984)

Story and Faith (Macmillan, 1986)

Ecclesiastes (Westminster, 1987)

Trembling at the Threshold of a Biblical Text
(Eerdmans, 1994)

Joel (Doubleday, 1995)

Urgent Advice and Probing Questions
(Mercer University, 1995)

Education in Ancient Israel (Doubleday, 1998)

Psalms (Eerdmans, 2001)

Defending God (Oxford University, 2005)

Prophets, Sages & Poets (Chalice, 2006)

Old Testament Wisdom, 3rd ed.
(Westminster/John Knox, 2010)

Dust and Ashes (Cascade, 2010)

Acknowledgments

This book, like the others I have written, owes much to Nita, who for fifty-four years has lived up to the proverbial patience attributed to Job in the Epistle of James.

All quotations from the Bible are my own. The abbreviation ANET refers to James B. Pritchard, ed., *Ancient Near Eastern Texts Relating to the Old Testament*, 3rd ed. (Princeton: Princeton University, 1969).

—*James L. Crenshaw*
December 2010

To Gail Chappell

Contents

Contents   xi

Editor's Foreword

Reading the Old Testament shares many of the aims and objectives of its counterpart series, Reading the New Testament. Contributors to the current series, like those to its predecessor, write with the intention of presenting "cutting-edge research in [a form] accessible" to a wide audience ranging from specialists in the field to educated laypeople. The approach taken here, as there, focuses not on the minutiae of word-by-word, verse-by-verse exegesis, but on larger literary and thought units, especially as they function in the overall conception of the book under analysis. From the standpoint of method, volumes in this series will employ an eclectic variety of reading strategies and critical approaches as contributors deem appropriate for explicating the force of the text before them. Nonetheless, as in RNT, "the focus [will be] on a close reading of the final form of the text." The overarching goal is to provide readers of the commentary series with an aid to help them become more competent, more engaged, and more enthusiastic readers of the Bible as authoritative Scripture.

The title of the series prompts several comments. For the editor, at least, the term "Old Testament" is a convenient convention, since any alternative seems either awkward or provocative. The Hebrew Bible is the shared heritage of Judaism and Christianity, the body of believers whom Paul once described as branches from a wild olive tree who have been "grafted contrary to nature into a cultivated olive tree" (Rom 11:24). Since the beginnings of Christianity, questions concerning how and in what sense the Hebrew Bible/Old Testament functions as Christian Scripture have perpetually confronted the church. Nonetheless, throughout its history, in the spirit of Paul, the church has insisted that the God of Abraham, Isaac, and Jacob is the God of the New Testament. Rather than impose a detailed doctrine of the unity of the two Testaments or specify a particular hermeneutical approach, the editor and the publisher have chosen to invite contributions to the series from scholars selected because of their learning and insight, again in the spirit of Paul we hope, without regard to faith tradition or denominational identity.

The books of the Hebrew Bible were the fountainhead for the faith of both Paul and Aqiba. May it be that through the scholarship presented in the pages of this series, the books of the "Old Testament" water the faith of another generation.

—Mark Biddle, General Editor
Richmond, Virginia
Christmastide 2010

Author's Preface

For nearly forty-five years I have taught classes on the book of Job. Most of the students were preparing for the ministry; the others were Ph.D. students who anticipated a career in teaching. The book continues to fascinate me after all these years. I have read and reviewed most monographs on Job that have appeared in print during my professional career, and each one has opened my eyes to something that had previously escaped my notice. There is no way I can acknowledge my debt to all who have preceded me in trying to understand the brilliant poet's complex images and intricate arguments. I do wish, however, to name the following scholars because of their commentaries and monographs that have always been within reach as I wrote: Samuel E. Balentine, David J. A. Clines, Edwin Good, Carol A. Newsom, Norman C. Habel, John E. Hartley, Ellen van Wolde, Yair Hoffman, Marvin Pope, and Raymond P. Scheindlin. In addition, I trust that the internal notes will suffice to express my appreciation for the many offprints that have been sent to me by friends and colleagues.

When the invitation to write a commentary on the book of Job was extended to me by P. Keith Gammons of Smyth & Helwys, I gladly accepted. First, I agreed because at the time I was translating Job for the *Common English Bible*, which will be published by Abingdon Press. Second, I had written the brief commentary for *The Oxford Commentary on the Bible* edited by John Barton and John Muddiman and prepared the annotations to Job for the *Harper Collins Study Bible*. These ventures planted within me a strong desire to attempt a reading of the biblical book that would enable non-specialists to explore the harrowing debate about the possibility of serving God without thinking about a reward or trying to escape punishment, to pose the issue in the way the provocateur does in the prologue to the book of Job. To state the issue another way, with this book I hope to help readers understand the stakes as God does in the epilogue, that is, how should we speak to or about the transcendent one?

At issue in the book of Job is the existential question, "Why does innocent suffering exist?" I have devoted my life to studying the vexing problem of theodicy—divine justice—that troubles most religious people in the Judeo-Christian tradition. The biblical poet who composed the book of Job exposes the enormity of this problem. Few individuals, I suspect, will come from reading the book unmoved. If they look for answers, they will be disappointed. Moreover, they will find the depiction of God troubling. If God were merely to meet our expectations, the creator would hardly be anything more than our own projections into the heavens. Perhaps the ancient poet serves later readers best by forcing them to face brutal reality, to wit that the world is not fair and that justice is a human project. If God is to be the object of veneration, worship must be an expression of gratitude for life and not the purchase of an insurance policy that will remove all angst.

For me, the angst does not lessen with age, as I explored in a recent poem in my book, *Dust and Ashes: Poems* (Eugene OR: Cascade Books, 2010).

What Job Might Have Asked God

Have you
seen a child's mangled body,
crushed like an ant
under a workman's boot?
Have you
felt the ache of a mother's womb,
emptied for naught?
Have you
surveyed tangled ruins
scattered by twisters
while children slept,
their last words
hollow as a broken promise:
"Now I lay me down to sleep;
I pray thee, Lord, my soul to keep"?
Have you
heard the screams
of drowning victims
when tidal waves rushed
through dikes into streets
once awash with life?
Have you
traced the path of lightning bolt

from golfer's head
to smoking shoes?
Yet
yours, the restless wind;
yours, too, the raging waters
and the thunder bolt.

In the end, I take comfort in the reminder from the divine speeches delivered in a tempest that human beings are not the measure of all things.

Finally, a word about the dedication of this book: For twenty-three years Gail Chappell has typed my handwritten material into a computer, making my life far less burdened than would have been the case without her excellent assistance. She has done all this work with a wonderful sense of humor and has always been a true friend. Truly, she has earned a place in my heart and on the dedication page of this book.

Part 1: Introduction

The Patience of Job

In western culture, who has not heard of the patience of Job? That is the virtue for which the author of the Epistle of James remembers him (5:11). Patience is not, however, what the oldest reference to Job outside the book that bears his name associates with this venerable character. That text, Ezekiel 14:14 and 20, links Job with two other notables, Noah and Danel, and highlights their exceptional righteousness (*ṣĕdaqah*). The larger context states that if God were to send four calamities (famine, wild beasts, sword, or pestilence) against sinful Israel, these three men would be able to save only themselves by their righteousness.

Who were these three men? The first, Noah, is best remembered as the survivor of the flood in the Bible, for which a Mesopotamian account served as inspiration. In the earlier version, the hero was named Utnapishtim (ANET, 72–99) or Atrahasis (ANET, 104–106). The second person, Danel, is the legendary king in a Ugaritic text whose son Aqhat was slain in a jealous rage by the warrior goddess Anath (ANET, 149–55). The spelling of the name Danel distinguishes him from the Daniel of late Hellenistic times whose exploits have been recorded in a canonical book bearing his name. The third person, Job, must have been renowned for righteousness, like the other two (see Spiegel). (The references within parentheses in this book are intended to alert readers to additional readings on the topic at hand. The readings do not necessarily confirm my own interpretation. Many of them offer alternative ways of viewing the text.)

Several things stand out in Ezekiel's use of these worthies to drive home a theological point. First, the intensification of a formula catches one's eye. (Renewed interest in literary features of the biblical text began to surface in the late seventies of the twentieth century with the publication of monographs on Samson by Crenshaw 1978, on God and the rhetoric of sexuality by Trible, and on David by Gunn. Alter 1981 ranges more widely than these three). The initial hypothetical instance, famine, is only reinforced by an oracular phrase, "utterance of Adonai Yahweh." In the following three instances—threats by wild beasts, sword, and pestilence—the oracular formula is preceded by a divine oath, "as I live." (Divine oaths, common in the ancient Near East where polytheism reigned, seem entirely out of place in Yahweh's mouth. Why would a deity who was thought to be trustworthy need to reinforce a remark by swearing on his life?) Second, the threat of famine concludes with the observation that Noah, Danel, and Job would only save themselves. The other three threats end with a specific reference to sons and daughters as being beyond their fathers' help. Even here, a variation occurs; the first two references to sons and daughters are plural, while the last one is singular.

The prophet Ezekiel has called on popular memory of three men whose goodness was believed to have saved the lives of others. Because of Noah's righteousness, so the story goes, his wife, sons, and daughters-in-law survived the flood. The ultimate destiny of Aqhat is not known because of the fragmentary nature of the text, but the story may have had a happy ending with the son's restoration to life because of the father's exemplary goodness. The mention of Job is even more problematic, but Ezekiel may have known a version in which Job's righteousness saved his sons and daughters. Apparently, an oral account of Job's trials that did not include his complaints, that is, the poetic dialogue (chs. 3–31), was known by an early Christian bishop, Theodore of Mopsuestia. Bruce Zuckerman (14) has even argued that the author of the Epistle of James had this oral version in mind, for he wrote, "You have *heard* of the patience of Job" rather than "You have *read* of the patience of Job." The argument presumes widespread literacy in New Testament times, which is highly unlikely (see the discussion of literacy by Crenshaw 1998 and Carr).

Ezekiel's rugged individualism was intended to combat a collective solidarity underlying a popular proverb, "The parents have eaten unripe grapes and the children's teeth are sensitive" (for the wide use of proverbial sayings in the ancient Near East, see Crenshaw, "A Proverb"). In Ezekiel's view, the fate of an individual and perhaps by extension an exiled nation was not determined by past actions of others but rested in one's own hands. In short, transferred virtue cannot alter one's destiny, even from such men as Noah, Danel, and Job, and skilled intercessors are completely helpless. Righteousness, not patience, is the virtue for which Job was famous, according to Ezekiel.

In this prophetic text, Job finds himself in company with a pre-Israelite and a Canaanite of primordial times. We may suppose, then, that in the early sixth century BCE someone who went by the name Job was popularly known for his righteousness. Beyond that, we cannot say. Conceivably, he was also remembered for his extraordinary patience, but Ezekiel omitted this quality because it did not support his particular argument. His name, Job, may offer a hint of patience in adversity, for it means something like "inveterate foe" and vaguely plays on the Hebrew word for an enemy. The name *'Ayyab* occurs in Amarna Letter 256 from c. 1350, and even earlier Akkadian documents from Mari and Alalakh attest the name *Ayyab-um* (Pope, 5–6).

The existential problems with which Job's name is associated—the suffering of the innocent, the problem of evil, the threat of chaos to cosmic order, the possibility of disinterested righteousness, and the nature of God—surfaced during the second millennium in Egypt and in Mesopotamia (above all, see Laato and de Moor; for a brief discussion of the problem, consult Crenshaw 2009a).

Texts of this nature are either the result of troubled times or a mode of intellectual debate, (in various publications [1973, 1976, 1980, 1992, 1992], Miriam Lichtheim has insisted that Egyptian texts that decry social turmoil are a form of intellectual debate and cannot be used to glean historical data indicating a societal collapse). Such discussions of these basic issues found their way into literature and influenced religious thought for centuries, if not millennia. All of them come down to a single issue: the character of God (Miles 1995 treats, among other things, the troubling description of Yahweh in the Bible; see also Seibert and Crenshaw 2005b). In short, has the creator lost control of things, leaving the world in danger of returning to its original chaotic state, and if so, can one continue to worship this deity from whom no reward is forthcoming? Philosophers and theologians recognize this problem as theodicy; the word, coined by Leibniz in 1710, is a combination of two Greek words, *theos* and *dike* (God and justice).

Related Texts in the Ancient Near East

The Egyptian exploration of this problem is best seen in "The Protests of an Eloquent Peasant" (ANET, 407–10). It tells about an abuse of power by a landowner that resulted in the imprisonment of a peasant whose eloquence was used to entertain a chief steward but who was eventually freed and compensated for his troubles. While suffering the deprivations of life in prison, this gifted speaker gave voice to injustice, societal chaos, the problem of evil, and dereliction of duty by rulers. The structure of this work, a prose prologue and epilogue that frames semi-poetic appeals for justice, in this case nine, is widely attested in the ancient world. Appropriately, that is the form the book of Job takes.

Dereliction of duty by the pharaoh as god finds expression in "The Admonition of Ipuwer" (ANET, 441–44). In it, the author refutes popular belief that the gods were good, even if tending small herds. He posits a pilot-less society, one in which the god has fallen asleep while confusion and murder run amok. Authority, perception, and justice, he grants, belong to the god, but these qualities are not established below, resulting in a chaotic society. A third text, "The Dialogue of a Man with his Soul" (ANET, 405–407), best demonstrates this condition. Here, too, a prose frame encloses poetry, with the man trying to persuade his soul to accompany him in suicide. This weary individual describes death in positive terms like recovery from illness, the aroma of myrrh or lotus blossoms, the cessation of rain accompanied by the return of clear skies, and the longing to see home after years in captivity. Refrains reiterate the reasons for desiring death: the loss of honor ("Behold, my name will reek . . .") and rampant evil ("To whom can I speak today . . . ?").

From Ugarit, a mythic text about a certain Keret, or Karitu, tells about the deaths of his wife and seven sons but has the god El communicate with him in a dream that shows him how to obtain a new wife and replace the dead sons with new ones (ANET, 142–49). Keret travels to a distant land and gains the Lady Hurriya as foretold in the dream. The story goes on to tell of an illness that struck Keret and of the successful intervention of Sha'taqat that brought healing and the return to his former state.

The intelligentsia in ancient Mesopotamia struggled with the same theological issues as those in Egypt and left a legacy that closely resembles the book of Job. That text, "The Babylonian Theodicy," consists of twenty-seven stanzas of eleven lines each and takes the form of an acrostic or alphabetic work (ANET, 601–604). A sufferer begins and ends the dialogue between him and a friend who responds courteously even when challenging what he has heard. Although the text is broken at some points, the argument can be summarized as follows.

Stanza 1: the sufferer complains about the death of his parents.
Stanza 2: the friend quotes a popular saying that we all die.
Stanza 3: the sufferer reports that his life has been turned upside down and wishes he could assure happiness.
Stanza 4: (fragmentary, but the friend urges the sufferer to seek justice, confident the gods will respond favorably.)

Stanza 5: the sufferer gives two examples from the animal world (wild onager and lion and a wealthy human; then he asks, "Did they give gold to the gods?" He contrasts his own scrupulous piety with their lack of it).

Stanza 6: the friend describes the plan of the gods as remote but points out that the two animals, onager and lion, will suffer a cruel end, as will the rich man.

Stanza 7: the sufferer observes that religion does not pay whereas the impious prosper.

Stanza 8: the friend warns against blasphemy and perverse thoughts.

Stanza 13: (9–12 are badly damaged; the sufferer vows to act as a rebel against the gods.)

Stanza 17 (15–16 are fragmentary; the sufferer complains that societal roles are reversed; princes wear rags, while nobodies are richly clothed.)

Stanza 20 (18-19 are damaged; the friend accuses the sufferer of being irrational.)

Stanza 22: (21 is damaged; the friend says that one who bears his god's yoke never lacks food, though it may be sparse.)

Stanza 23: the sufferer complains that the gods let evil flourish and have not rewarded him for loyal worship.

Stanza 24: the friend describes the divine mind as remote.

Stanza 25: the sufferer laments a brutal fact that people exalt murderers and bring down the innocent.

Stanza 26: the friend states that the gods who created humankind endowed them with lies.

Stanza 27: the sufferer characterizes himself as humble, wise, and pious but abandoned by the gods, who he dares to hope will show mercy, pasturing their flocks as a god should.

It should be noted that this text differs from the book of Job in several ways despite the remarkable similarities: (1) it has only one friend while Job has three, plus Elihu; (2) it lacks a prose framework; (3) it has no divine speeches; (4) the friend is both courteous and firm, whereas Eliphaz, Bildad, and Zophar, as well as Elihu, disparage Job, sometimes mercilessly; and (5) it is an alphabetic poem and the book of Job is not. (Alphabetic poems may have been written as a way of indicating complete coverage, like our "from A to Z." Several psalms (e.g., 9–10, 25, 34, 37, 111–112, 119, and 145 and Lam 1–4 attest this practice in ancient Israel.)

At least two additional texts from Mesopotamia resemble Job to some extent. The Sumerian "Man and His God" tells about a sufferer whose life has been turned upside down like Job's and quotes the sages' answer as true:

"Never has a sinless child been born to its mother; a sinless workman has not existed from of old" (ANET, 589–91). In short, humans cannot be innocent, even if the fault points beyond them to the gods. The other text, "I Will Praise the Lord of Wisdom," often called "Ludlul" from its first word, is more properly compared with the psalms of lament than with the book of Job, although a strong argument has been made for classifying the biblical book as a paradigm of an answered lament (ANET, 596–600). In "Ludlul," the sufferer laments his loss of status and health, complains that it is impossible to know the will of the gods, experiences three dream visions that announce a turning, and is restored as a result of correct ritual. Praise of the Babylonian high god Marduk, the text teaches, is the proper response to suffering.

One additional text is sometimes compared to Job, but with less justification than the other two. "The Dialogue of Pessimism" is a conversation between a master and his slave in which the former proposes to engage in various activities and is urged to do so, but when the master changes his mind the slave praises that particular activity with equal enthusiasm (ANET, 600–604). In the end, the master mentions suicide and the slave describes its good points, whereupon the master says he has decided to kill the slave. He in turn responds that the master would not last three days without him. Whether humorous or deadly serious, this text depicts a certain tiredness of life, ennui that finds its fullest expression in Ecclesiastes. In contrast, Job's exhaustion stems from a conflict between reality and religious belief, not from a jaded existence (Weinfeld).

Genre

If nothing else, this list of literary compositions that have something in common with the book of Job suggests that a single genre does not do justice to the biblical work (see Good, Habel, Hartley, Newsom 1996 and 2003, Balentine 2006, and Crenshaw 1992 and 2001). For this reason, it is often said that the book of Job is *sui generis*, unique unto itself. That may be true, but the same can be said of every literary work, unless it is an exact copy of another composition.

What, then, best describes the book? The first thing that comes to mind is its disjointed nature; at the very least, the book of Job is at odds with itself. It consists of prose and poetry that have not been fully integrated. The two forms of discourse point in opposite directions. The prologue and epilogue, in epic prose (Sarna), comprise a folktale about a good man who lived in days of yore far off in a fantasy land and was tested twice (we expect three tests in such stories) but successfully withstood the test and was richly rewarded. A missing middle must have told how his friends advised Job to curse God. (For an astute analysis of the prologue, see Weiss.)

That story frames a philosophical debate in poetry between Job and three friends about the fundamental character of God. Does God permit suffering by innocent people, or has a web of causality been spun over the universe that rewards goodness and punishes wickedness (this apt phrase comes from the stimulating interpretation of the book of Job by van Wolde 1997)? Job begins the debate and responds to each friend in turn. The debate consists of three cycles, the last of which is broken off (Bildad's speech is brief and Zophar's is missing altogether). At this point, an elegant poem about wisdom's hiddenness to all but Yahweh interrupts the flow of the debate (on Job 28, see especially Geller, the collection of articles edited by van Wolde 2003a, and Lo). It is followed by Job's monologue about the difference his suffering has made in his daily existence. Almost abruptly, Job swears an oath of innocence and challenges God to meet him in a court of law.

Then, from out of the blue, a new debater appears and offers his answer to Job and his three friends, quoting them loosely and claiming full knowledge. No one responds to him, so he rambles on incessantly, concluding with praise of the deity who wraps himself in a storm. When this intruder finally shuts up, Yahweh does appear in a tempest. After giving a lecture on cosmology and meteorology, he turns to discuss the animal kingdom living beyond human observation, and then lavishly praises two semi-mythical creatures, the one bovine and peaceful, the other a violent sea serpent. Both Yahweh and Job speak twice, but Job's responses combine brevity and enigma (Kubina, Ritter-Müller, and Brenner).

The book of Job is more than a combination of a folktale in epic form and a philosophical debate, sometimes called a dialogue. It has a number of sub-genres, the most notable being lament (Westermann). Similarities between Job's complaints and other laments in the Bible and elsewhere can scarcely be missed, but one feature of virtually all biblical laments outside the book of Job is lacking—the confession of confidence that turns laments into expressions of hope. (For example, Psalm 13 begins with the question, "How long? Will you forget me forever? How long will you hide from me?" but ends with confidence that Yahweh has bestowed kindness on the supplicant. Scholars have explained the sudden shift in psalms of lament from questioning Yahweh's concern to assurance in his help as the result of a favorable priestly oracle.) A second genre that occurs several times in the book of Job is the hymn. Participles with God as subject laud the deity as creator and mighty ruler (see Wahl). A third genre, theophany, allows readers to grasp the perspective of the deity. A fourth genre, lawsuit (*rib*), lies behind much of what Job says and prompts him to issue an ultimatum to God in the form of an oath of innocence. A fifth, meditation on wisdom's inaccessibility, ironically enunciates the basic theme of sages that the fear of God is the beginning and first principle of wisdom, and this wisdom is available to those who worship Yahweh. Finally, some features of prophetic literature are detectable, beyond the affinities between laments by Job and Jeremiah, above all language akin to that of Deutero-Isaiah (Isa 40–55; see Bastiaens and Terrien 1966).

Composition

How did a book with such diverse components come into being? We can only speculate, but the following compositional history seems probable. A gifted poet used a well-known story about the trials of a good man (perhaps transforming it into "epic prose") to frame a poetic critique of its underlying premises about a principle of reward and retribution, one that is already compromised by the deaths of the hero's ten children and an unknown number of servants. The sophisticated critique consisted of a debate between Job and three learned friends, which comprises three cycles, the third incomplete, followed by a monologue by Job and two divine speeches with an equal number of brief responses by Job.

Either the author of the speeches, or someone else, added a poem about the inaccessibility of wisdom and placed it immediately before Job's long monologue. This poem, written in a different style and language, served as an interlude for reflecting on the progress of the debate to this point. Sometime later, perhaps in the Hellenistic era, a different author composed four speeches and put them in the mouth of an angry youth with an Israelite name, Elihu. Finally, a copyist who considered the last speech of Job theologically unacceptable removed it and attributed some of Bildad's remarks to him (Newsom 1996, 320–25, has conveniently summarized this view of composition, which closely corresponds to my own). Alternatively, the last speeches of Job, Bildad, and Zophar were accidentally disturbed and parts were lost. The hypothesis that Zophar's missing speech indicates defeat is less persuasive, given the inappropriateness of words placed in Job's mouth at the end of the debate with the three friends.

Date and Social Worlds

When did this literary activity take place? We do not know, partly because wisdom literature prior to Ben Sira in the early second century BCE completely avoids anything specific to Israel (Crenshaw 2009b). The language of the folktale may be intentionally archaic, and the earliest date for the poetry is, according to the most thorough investigation thus far, the sixth century (Hurwitz). If that assessment is correct, the most likely date of composition is between the sixth and fifth centuries BCE with Elihu's speeches being as late as the third century. They can hardly be later than this, for the earliest witness to the book, the Aramaic Targum discovered at Qumran, includes the speeches of Elihu.

A sixth/fifth century date of composition accommodates the meager data other than language: a possible allusion to the Behistun rock on which the Persian king Darius's exploits were inscribed with lead inlay (Job 19:23-24), the mention of caravans from Teman (Job 6:19), and the influence of Persian concepts (the watchful eyes of the emperor, and the development of the figure of the *śaṭan*, still an office in the book of Job but on the way to becoming a proper name in Chronicles; see Day. In the prose tale of Job, the article is used with *śaṭan*, as in Zech 3:1, but 1 Chr 21:1 lacks the article. By the time of the Chronicler, the word had become a proper name).

Such data contrast with the fictional world of the book. In it, Job is a pastoralist like the patriarch Abraham, a fiction created by linguistic associations, especially the preferred names for the deity, El Shaddai and Eloah; the name for a monetary unit, *qesiṭah*; and Job's possessions, herds and servants rather than silver and gold. The real world of the author is quite different from this fiction. In it, Job is an agriculturalist who lives in a house, as do his children, rather than in a tent, raises wheat and barley, participates in judicial decisions at the gate of a village, and endorses moral values such as the necessity of returning clothing used as collateral before nighttime and caring for widows and orphans, values shared by Israel and her neighbors (see Coogan 2009).

Structure

What is the structure of the book? The answer to this question depends on how one interprets the relationship between the prose and poetry. At least three different ways of reading the book have arisen as a response to this problem: (1) on the basis of diction; (2) on the basis of dramatic movement;

and (3) on the basis of individual components (see James L. Crenshaw, "Job, Book of," for further elaboration of this view).

On the Basis of Diction

The most notable feature of the book of Job, its use of a story to frame a poetic center, is baffling to many readers. Modern authors choose the medium that best suits their purposes, either prose or poetry. They do not move back and forth between the two. Even when poets write a brief introduction to a book of poetry, they do not intersperse prose sections with the poems, nor do they revert to story form to bring the book to a close. (In my latest book, *Dust and Ashes* [Eugene OR: Cascade Books, 2010], I introduce the book of poems by writing prose.)

As we have seen, the use of a story to frame a poetic center is not unique to the book of Job. Ancient Near Eastern parallels use this framing device to enclose conventional proverbs and philosophical discussion of existential questions. The principle can be illustrated by the practice of framing a painting, which, if done right, highlights individual features and focuses viewers' eyes on the art itself. Ancient teachers like Ahiqar (Lindenberger and Kottsieper) and Anksheshonqy (Lichtheim, 159–84) use stories that make the enframed poetic sayings more persuasive, and the author of "The Tale of the Eloquent Peasant" puts the device to effective use when struggling to understand the lack of social justice at the time. Without the stories, readers would have no insight into the adversities that contributed to the teachings condensed in the proverbs and intellectual debate. They would also know nothing about each author's character and educational development.

We should note that ancient Israelites knew how to tell a moralizing story without resorting to poetry. Two examples suffice. When the prophet Nathan rebuked David for his adulterous affair with Bathsheba and the murder of Uriah, her husband, he chose a story about a pet lamb to convict the powerful king (2 Sam 12:1-7). In light of the tradition about David as a shepherd, one can hardly imagine a more damning indictment than the simple statement, "You're the man!" Consider another story. When two prostitutes claimed to be the birth mother of the surviving infant after one was smothered accidentally during the night, Solomon listens while each tries to persuade him to rule in her favor. By a clever ploy, threatening to cut the child in half and give each one an equal share, Solomon learns which woman has a mother's heart (1 Kgs 3:16-27; this story appears to have been nearly universal, with the wise hero varying from country to country).

An author could have combined prose and poetry in a way that improved on either one of them by itself, but that does not happen in the book of Job. The poetry interrupts the story and suspends Job's destiny in midair for an interminably long time. Only after the poetry has achieved closure of a sort does the story resume with the anticipated happy ending (Ngwa). In a sense, this resumption of prose marks a return to reality, at least to a world that the average person understands. That is, it returns to a realm where the motto, "I give so that I may receive," flourishes. In short, the story's plot has run its course; Job endured the test successfully, and God rewarded him as expected.

The narrator of the story intrudes twice to pass independent judgment on the hero (1:22 and 2:10) but fades into the background so that other voices can be heard in the poetry. His withdrawal gives place to the hero's threatened ego fighting for survival against overwhelming odds, the confident assurances of Eliphaz and his two companions, the brash rebuttal of all four by an angry Elihu, and interrogation from Yahweh in a tempest. By this means, the author creates a story within a story, but not without frequent prosaic interruptions that provide transition between speakers and introduce each one. These comments range from simple formulas such as "Then Eliphaz the Temanite replied" (4:1) to six verses (32:1-6), from three words in Hebrew (23:1) to fifty-nine (2:11-13). Even when the speaker remains the same, the narrator sometimes interrupts, as in 27:1 and in 34:1 (cf. 36:1; 29:1 is different because a poem on wisdom's inaccessibility breaks the rhythm of Job's complaint).

The book is a bundle of colliding views; the framing story depicts a world in which retributive thinking is taken for granted, at least in the case of its hero, but this concept is refuted by Job and Yahweh in the poetic center while defended by the other four friends of Job. The force of anti-wisdom within the poetry is muted by the heavy hand of the narrator in the epilogue. Prologue elicits dialogue, and the epilogue terminates it. The śaṭan, or adversary, the catalyst of the prologue, mysteriously vanishes when the epilogue ties up all loose ends of the folktale.

On the Basis of Dramatic Movement

Introductions at 1:1-5, 2:11-13, and 32:1-5 suggest another way of dividing the book. The first of these introduces Job and gives essential insights into his character, which will soon be assailed mightily. The second introduction identifies Job's three friends and sets up expectations about their role as comforters, expectations that will be quickly dashed in the debate. The remaining introduction describes Elihu's boldness in venturing to address his elders without being invited to do so and justifies his anger over the blasphemous remarks of Job and the friends' inability to offer a cogent refutation.

On this reading, the book is a drama comprising three acts: (1) God afflicts Job; (2) Job challenges God; and (3) God challenges Job (Habel, 25–35 and 70–73). In different words, the drama consists of a hidden conflict, the exploration of this conflict, and its resolution. Such an understanding of the book depends on narration by means of dialogue, with prose being its fundamental category. Thus understood, the dialogues retard the movement of plot and heighten emotional pitch.

Nevertheless, this attractive approach requires the reader to ignore several things that do not easily accord with such an interpretation. One can argue that the brevity of the first part is balanced by the short confessions in the third part, while the middle section has a lengthy outpouring of resentment, but indications of closure within a single section should raise a red flag. For example, the narrator's commendation of Job's conduct in 1:22 and 2:10 marks two closures, and Yahweh's first speech evokes Job's final words, or so he says (40:45), only to give way to a second divine speech and another response from Job (42:2-6). The second section alone ends appropriately ("The words of Job are ended," 31:40). It seems that each indecision necessitates further brief introductions of speakers, but these comments by the narrator play no role in the suggested structuring of the book.

Above all, the speeches by Elihu prolong the conflict between Job and God and, except for summarizing the arguments he has heard, add nothing substantial to plot development. The epilogue alone describes the resolution of the conflict that first comes to expression in the poetic debate among friends and intensifies with each cycle, then reaches a peak with Yahweh's two speeches from the whirlwind.

On the Basis of Individual Components
A third way of structuring the book derives its clues from the distinctive components in it. They are (1) a story about Job's affliction; (2) a debate between him and three friends; (3) the speeches of Elihu; (4) divine speeches punctuated by Job's submission; and (5) a story about Job's restoration. Even here, inconsistencies abound. The second division breaks off abruptly without completing the third cycle of debate, with Job unexplainably uttering views held by the friends he has vigorously opposed. Moreover, Job then falls into a nostalgic monologue of self-pity before issuing a direct challenge to God, the enemy.

On this reading, the development of plot is both psychological and spiritual, with movement being measured in emotional heights and depths as well as in imagination. The latter can be seen in Job's fantasy about possible help from someone who will intervene between him and God. He imagines three possible helpers: an advocate, a mediator, and a *go'el* (one who will ransom him from bondage). In the end, however, he abandons all hope from them. Throughout the book, opposing forces fail to cancel one another; the poetic debate retards the development of plot but emotional changes take place anyway. Hence movement toward an unnamed goal occurs, despite the appearance of mounting irreconcilable differences between Job and God, who has become an enemy in Job's eyes. In one respect, however, entrench-ment sets in. The intellectual positions represented by the several characters harden the longer they speak, and no real change of view seems to have occurred. Whether or not Job actually acquiesces in the end remains a hotly contested point (contrast the opinions of Good and Habel, 575–83).

This last way of dividing the book has no convenient explanation for the poem about wisdom's inaccessibility. That is why it may be wise to adopt the simple explanation of the book as a triptych consisting of prologue, dialogue, and theologue (van Wolde 1997a, 88–89). The hinges connecting the three panels, on this reading, are Job's two monologues, chapters 3 and 28–31. The advantage of this approach, that it finds a place for chapter 28, is never-theless negated by the inability to explain the speeches by Elihu. One could, however, extend the debate to include the poem about wisdom and Job's monologue in 29–31, making Elihu's speeches function as the second hinge. The structure would then consist of (1) prologue, chapters 1–2, with chapter 3 serving as the first hinge; (2) dialogue, chapters 4–31, with chapters 32–37 as the second hinge; and (3) theologue, chapters 38–41:26. The weakness of this hypothesis is that it fails to account for Job's brief responses in 40:4-5 and 42:2-6 and the epilogue.

Main Themes

Clearly, the structure of the book can be viewed in several different ways. Is that also true of its main arguments? Exactly what did the author, or authors, hope to accomplish? The answer depends on who is believed to represent the author's view: a single speaker or the combined voices of them all, a rich polyphony created by clashing viewpoints, each one defended with eloquence and passion (Newsom 2002 and 2003; Good has brilliantly traced the rhetoric of each speaker, while Hoffman highlights irony within the book of Job).

The *śaṭan*, or adversary, of the prologue identifies the issue under dispute as the motive for piety (1:9-11). Stated simply, can religion exist without any expectation of benefiting from its rituals and ethical practices? Is the world governed by the principle of *do ut des*, "I give so you can give back"? The adversary asked the perennial question of the powerful: do I have true friends or merely bargain hunters who are looking out for their own interests? Even the mighty must ask whether mutual back scratching makes them guilty of using others. This necessity for self-examination applies to God, who has something to gain from Job's piety, if nothing else confirmation of his positive view of Job. The adversary thus exposes the uncertainty deep within God, almost as an alter ego (Weiss and Jung).

Spontaneous and unmotivated love is precisely what the adversary has not been able to locate while wandering about from place to place, and that lack of success has made him skeptical. When Yahweh calls his attention to the devout Job, a test is born. Will Job worship God in all circumstances, or will he buckle under adversity and curse God? According to the epilogue, Job passed the test with flying colors, since Yahweh approved of what he said under duress.

An adverb, *hinnam*, and a verb, *barak*, focus the issue as defined by the provocateur, who genuinely seeks to promote divine interests. The first word, "without cause," strikes at the heart of ancient thinking that will dominate the speeches of the debate prior to Yahweh's appearance. Causality, the correspondence between deed and consequence so cherished by Job and his friends, was crushed when Yahweh broadened the human vision (Tsevat nicely sums up this understanding of the book, to wit that Yahweh completely demolishes the human illusion that the world is just). The second word, the open-ended "bless/curse," is like a door with two panels, each leading in different directions. Job is presented with a choice, and his decision must be made "without cause," *hinnam*.

We expect the epilogue to confirm Yahweh's belief that Job will pass the test, thus showing that Yahweh had not been duped by acquisitive piety. Instead, it redefines the issue, stating what is under dispute from Yahweh's perspective. The three friends are rebuked because they did not speak about God reliably (*nekonah*) as Job did (on the meaning of *nekonah*, see Pyeon). Nothing is said in the epilogue about a test, and the adversary is not even mentioned. In Yahweh's eyes, the disputed issue is how to talk about God, and Job's exemplary remarks in the prologue have pleased Yahweh. What about Job's altogether different words about God in the poetry? The present form of the book requires that those blasphemous outcries be included in Yahweh's approbation of his servant Job, unless Job's obscure response in 42:2-6 qualifies as *nekonah*. If so, why does Yahweh say nothing about Job's extreme views prior to this?

So much for the central themes as stated in the folktale. What are the fundamental problems being addressed in the poetry? They appear to be these: (1) disproportionate suffering and (2) the nature of God. Both problems grow out of the story, for it describes a good man whose suffering is out of proportion for one who has lived an exemplary life, and it depicts a deity who allows an agent to provoke him into subjecting Job to a diabolical test that has considerable collateral damage (I have studied the role of divine testing and its undesirable consequences in Crenshaw 1984 and 2005b).

The problem of disproportionate suffering usually goes under the topic of "innocent suffering," and the nature of God is basically a question about the relationship between heaven and earth. At issue in the first is divine justice. The second concerns how God relates to human beings, if at all. (For a discussion of revelation in Israelite wisdom, see Crenshaw 2010, 207–28, and van de Toorn.) Each participant in the debate has much to say about these two disputed matters, and no consensus is reached. In the end, the participants in the debate are just as divided as before, with the possible exception of Job and Yahweh, who may have reconciled.

Should the two issues be related at all? The story brings them together as an integral problem. Job's suffering for no discernible reason except divine caprice casts doubt on the possibility of a genuine relationship with God, for what sane individual would worship a cruel deity? The poetry brings the two ideas together in quite a different way. Although Job and his friends presuppose a world under the sway of a retributive system, even if in Job's mind momentarily suspended, Yahweh describes a universe in which no such principle exists. Justice, that is, applies only to society, and the rules of human logic stop at heaven's gate. Furthermore, the creator is said to have fashioned a world in which everything can be itself, both predator and prey, and human beings are no more special than other creatures inhabiting the earth. Even though Yahweh deigned to speak to Job, it was by no stretch of the imagination comforting. In the end, mystery abounds, as does fear in the presence of transcendence. Ours is a universe with a delicate balance between chaos and order, like life itself, and Yahweh makes it all possible. That is the essence of the divine speeches, which completely ignore the perplexing issues that were so troubling to Job and his friends. Yahweh does not even mention disproportionate suffering and the bond between mortals and deity.

Such silence about the disputed issues contrasts with Job's frequent accusations that God has become his enemy and thereby encourages injustice. In short, a rupture in the relationship between him and God has taken place and the cause of that breach is God. Job's miserable condition bears witness to God's failure and can only be set right, Job comes to believe, in a court of justice. (An eminent lawyer, Robert Sutherland, has approached the book of Job from this perspective, as have a survivor of the Holocaust and any number of biblical scholars; see Sutherland, Wiesel, Scholnick, and Habel. The difficulty of this rhetorical strategy is the lack of anyone to enforce punishment for a sentence of guilty, given divine power.)

Job's friends see the problem quite differently from him; they think Job adds rebellion to transgression and needs to repent. The primary issue for them is admission of wrongdoing and humble submission to God. Suffering, in their eyes, is divine pedagogy. Through diversity, an individual learns humility. Unlike his friends, Job believes he will be vindicated by meeting God face to face, not by repenting ("This also will be my vindication: that a lawless person cannot come into his presence," 13:16).

Warrants for the Arguments

Other than logic, what warrants for their arguments did the debaters call upon (Crenshaw 2010, 110–12, and 1998b)? The friends argued from universally accepted beliefs about the brief duration of a wicked person's prosperity. In addition to consensus, they appealed to personal experience and to careful inquiry ("See, we have searched this out; it is true; hear, and know it for yourself," 5:27). Tradition also played a huge role in their argument, but a surprising move is taken by Eliphaz, who cites revelation as the authority for his teaching (4:12-17), a point also made by Elihu and to some degree Zophar. Seniority, the wisdom of a long life, was an important factor to Bildad and Eliphaz (15:10) but rejected by Job and Elihu.

For his part, Job appealed to universally acknowledged truth when applying insights gathered from the animal kingdom to human behavior, and he boldly relied on what he knew to be true. He freely borrowed the language of sages about personal validation of information ("I have seen, heard, and understood"). He, too, relied on analogy between animals and humans, while an international interest led him to reinforce certain points by appealing to information gleaned from travel to distant lands, what moderns refer to as exposure to different cultures.

Elihu's primary warrants combined personal experience and divine inspiration. In his view, God bestowed his spirit at birth and kept it accessible through visions and dreams. Elihu also relied on universal truth and wisdom derived from observing nature, while disparaging what can be learned from birds and beasts.

The interrogatives that Yahweh hurls at Job emphasize divine authority. That is why the deity did not need to appeal to any external warrant for validation. The syntax underscores this fact. "Were you present when I established the foundations of the world?" really means "You weren't there when it took place." The futility of arguing with one who is not subject to law quickly dawns on Job and justifies his reticence when called upon to respond. As van Wolde writes, "Justice has not been woven as a pattern into the garment of the world, nor is God burdened with its administration. It is an ideal that must be realized by human beings within their society, through them and for them, and it cannot be put to God's account" (1997a, 129).

Why Poetry?

With chapter 3, the language of discourse shifts to poetry. Surely debates could have been carried out in prose. They were not. Why? Perhaps the intense emotions could be expressed best in poetry, but this shift away from prose turned a relatively simple story into the most difficult book in the Bible. The abundance of *hapax legomena*, words occurring only once in the entire canon, and complex images make translation into a modern language almost impossible. There are many places where honesty requires a translator to leave a blank space. (Having just completed the translation of the book of Job for the *Common English Bible* that will be published by Abingdon, I am acutely aware of the difficulty of understanding the poetic images and successfully accomplishing the "translator's turn.")

As is well known, Hebrew poetry is marked by parallelism. In synonymous parallelism, the second half line of a bicola (two-line sequence) restates what is said in the first but in different words as in "Perish the day I was born, the night someone said, 'A boy's been conceived'" (3:2). In antithetic parallelism, rare in the book of Job but the prevalent form in Proverbs 10–15, the two halves utter contrasting observations ("If he restricts water, they have drought; if he lets it loose, it overturns the land," 12:15). Synthetic parallelism (see Alter 1985, Kugel, and Berlin) is largely additive, as in "His anger tears me; he holds a grudge and gnashes teeth against me; my foe whets his eyes on me" (16:9).

Hebrew poets seldom employ rhyme, and the meter is so complex that no satisfactory scansion has been found. Even its form varies from the occasional single line to the more usual two lines, but three lines are a regular feature as well. It has been argued that the so-called synonymous parallelism is better understood as additive, amounting to something like "This is true, and what's more, so is this."

In the book of Job, the images often resemble a kaleidoscope, spiraling round and round to form dazzling figures that tease the imagination but defy comprehension. The dominant images are taken from warfare, hunting, and nature. (Brown surveys metaphors in Psalms concerning refuge, pathway, a transplanted tree, the sun of righteousness, the voice of many waters, the song of Leviathan, birthing, and protection. I know of nothing comparable on the book of Job, although Perdue 1991 comes close.) Poisonous arrows, swords, ramparts, prisoners, the slain, and the tumult of battle remind readers that the author lived in a violent time. Frequent references to the pursuit of lions, to nets and traps, and to fishhooks indicate a society known for royal sport as well as one dependent on hunting for food and to rid the land of dangerous beasts. Images from nature point to the importance of rain for a bountiful harvest, the perils associated with storms and earthquakes, and celestial wonders. Above all, images of light and darkness, life and death, heaven and the abyss, corporeality and psychic states, fantastic mythical creatures, crafts such as weaving and pottery making, and land and sea lend vitality to the poetry and enhance its exquisite beauty and power. Rarely is the poetry in this book matched elsewhere in the Bible, and never in scope.

Related Texts in the Bible

The closest canonical text to the book of Job marks the transition from Book II to Book III in Psalms. The seventy-third psalm explores the near-crippling effect of a failed retributive system on belief (Crenshaw 2001b, 109–27, and 1984, Buber, and Nielsen). The psalmist begins by confessing that God is good to the upright but admits that daily experience fails to confirm that creed. Tempted by the prosperity of the wicked, the psalmist almost abandons his faith but at a decisive moment enters a holy place and "sees" their untimely demise. His confidence restored, the psalmist reflects on the permanency of divine presence and reaffirms the belief in God's goodness, which has come to mean divine presence.

The spiritual angst created by the belief that God has turned against a faithful servant links Job and Jeremiah as portrayed in the so-called confessions (Jer 11:18–12:6; 15:10-21; 17:14-18; 18:18-23; 20:7-12, 14-18) (Crenshaw 1984, 31–56, and von Rad). Here the prophet complains that sinners prosper while he suffers from false accusations, but more important, Jeremiah accuses Yahweh of seduction and rape. In Jeremiah's eyes, the deity had betrayed loyalty, repaying it with contempt. Like Job, he thought God had become a personal antagonist, treating a righteous person like a sinner.

A common thread runs through these three works: the failure of justice. The consequence of a universe where chaos reigns is felt in the lives of Job, the psalmist, and Jeremiah. Above all, a cherished friendship has been broken. In all three instances, the breach was God's doing. Suffering, both physical and psychic, tormented all three while they waited for relief. In

Jeremiah's case, the torment persisted to the end. Of the many laments in the book of Psalms, only Psalm 88 concludes with similar despondency ("You [Yahweh] have thrust far from me lover and neighbor; my intimates you have cast into darkness," 88:19). One may compare the haunting ending to the fifth chapter of Lamentations ("Have you utterly rejected us; are you exceedingly angry with us?" 5:22).

Dissent in the Bible

These texts and others of similar content attest a presence in ancient Israel of a dissenting voice that vigorously challenges simple answers to life's perplexities (Crenshaw 1977). The comforting assurances in Psalm 37:25 that the righteous are never forsaken by God and always have plenty to eat do not represent life as experienced by many good people. Such truisms cause enormous harm when used to explain tragedy, sickness, and deprivation. In these circumstances, poets like the author of the book of Job lifted their voices in protest.

Voices of dissent met strong resistance, just as Job did. The retributive view of moral conduct was etched into the very soul of ancient peoples. Perhaps its clearest expression can be found in the book of Deuteronomy and in the historiography that its views influenced, especially Joshua, Judges, Samuel, Kings, and Chronicles. At first the principle of reward and punishment commensurate with the deed was applied to the nation and its rulers, but Chronicles took it a step further to cover every single individual.

Prophets and priests took the principle for granted, vigorously threatening the wicked with disaster and promising divine blessing for the righteous. Together with a slanted interpretation of historical events, prophetic and priestly oracles raised expectations in ordinary people that were seldom fulfilled in real life. The resulting disappointment became a seedbed for apocalyptic thinking that delayed the expected reward until after death. Under Persian influence, heaven and hell came to prominence as a viable answer to apparent failure of the retributive principle. Because nobody knew anything about what takes place beyond the grave, such solutions could neither be refuted nor confirmed. In a word, they solved nothing, and yet apocalyptic thought flourished in the period from the early second century BCE until the late second century CE (Collins 1984 and 1992). Its special place in the early church eventually led to a decline of apocalypticism in Judaism as the two religious communities distanced themselves from one another.

Canonization

Given the pervasive presence of Deuteronomistic thinking, how did the
book of Job enter the canon? Modern fascination with rebels makes us think
its selection as canonical was a "slam dunk," but textual alterations to accommodate the book to traditional piety suggest otherwise. Undoubtedly, the
happy ending made it more palatable to those who tenaciously held on to
ancestral teaching, but something more was needed.

The decisive factor may have been the author's decision to make the
hero an Edomite (J. Day). As a non-Israelite, Job was free to vent his anger
against the deity and to practice sacrifice on his own rather than leaving it to
priests. The latter also can be explained as a feature of placing Job in pre-
patriarchal times. The names for deity (El, Eloah, Shaddai, Elohim) were
general designations in Syria-Palestine, and only the author of the folktale
and the narrator use the special name Yahweh (with one exception, 12:9).
The avoidance of the Tetragrammaton, Yahweh, by foreigners was an established tradition in canonical literature. The choice of a foreigner as a paragon
of virtue illustrates the internationalism of sages, even if Edomites were
powerful rivals to Israelites after the exile.

Perhaps the popularity of the folktale and the poet's brilliance combined
to make the book worthy of inclusion in the canon. The exploration of two
great mysteries—suffering and God—gave people who refused to accept
simple answers a means of examining reality in the raw. The canonization of
the book of Ecclesiastes demonstrates a readiness to question everything and
even to deny meaning in life (scholars' fascination with Ecclesiastes appears
to be endless, on which see my recent articles, with extensive bibliography,
especially Crenshaw 2007, 2006c, 2006d, and 2006e). The book of Job has
benefited from such generosity and openness among the intellectually elite in
society.

It helped also that Job's final response to Yahweh is ambiguous. Those
who were inclined to interpret his words as submission were free to read the
book as a depiction of a journey of faith from God the enemy to God the
friend and companion. Stated differently, Job teaches three things (Gordis,
156): (1) *ignoramus* ("we do not know"); (2) *ignorabimus* ("we may never
know"); and (3) *gaudeamus* ("let us rejoice"). The darkness and mystery
remain, while the beauty of the natural order throws dazzling light on
human existence and evokes gratitude.

Then, too, the teachings of Ben Sira at the turn of the second century
reaffirmed the retributive scheme that was largely taken for granted by the
various composers of aphorisms collected within the book of Proverbs

(Crenshaw 2009a and 2005c). It appears that his views prevailed over less traditional ones promulgated by the skeptical authors of the books of Job and Ecclesiastes. Denying retributive justice was nothing less than trying to stop a rushing torrent. That is why interpreters sometimes think Qoheleth's word about swimming against the current is an indirect indictment of Job's open resistance of God.

The Testament of Job

It did not take long for speculation about the book of Job to take a new form. The popularity of testamentary literature prompted an unknown author in the first century BCE to the first century CE to compose "The Testament of Job" (Spittler). In literature of this genre, a wise father gives final words of ethical advice to his children (see, for example, Tob 4:5-21, to which may be compared the advice given by Raphael, the angel in 12:6-10). Variations occur, as in the enormously popular "Testaments of the Twelve Patriarchs," which offers teachings to foreigners (Kee). The genre was so well liked among Romans that schoolboys were entertained by a humorous account of a testament by a pig, Grunnius Coroccota, before it was slaughtered (Spittler, 832).

In some ways, "The Testament of Job" develops themes already found in the Septuagint translation of the biblical book. The Greek of the book is twenty percent shorter than the Masoretic Text, although the author expands the Hebrew at some points. For example, the two sentences of Job's wife, "Do you still hold on to your integrity? Curse God and die," become a long paragraph in the Septuagint:

> After a long time had passed, his wife said to him, "How long will you endure and say, 'See, I will wait yet a bit longer, looking for the hope of my salvation.' Look, your memory is already blotted out from the earth [along with] the sons and daughters, the travail and pangs of my womb, whom I reared in toil for nothing. And you, you sit in wormy decay, passing the nights in the open, while I roam and drudge from place to place, and from house to house, waiting for the sun to go down, so that I may rest from my toils and the griefs which now grip me. Now, say some word against the Lord, and die." (2:9)

Similarly, the Greek version concludes with information about Job's place of birth and ancestors. He is said to have lived on the borders of Idumea (Edom) and Arabia, to have been named Jobab, to have taken an Arabian wife, and to have had a son named Ennon. Jobab is called a descendant of Esau, five generations after Abraham; he ruled over a city in Edom, as did others in the region. The three friends who came to console him are identified as kings. Their names are Eliphaz, Baldad, and Sophar.

More importantly, the Septuagint has Job express confidence that the eternal one will raise him up to the earth (19:25-27). This optimism fills to overflowing in "The Testament of Job," for in the years between the translation of the book of Job into Greek and the time of the Testament, belief in the resurrection of the body flourished, particularly among Christians, but also in Pharisaic Judaism (see the collection of articles in Charlesworth; the evidence in the Hebrew Bible is discussed in Crenshaw 2006c).

The essential theme of "The Testament of Job" can be found in a single statement: "Now then, my children, you also must be patient in everything that happens to you. For patience is better than anything" (27:7). Possibly the most striking feature, beyond the haggadic magnifying of Job's piety, is the emphasis on women. This glorification of females takes two forms: (1) the depiction of the suffering of Job's wife, Sitis, and (2) the development of the biblical observation that Job gave an inheritance to his three daughters.

Sitis not only suffers from the loss of her children; she also endures the discomforts of privation, which force her to work to support her sick husband and even to sell her hair to Satan for three loaves of bread. In the ancient world, the sale of a woman's hair was a last resort, so shameful was the act thought to be. Furthermore, Sitis mourns her unburied children until comforted by her husband's assurance that they have been resurrected.

The account of the daughters' inheritance combines magic and charismatic prophecy, the special gifts bestowing prophetic ecstasy on the females, enabling them to speak the language of angels. The charismatic sashes, when worn by the daughters, magically changed their hearts so that they only cared for heavenly things (on the relationship between this section about the daughters' inheritance and biblical precedents, especially the daughters of Zelophahad, see Machinist).

Another feature of the Testament is its advanced development of the adversary, who at this late date has become a proper name, Satan. He is no longer in the service of Yahweh but a foe whose aim is to destroy Jobab, whose name was changed to Job by God. The struggle between Job and Satan is described as a wrestling match; such athletic language was especially popular among Greek writers. Although Satan disguises himself, Job recognizes him and easily defeats his opponent. Job's wife is not so fortunate, which leads to the sale of her hair. This act becomes the occasion for a hymnic insert contrasting her earlier opulence with her present misery. A refrain punctuates the change in her life, its variations all the more poignant.

> Now she exchanges her hair for loaves! . . .
> Now she gives her hair in return for loaves! . . .
> Now she sells outright her hair for loaves! . . .
> Even her hair she gives in exchange for loaves! . . .
> But now she bears rags and gives her hair in exchange for loaves! . . .
> But now she sells her hair for loaves! (25:1-8)

Gone are the draperies, camels, tables laden with food, gold and silver objects, and linen clothes with gold embroidering.

There is also a hymn against Elihu in the Testament. Because he is not included in those who were saved from Yahweh's wrath by Job's intercession in the canonical version, Eliphaz curses Elihu as evil and says that darkness will envelop the one who loved the beauty of the snake and has the poison of asps in the tongue (43:5-17). This reference to snakes appears to be an attack against Ophism, a popular form of worship in Greco-Roman times. As in the hymn attributed to Sitis, this one seems to have had a refrain in alternating verses, but only its opening and concluding verses remain:

"Our sins were stripped off, and our lawlessness buried. Elihu, Elihu—the only evil one—will have no memorial among the living" (43:5).

"Gone is our sin, cleansed is our lawlessness. And the evil one Elihu has no memorial among the living" (43:17).

The sequence of events in the Testament begins with Job gathering his ten new children to his bedside so he can tell them the story of his suffering. The children's names are given—Tersi, Choros, Hyon, Nike, Phoros, Phiphe, Phrouon, Hemera, Kasia, and Amaltheia's Horn—and their mother, Job's new wife, is said to be Dinah from the tribe of Esau (ch. 1).

The cause of Job's calamities is his destruction of the holy place at which offerings to Satan were made, even though an angel had warned him of serious consequences while encouraging him by promising renown and resurrection for patient sparring with the devil. Disguised as a beggar, Satan seeks entrance to Job's house. Knowing his identity, Job hands a burnt loaf to his maid and instructs her to give it to Satan. Ashamed to do so, she gives him a good loaf and is promptly rebuked by Satan, who sends her to inform Job that he will be burnt like the bread (chs. 2–8).

The next section is a haggadic glorification of Job's piety. Of his 130,000 sheep, he designated 7,000 to be sheared for clothing the poor. He had 80 dogs guarding his flocks and 200 guarding his house. He sent 3,000 camels laden with goods for the needy, and of his 140,000 she-asses he set aside 500 and ordered that their offspring be given to the poor. Four doors of his house were always open so people from north and south, east and west, could enter directly. Thirty tables were spread daily for strangers and twelve others for widows. Of his 3,500 yoke of oxen, 500 were free to be used by anyone for plowing and their produce given to the poor. His fifty bakeries supplied the bread for daily meals. If servants tired, Job entertained them with music, and in case his sons had sinned, he offered 300 doves, 50 goat's kids, and 12 sheep (chs. 9–15).

Next comes an account of Job's losses. Satan torches Job's animals and then disguises himself as king of Persia to learn of Job's children, whom he slays. Coming to Job while he sits on his throne and mourns the loss of his children—which he never does in the canonical version—Satan becomes a whirlwind and overthrows Job's throne. Sickness follows, along with sores and worms. When a worm falls off Job's body, he picks it up and places it where it had been (chs. 16–20).

For 48 years Job sits on a dung heap and Sitis carries water to a nobleman like a servant to earn bread, and after eleven years they are so poor she has to share her bread with her husband, finally selling her hair to Satan, who has disguised himself as a bread seller. Sitis thinks, "What good is the hair of my head compared to my hungry husband?" Whereupon she makes a passionate speech, which is interrupted by a lament for her, and then urges Job to eat the loaves, curse God, and die. Shocked, Job says he has lived seventeen years in misery but nothing has been so painful as her words, which if followed would lead to loss of the one true wealth. Then Job asks Sitis if she cannot see Satan standing behind her and destroying her ability to reason (chs. 17–26).

At this time, Job demands that Satan come forward and engage him in a wrestling match. Satan does and gains the top position, but Job defeats him anyway. Ashamed, Satan leaves Job for three years (ch. 27). The three kings visit Job and offer words of advice. Eliphaz concerns himself with confirming Job's identity and uttering a lament for him (chs. 31–34). Baldad's argument runs as follows: In whom do you hope? [Job: in God]. Who destroyed your goods and inflicted you? [Job: God]. How can you call him unfair? No king dishonors a faithful soldier. Who can understand the Lord's mysteries or who dares ascribe injustice to him? Explain, if you can, the sun's rising and setting. Tell me how the body separates food and water that enter the same mouth. If you don't know, how can you understand heavenly things? (Chs. 35–37; this type of reasoning is typical of the angel's response to Ezra in Fourth Ezra [II Esdras].) Sophar urges Job to be treated by royal physicians they have brought with them, but he declines, saying that his God created physicians (ch. 38).

Emotionally and physically exhausted, Sitis laments her dead children and dies, having been told by Job that they have been taken up into heaven. A lament for her is said to exist in "The Miscellanies" (chs. 39–40). Job now recovers and is vindicated after praying for his three friends. Elihu, however, is inspired by Satan and speaks insulting words against Job that are said to be preserved in "The Miscellanies of Eliphas." Job's friends bring him a lamb and a gold coin, Job warns his children against marrying strangers, and then he divides his possessions among the ten children. Job explains to his daughters that the sashes will give them a better life on earth and lead them to live in a better world, heaven. These protective amulets will also bestow angelic dialects on them. (Compare the pious explanation for fallen Jews in 2 Macc 13:40. Each one was wearing a sacred token of the idols of Jamnia under his tunic. The author of "The Testament of Job" was not troubled by sacred objects as a feature of clothing.) The hymns of the three daughters are said to be written down by Job's brother, Nereus (chs. 41–51). Job dies, and the daughters experience *merkabah* mysticism, seeing gleaming chariots that have come for his soul (the word *merkabah* means "chariot" in Hebrew and is taken from Ezekiel's vision of the throne chariot in 1:4-28a). People who have been the object of Job's generosity now prevent his burial for three days, then relent, and his body is buried. Nereus and the children join the poor and orphans in song:

> Woe to us today! A double woe!
> Gone today is the strength of the helpless!
> Gone is the light of the blind!
> Gone is the father of the orphans!
> Gone is the host of strangers!
> Gone is the clothing of widows!
> Who then will not weep over the man of God? (chs. 52–53)

Job in the Koran

Muslim tradition about Job and his wife has been summarized in the following way (Pope, *Job*, 22–23, who quotes G. Sale, *The Koran*, 1889, 247–48, as the source of the account that follows). A descendant of Esau, greatly blessed with riches and family, was tested by God and lost everything but remained faithful. Physically afflicted, he lay on a dung heap and was so loathsome no one came near, except his wife (called by some Rahmat

[Mercy], the daughter of Ephraim, Joseph's son, but by others Makhir the daughter of Manasses). She worked to support her husband, and one day the devil appeared to her and promised to restore all if she would worship him. Tempted, she told Job about the proposal and asked his consent. An angry Job swore that if he got well he would beat her with a hundred stripes. After Job prayed the words, "Verily, evil hath afflicted me, but thou art the most merciful of those who show mercy," God sent Gabriel to raise Job. Simultaneously, a fountain sprang up at his feet and Job drank from it, whereupon the worms fell off his body. Upon bathing in the fountain, Job was made healthy again. He then received double what he had before, and his wife bore him twenty-six sons. To satisfy his oath, Job was instructed by God to strike her one blow with a palm branch having a hundred leaves (cf. Koran xxxviii 43 and Sura xxi 83).

Like "The Testament of Job," Muslim tradition restricts the devil's activity to the earth, pitting him against humans rather than God. In both accounts, the wife is deemed more vulnerable than her husband. New features in the Muslim tradition highlight Job's tender treatment of his wife, while at the same time emphasizing divine mercy, and stress the healing power of a miraculous fountain. New, too, are the names of Job's wife and the number of sons born to replace the dead children. The silence about daughters contrasts with their prominence in "The Testament of Job."

The Flourishing of the Interrogative: Fourth Ezra and Second Baruch

While "The Testament of Job" and Muslim tradition about him were influenced primarily by the folktale as recounted in the prologue and epilogue (just like the author of the Epistle of James), a sizable number of literary works took up the questioning of God that plays such an important role in the poetic center to the book of Job. The most significant of these works is Fourth Ezra, or Second Esdras (on Fourth Ezra, see the magisterial commentary by Stone). Second Baruch also addresses some of the same issues and probes them with equal tenacity (Wright).

Both of these apocryphal works belong to the literary genre of apocalyptic. Some of its chief characteristics are (1) bizarre images, often taken from the world of animals; (2) pseudonymous authorship by figures chosen from the remote past such as Adam, Enoch, Abraham, and Elijah; (3) heavenly journeys during which angels convey valuable knowledge to the supposed author; (4) description of the earth and its inhabitants as having fallen under the control of cosmic evil forces; and (5) eschatological dualism, with a strong belief in the resurrection of the righteous and eternal damnation of the wicked.

Fourth Ezra takes the form of seven visions. In the first of these, Ezra is distraught over God's elevation of Babylon, which symbolizes Rome, and suppression of Israel. In short, Ezra questions divine justice just as Job did; the basic difference between him and Job is Ezra's nationalizing of the problem as opposed to Job's individual focus. An angel tells Ezra that he is not able to understand the ways of God. To drive his point home, the angel gives a series of impossible tasks for Ezra to contemplate: weigh fire, measure the wind, conquer time (Crenshaw 1980). And the angel inquires about Ezra's knowledge about the exits of hell and entrances to paradise. Two illustrations—the sea and the forest—serve as a warning against hubris, and an allusion to the duration of pregnancy reminds Ezra to be patient.

The second vision emphasizes God's predilection to choose one of many (vine, land, flower, river, city, dove, sheep, people, Torah) and also lists several impossible tasks (count those yet to come, gather scattered raindrops, make withered flowers bloom, open closed chambers, bring forth winds, show me a picture of a voice). Earth's increasing senescence is also mentioned. (Compare the use of gold, silver, bronze, iron, and clay to imply the gradual deterioration of things. The author of Daniel 2:37-43 describes competing empires [implied by "another kingdom, inferior to you"] as gold, silver, bronze, iron, and a mixture of clay and iron.)

The flaws in the created world occupy Ezra's attention in the third vision, leading to the question, "Why doesn't Israel own the world, since the nations are spit?" The angel answers that the entrances are both broad and narrow, with contrasts between the many and the few. This response evokes in Ezra the comment that it would be better not to have been born, or better still, that Earth had not birthed humans. The avoidance of God as the source of human life here is remarkable. Even more surprising is the comment that the fault is Adam's (Ben Sira chose to blame Eve for originating sin: "From a woman sin had its beginning, and because of her we all die," 25:24; contrast 2 Esd 8:48, "O Adam, what have you done? For though it was you who sinned, the fall was not yours alone, but ours also who are your descendants"). The angel reminds Ezra that all have free will, and a midrash on Exodus 34:6-7, the divine qualities of justice and mercy, follows. After all, says the angel, this world is for the many, but the next world is for the few. Free will means that God's justice is secure.

In the fourth vision, Ezra confronts a woman who is mourning the death of her only son; Ezra tells her that the nation's loss is greater than hers, and he promises her that she will get her son back if she will confess God's justice. Both Ezra and the woman are transformed, he in his acceptance of divine justice and she in appearance. Amazingly, she is changed into Zion, the holy Jerusalem, before his very eyes.

Visions five and six abound in images of animals, like the canonical book of Daniel, representing foreign kingdoms and the messiah. The last days are imminent, and Ezra must teach secret wisdom to others. The final vision comprises a theophany similar to Genesis 18 and Exodus 3. Ezra then restores the Torah by dictating it for forty days, just as Moses dwelt on Mt. Sinai the same duration when receiving the law. In addition, Ezra dictates seventy books that are to remain the sole property of the intelligentsia. These Apocryphal books are praised above the canonical twenty-four books that are to be made available to everyone.

The essential teaching of Second Baruch is the incomprehensible God of unfathomable grace. Because of free will, everyone is his own Adam—one might add, and her own Eve. The author is perplexed by the disclosure that the earth will remain even after all humans have departed. How can this be, he asks, if the earth was created for use by human beings? The fall of Jerusalem to invading soldiers from Babylon also puzzled this author, given the supposed protection of Zion by God. The answer relieves the deity of charges of weakness; it is said that God breached the wall and departed, leaving the city vulnerable to attack. Like Ezra in the end, Baruch praises the God he cannot understand. It would be difficult to improve on Baruch's devotion, which can be summarized in a brief statement: "If my members and hair were voices, I still could not praise God enough." With little basis other than the confidence of trust, Baruch firmly believes that God will eventually set things right.

Both Fourth Ezra and Second Baruch ask serious questions about divine justice, just as Job did, but in the end the writers come to believe that God will establish a just order so those who have remained faithful will be rewarded. In this regard, they have gathered inspiration from the biblical folktale about Job's restoration. Such confidence, however, resides alongside a strong conviction that God's ways are inscrutable, like the mysteries of the universe. This knowledge of the limits imposed on the human intellect does not make the injustices of everyday life any less vexing. The result is existential angst.

Saadiah Ben Joseph Al-Fayyūmī

Jewish speculation about Job tended to blunt his rebellious side. A Midrash on Psalms states that four men were smitten—Abraham, Job, David, and

Hezekiah. Abraham laughed (Gen 17:17), Hezekiah prayed to God (Isa 38:2), David asked for more (Pss 94:12; 26:2), but Job complained bitterly and rebelled, challenging God (10:1-3; 13:23; 16:17-18). Abot de Rabbi Nathan accuses Job of sinning with his heart while remaining discreetly silent; naturally, this reference applies to the narrator's observation that in all this adversity Job did not sin with his lips (2:10).

Job's presumed faults vary with the interpreter (Glatzer 1966 and Baskin). Rashi accused him of talking too much, Ibn Ezra and Nachmanides considered him a rebel, Sforno added dualism to Job's sins, Maimonides said Job lacked the love of God, Gersonides believed him an Aristotelian denier of providence, Simeon ben Semah Duran said Job confused the work of God and Satan, and Joseph Albo thought him a determinist. The mystical Zohar depicts him as one who failed to pacify Satan, a scapegoat, and an isolationist. A Jewish legend has God turn Job over to Satan, called Samael, to keep him occupied while Israelites cross the Red Sea, then rescue Job at the last moment. It appears that later Jewish interpreters agreed with the Midrashic assessment that, when tested, Job was found wanting. That was not Saadiah's view, however; instead, he stressed Job's spiritual growth through questioning in adversity.

The founder of modern interpretive method, master of Hebrew grammar and lexiocography, and first systematic philosopher of Judaism, Saadiah (882–942) wrote an important commentary on Job in Arabic. It has been translated as *The Book of Theodicy*; the translator, L. E. Goodman, has written a valuable introduction. Saadiah's central argument was that creation is an act of pure grace and therefore God cannot "shortchange" humans. In his view, the answer that Job sought came from a better understanding of nature. Refreshing showers may be either a reward or an act of grace, a miracle. Much of the power of the book of Job, Saadiah avers, is found in divine silence, the fact that we do not know we will be tested and are not told of its nature, outcome, or meaning.

According to Saadiah, evil can only be explained by countervailing good, that is, life itself. Vindicating the central thesis of God's justice in and through nature is Saadiah's goal. He anchors the necessary explanations of suffering in three things: (1) the pure grace of creation; (2) the nature of life that allows for self-help, cure, and restoration; and (3) the providential provision of each creature with its own place in the universe.

For Saadiah, suffering was the spark igniting Job's soul, the means by which he was changed for the better. The divine speech, however, is troubling to Saadiah, a fiction within a fiction. For God to articulate the answers humans must apprehend would trivialize Job's trial and render meaningless the very act of creation. God acts through nature and takes no sides. This means that God is not a moral being, a creature. Because God's grace through his creative act extends universally, God is just. Like <u>God, nature is impartial;</u> it cannot "wear a friendly face."

One other feature of the biblical book bothered Saadiah: its rhetoric. He considered rhetorical flourish an impediment to discovering the true line of argument. (Contrast Saadiah's view of rhetoric with the first use of Greek and Roman authorities on the topic by Judah Messer Leon, *Sefer Nofet Sufim* [*The Book of the Honeycomb's Flow*] that appeared in 1475 or 1476. Messer Leon examines the structure of persuasion and identifies eighty-two figures of speech. On biblical rhetoric, see Crenshaw 1998b.) The divine speeches, however, are said to be the poet's speaking for God, "prophecy of the highest and truest kind." Far from troubling Saadiah, Elihu's speeches prepare the way for Yahweh, who expands on them and confirms Elihu as a truthful witness. Saadiah believed that the speeches in general have dialogic unity. For example, Elihu's four addresses respond to Job's three speeches in sequence and then offer something additional. Interestingly, Saadiah rejects all mythological projection. The adversary is thus considered a human being.

Job's Continuing Influence

Bontsye Shvayg

A strong case has been made for viewing Y. L. Perets' *Bontsye Shvayg* as a satire inspired by Job (Zuckerman, 87–92, and his appendix, "The Text and Translation of Y. L. Perets's 'Bonstye Shvayg,'" 181–95). This Yiddish short story was published in 1893 in the wake of the pogroms against Jews following the assassination of Tsar Alexander II in 1881. It tells about a man whose entire existence consisted of suffering but who never uttered a word of complaint. Heaven quaked at the thought that Bontsye might call in the debt owed him for his suffering, a moral debt greater than heaven could cover. On earth, he made no impression; but his death resounded in the heavens, as angels pondered why he would need to come before the Supreme Assembly (behind this reference lies the belief that everyone will be judged in the next life to determine whether it will be spent in heaven or hell). "The case will last but five minutes," they said. Hearing that a crown of gold was prepared for him, Bontsye was struck silent. Was it a dream? A slipup? He was used to both.

The presiding officer pronounces his name and says to the defense, "Keep it short." The chief argument in Bontsye's favor is the fact that he was always silent, even in the face of all kinds of mistreatment. A refrain makes the point: "He kept silent." Indeed, he kept silent at the moment of death. He spoke "not a word against God, not a word against man. The defense rests."

The prosecutor begins to speak two times before saying, "My lords! He was silent! I will be silent, too!" Thereupon, the presiding officer offers Bontsye anything he wants. "Are you sure?" he asks. "Absolutely" is the answer, and everyone agrees. "Gee, if you mean it," says Bontsye. "What I'd really like is, each and every morning, a hot roll with fresh butter." At this, judges and angels lower their heads in shame; the prosecutor bursts out laughing.

Like Job's second response to God, the ending to Perets's short story can be read two ways. A truly pious man has put heaven to shame, or the hero is a simpleton whose only care is for bodily sustenance. The final comment about the prosecutor's laughter leaves a jagged edge and strongly suggests that the author is parodying the piety of his day. Later events, however, circumvented his original purpose, for suffering became a grim reality for the Jewish community in Russia. The story of Bontsye then became a celebration of the virtue of silent acceptance of one's lot rather than mockery of belief that in spite of so much evil in this world, good people will be compensated in the next life.

Blake's Illustrations

The lone reference in *Bontsye Shvayg* to the biblical Job contrasts with William Blake's engravings that were published in London in 1825. (The following treatment relies heavily on Damon.) This series of twenty-one illustrations of the book of Job is the product of a gifted poet with a creative imagination. Blake insists that they are symbolic: Job's children are not really dead, the devil is the accuser in Job's mind, and the boils on Job's body are a disease of the soul. The entire drama, that is, takes place in Job's soul. The friends are Job's inner guilt, and God is Job's own creation, made in his own image. Left and right symbolize evil and good respectively; Job gives a loaf to a beggar with his left hand, showing no compassion, but God arrives to Job with right foot first. The cross is a symbol of false religion, and the seven eyes on the title page are the seven spirits of Revelation 5:6. Of the seven angels, only Jesus appears outside the title page. The other six are Lucifer, Molech, Elohim, Shaddai, Pahad (fear), and Jehovah. The twenty-one illustrations are divided into three cycles. Man is born a Lucifer, inherently proud. He must conquer pride to become truly human. Job's mistake was in letting his accuser into his heaven, and only a false god would have listened to him. Job's misery is educational, not punitive, and only by overcoming the traditional view of disasters as punishment does he begin to search for the true God. Job's progress is depicted as follows:

1. Job and his family sit in a state of innocence, but Job fears God rather than loving him, hates evil, and thus half of life, and counts on the letter of the law. Above all, he is proud.

2. God, Job's own ideal, is like him and hence can call Job perfect. Job sits with his mistress but does not really know how his sons behave.

3. Job is angry that his sons have taken mistresses; after a quarrel, they are dead to their parents.

4. Two messengers bring bad news.

5. Job shares his last loaf with a beggar, a scene that is not taken from the Bible.

6. Satan attacks Job, especially his guilt over sex, and destroys four of his senses, corrupting the fifth, touch.

7. Three friends arrive; their arguments are Job's third test.

8. Job's spiritual revolution begins; his wrath erupts.

9. Eliphaz's vision: God must reward according to one's just deserts.

10. The friends ridicule Job as he had condemned his children.

11. Scary dreams show Job that his god is the devil.

12. Elihu's traditional view leaves an impact on Job.

13. Jesus appears in the whirlwind; he is the divine imagination and the forgiveness of sins.

14. The vision of the universe has the divine imagination supporting brain and heart and is the portal to the spirit world.

15. Behemoth and Leviathan exist within man as the unredeemed portion of the psyche.

16. The wicked are judged and Satan is cast out of heaven.

17. God has brought Job and his wife back to heaven.

18. God, now in the form of the sun, accepts Job's prayer.

19. Job's friends bring gifts to him; a woman offers an earring.

20. Job sits with his three daughters, who represent poetry, art, and music.

21. Job and his family worship God with musical instruments.

The beauty of these illustrations is captivating, as is Blake's view of the entire drama as Job's inner struggle. Behind the symbolism rests Blake's own view of the universe as an organism with different parts, each relating to the other, and every single one with a function and meaning. Job's fundamental flaws, pride and a legal understanding of God's relationship with humans, are based on the canonical account, especially the divine speeches. The chief problems of the biblical book, however, fade into the background: the nature of God, the problem of innocent suffering, the correct way to talk about God, and the possibility of disinterested righteousness. Job's troubles teach him that God does not judge humankind on the basis of law. It is a mistake, therefore, to assume that calamity comes as punishment for transgressions.

C. G. Jung's *Answer to Job*

While Blake believed that the Joban drama was enacted in Job's psyche, the psychologist C. G. Jung considered the adversary to be the dark side of God's being, a nagging uncertainty about his own character (Jung). As an unreflecting sovereign, God holds together competing natures, total justice and its total opposite. He is jealous of Job and secretly resists one who is self-reflective from vulnerability. In a ruthless display of power, Yahweh slays Job's children and ultimately thunders reproaches at Job, who is "no more than the outward occasion for an inward process of the dialectic of God." Job discovers that his God is less than human. Unwittingly, God raises Job by humiliating him, at the same time pronouncing judgment on himself.

Yahweh has no eros, no relationship to humans, but wisdom becomes an advocate for Yahweh, revealing his kind side. The incarnation objectifies God, and thus is a world-shaking transformation of God. In short, the answer to Job is a changed God, one who has acquired wisdom and rejected power as the manner of relating to human beings. This interpretation of the book of Job relies on the assumption that psychic facts are just as real as physical ones. Deep within the subconscious, these truths attest humanity's attempt to come to terms with evil, the mysterious, and the ineffable. Jung gives voice to the shattering emotion caused by the divine savagery in the book of Job.

In Jung's view, Job never doubts the unity of God. That is why Job still believes that, despite the cruelty, God will become his advocate. God needed mortals in the same way they needed him, for existence is only real when it is conscious to somebody. Yet because of Yahweh's ruthless nature, Job can only fear him. Tempted to divorce his wife Israel and take on *hokmah*, Yahweh seeks out similar unfaithfulness but makes the mistake of charging his most loyal subject, Job.

Now Yahweh needs wisdom. Since in Jewish legend Adam had two wives, Lilith and Eve, his heavenly prototype did too. The former represented the male principle of perfection, the latter the female principle of completeness. From this marriage to Wisdom, a new creation is born, God-man. And Mary is said to be free from sin, an everlasting virgin, two doctrines that throw into question the human side of Jesus. Jung's extensive analysis of Christian apocalyptic takes him far away from the book of Job, although some modern interpreters think the character of Job's God has certain affinities with late apocalyptic. (The chief similarities between the character of God in Job and apocalyptic are the distance separating the creator from humans and the dominance of evil in the world.)

Archibald MacLeish's *J.B.*

J.B., a Pulitzer Prize-winning play by Archibald MacLeish, is perhaps the most effective modern interpretation of the book of Job (MacLeish). In an earlier work, *Panic*, MacLeish experimented with the book of Job as a way of dealing with the problem presented by the Great Depression, his Job figure being an honest banker named McGafferty who ultimately committed suicide. The love of his mistress, Ione, was not sufficient reason, in McGafferty's view, to make life worthwhile. *J.B.* contrasts sharply with *Panic* in this regard, for the popular Broadway play ends with J.B. and Sarah taking comfort in blowing on the coals of the heart and in anticipated sight and knowledge, now that religion has failed.

The plot of *J.B.* is simple. Two bygone actors, Zuss and Nickles, decide to play God and Satan respectively, with "everyone" playing Job. At a Thanksgiving dinner, J.B. and Sarah discuss divine justice ("A man can count on him"), and this idyllic scene is quickly shattered as the children are slain (a soldier son is killed, two children die in an automobile accident, and a child is raped and murdered). J.B. responds as Job did, but Sarah accuses God of killing their children. Injured in the calamities that follow, she leaves J.B. Then a doctor, a banker, and a priest counsel J.B. Above all, they discuss guilt, which they identify as a sociological accident, a psychophenomenal situation, and an illusion. When J.B.'s situation is reversed again, Zuss is furious because J.B. forgives God, not the other way around. J.B. asks Sarah why she left him and learns that it was because she loved him. Then she says, "You wanted justice and there was none—Only love," to which J.B. responds, "He [God] does not love. He Is." Sarah answers that we love, which she thinks is cause for wonder.

Some of the most provocative lines are given to the actors playing God and Satan: "God never laughs!—In the whole Bible"; and "If God is God He is not good, If God is good He is not God." While Nickles wears a mask of loathing that lets him see awful things, Zuss wears an impermeable one of cold complacency, leaving God blind. J.B. and Sarah also have opposing views. He thinks nobody deserves the world, which is a gift of grace, whereas she insists that everyone gets what she or he deserves.

The cogency of MacLeish's modern version of the Joban drama explains the popularity of *J.B.* on Broadway for so long. *J.B.* also illustrates the power of humanism to bring warmth and light when disaster strikes. Still, it is far removed from the biblical drama where God cannot be characterized by the verb "to be," despite the enigmatic "I am that I am." Job's God was passionate; that much is certain. Perhaps he also had a tiny element of compassion as well.

Another modern adaptation of the Joban dilemma, Neil Simon's play, *God's Favorite*, lacks the grandeur of *J.B.* but emphasizes the endless nature of Job-like suffering (Simon). The punch line comes once David, the Job figure's favorite son, has renounced his atheism and returned to the family. "Guess who is God's favorite now" implies that the son is destined to repeat his father's story. In other words, he too becomes a Job, and the cycle never ends.

Conclusion

So many great minds have been moved to grasp the mystery of the book of Job, and yet it remains the most enigmatic of books. It has been called "the greatest thing ever written with pen" (Thomas Carlyle), and even Ernst Bloch, a Marxist philosopher, considered the book rare truth in the Bible—naming God for the tyrant he is. In a horrendous anti-Semitic comment, the French critic Ernst Renan considered the book of Job the only beautiful book ever written by a Jew, and Johannes Hempel wrote, "The book of Job is the struggle for the last truth about God" (Hempel; see Murphy 2002, Crenshaw 2002, and Janzen 2002). Yair Hoffman has compared the book to the statue of Venus de Milo, a blemished perfection, and David Wolfers has accused critics of totally misreading a myth about the nation Israel. More to the point, Mattiahu Tsevat's view strikes the right note. The book demolished the pious belief that the world is ruled by a just God, to which may be compared Robert Frost's "The Masque of Reason," a dialogue featuring God, Job and his wife, and Satan. At the beginning, God praises Job for freeing him from the necessity of rewarding virtue and punishing vice.

By contrast, the early church saw Job's suffering as educative and had readings from Job in the liturgy of the dead, readings recently removed by the Catholic Church (Tilley and Rouillard). Gregory the Great composed thirty-five books of sermons on Job, and Augustine read the book as an example of divine grace. For Thomas Aquinas, the book was the starting point for a discussion of divine providence, and Calvin wrote 159 sermons on the book, mostly about providence. In the seventeenth and eighteenth centuries, a shift occurred in which Job was celebrated as a rebel and thus a true representative of the human condition.

A modern physician, Jack Kahn, uses modern psychiatry to understand the grief process through which Job passed; an anthropologist, René Girard, has developed a theory that society needs to sacrifice a scapegoat to establish order (in Girard's view, the book is a sacrificial drama; a different type of drama is envisioned by Luis Alonso-Schökel [1977] and H. M. Kallen); and a liberation theologian, Gustavo Gutierrez, has emphasized Job's identification with the causes of the poor. A Yiddish interpreter, Chaim Zhitlowsky, uses Goethe's *Faust* as a lens through which to view the book of Job, a Nobel Prize-winning novelist, Eli Wiesel, has compared the fate of Jews under Hitler with Job's affliction, and William Safire considered Job the first dissident.

Regardless of the lens one uses when reading the book, Job's God transcends morality. For this reason, the book does not depict a comforting deity or an accommodating universe. Without postulating such a worldview, how could the author have explored the issue of disinterested righteousness? That examination enables the book to "crash into the abyss of radical aloneness" (Susman), but also to evoke high praise: "Here, in our view, is the most sublime monument in literature, not only of written language, nor of philosophy and poetry, but the most sublime monument of the human soul. Here is the great eternal drama with three actors who embody everything: but what actors! God, humankind, and Destiny" (Alphonse de Lamartine, cited in Hausen, 145).

Part 2: Commentary

The Prologue (1:1–2:13)

A good story draws us into its twists and turns like nothing else. Forgetting present reality, we freely throw ourselves into an imaginary world peopled by characters we come to admire, or loathe, as the plot develops before our eyes. We feel their emotions as our own, rejoicing when our favorites rejoice and crying when they are overwhelmed by sorrow. We quickly become participants in events over which we have no control (Cooper).

Such is the power of the biblical story about Yahweh's servant Job. It gives flesh and blood to a philosophical debate about the possibility of being religious without considering the reward for such behavior. Stated differently, can virtue exist apart from incentives? Because the issue cannot be resolved without introducing the problem of innocent suffering, the story includes pathos as well as mind-boggling events. Putting difficult thoughts into appropriate words becomes an integral part of the total story, for speech discloses character.

According to irrefutable evidence, the testimony of an omniscient narrator and of Yahweh, Job's character was flawless. He was perfect and just, religious and moral. The word *tam*, which I have translated "perfect," indicates wholeness rather than moral perfection, and *yašar* suggests fair treatment of others. The third adjective, *yere' 'elohim* means one who fears God, which in modern parlance is best rendered "religious." The fourth expression, *sar mera'* ("turns away from evil"), places Job squarely in the camp of moral people.

Such "larger than life" characters only exist in the human imagination. That is why Job is located in far-off Uz and in remote antiquity. The unknown country was perhaps invented because of its similarity to *'eṣah*, "counsel." Like the patriarchs Abraham, Isaac, and Jacob, Job possessed cattle and servants as symbols of wealth; counted money that was called a *qeśiṭah*;

had dealings, both positive and negative, with Sabeans and Chaldeans; practiced sacrifice on his own rather than employing priests; and enjoyed a lengthy life span.

His name, attested from early times both in Egypt and in Mesopotamia, can mean "Where is the (divine) father?" and "Inveterate Foe/Hated One." It belongs to a folk hero like Noah and Danel, with whom he is associated in Ezekiel 14:14 and 20. The Canaanite Dan'el rather than the later Daniel in the Bible is the probable hero behind Ezekiel's remark. Typical of wisdom literature, which emphasizes knowledge accessible to everyone, the story pushes no national agenda. Its main character is an Edomite, and his three friends are also non-Israelites. Although his god bears several names, he is identified with the biblical Yahweh, both in the prologue and epilogue and in the divine speeches. This god's conduct, however, is morally more questionable than elsewhere except in a few strange episodes such as the command to Abraham to sacrifice his son, the attempt to kill Moses, and the legislation of genocide directed against various foreign peoples.

Not only is this story about a hero who is like no one we know and about an alien deity, but it also has a heavenly provocateur who is called *haśśaṭan*, the adversary. The definite article on the word indicates a profession, not a proper name as in 1 Chronicles 41:6-7. This predecessor to the later figure called Satan is in the service of the supreme deity who rules over a divine council, familiar to readers of the Bible (cf. 1 Kgs 22; Isa 6:1-13).

As so often is the case in compelling dramas, the villain initiates the action. After what appears to be an intrusion in the assembly of celestial beings, the provocateur hurls a question at Yahweh that strikes at the heart of genuine religion. "Will anyone serve God for nothing?" he asks. Later, when pressed, he voices the creed by which he lives: "Everything a person has he'll give for his life." With that, the stage is set for a struggle of gigantic proportions. Through it all, Job must not be told what readers know, for that would render the outcome of the test meaningless, mollifying the universality of the paradigm (Fox, esp. 355).

Curiously, this figure whose office resembles that of a contemporary CIA agent has not noticed Job while traveling hither and yon in search of a truly virtuous person. He has definitely been affected by the nature of his job, adopting a suspicious attitude that has gradually turned cynical. Yahweh's readiness to accept his servant Job's goodness may extend to this intruder as well. That possibility for delusion opens a door for critics who view the provocateur as the dark side of the deity! Has access to supreme power made it unnecessary for this god to develop cognitive faculties that would hold might in check? This question leaps to mind because Yahweh permits the adversary to create havoc in Job's serene existence.

Five scenes make up the drama. They alternate between earth and heaven, beginning below (1:1-5). We are first permitted to hear the narrator's voice, which shapes our opinion of Job as a good man deserving the very best. One almost reads the conjunction in the connected verb "and there were born to him" as the reward for his virtue. His life was just as complete as his character. He had seven sons and three daughters, both perfect numbers in biblical reckoning, as well as huge numbers of cattle and servants. Even in the area of property, the perfect numbers prevail (seven thousand sheep and three thousand camels, five hundred yoke of oxen and an equal number of asses). In fact, he is said to have been greater than anyone else in the east, just as Solomon was thought to have surpassed all others in wisdom.

Job's seven sons celebrated their birthdays, the probable meaning of *yom* in 1:4 and definitely its sense in 3:1, and invited their sisters. Into this happy setting of brothers and sisters eating and drinking together creeps a sinister note. It is signaled by the age-old struggle between the generations, as seen in a loving parent's anxiety. This is not the first episode where the revelry of the young troubled the parents. The Babylonian creation account "Enuma elish" tells of a clash between the gods and their children, but hardly one tempered with love like Job's action. Thinking his children may have sinned inadvertently and then cursed God, he offers atoning sacrifices for them all. The verb translated as cursing is a form of *barak*, "to bless," which seems to be used euphemistically in at least two of its seven appearances in the story (1:11 and 2:5); 1:5 and 2:9 can have the usual meaning "bless" (Linafelt 1996). The first scene ends with the observation that Job's protective conduct was habitual.

Scene two describes events in the celestial realm that will soon bring an end to Job's tranquility (1:6-12). While Job's children gathered to eat and drink, Elohim's children assembled in the divine council for the purpose of presenting themselves before Yahweh. Among them, only the provocateur is singled out and asked about his activity. Asked whence he came, he answers brusquely with a pun on his office (*haśśaṭan: miśśuṭ*), "Walking about on earth." Eager to have his own assessment of his servant Job confirmed from a knowledgeable source, Yahweh inquires whether Job had appeared on his radar screen.

This probing question first introduces the subservient relationship in which the exemplary Job found himself. He is a servant, a fact that puts the divine treatment of him in a special light, for masters had considerable

freedom over their property. At the same time, *'abdi* in this context is a badge
of honor, for Yahweh clearly takes pride in Job when repeating the exact
words of the narrator (1:8; cf. 1:1). The response is cynical beyond belief:
"For naught (*haḥinnam*) does Job fear Elohim?" Reminding Yahweh that he
has built a protective hedge around Job and his possessions, the adversary
challenges Yahweh to take away everything and see "if he doesn't curse you to
your face." The gauntlet has been thrown down and Yahweh takes it up. A
single condition is mandated: "Touch only what he owns." In other words,
leave Job unscathed. All heaven watches and awaits the outcome of this test.

The third scene takes place on earth, the place where the provocateur
had been roaming prior to his confrontation with Yahweh (1:13-21). It
opens with a false sense of security, Job's children eating and drinking in the
house of the oldest brother. Four messengers in succession arrive at Job's
doorstep with refrains that drone on like a funeral march. "I alone escaped to
tell you," and "while he was speaking, another messenger came and said."
Four decisive blows have struck against Job's protective hedge, two from
heaven and two by earthly powers. Sabeans stole Job's oxen and asses; divine
fire consumed the sheep; Chaldeans made off with the camels; and a mighty
wind felled the house on Job's children. Confronted with such colossal loss,
Job grieves outwardly but blesses Yahweh in unforgettable words: "Naked I
emerged from the womb and naked I'll return there; Yahweh has given and
Yahweh has taken. May Yahweh's name be blessed" (1:21). The *šamah*
("there") is no Freudian desire to return to the womb but a euphemism for
Sheol, the land of no return. Lest anyone miss the point of Job's response to
the loss of all his possessions, the narrator returns momentarily and under-
lines Job's integrity: "In all this Job didn't sin or attribute wrongdoing to
Elohim" (1:22).

The fourth scene (2:1-6) returns to heaven where one expects to see
rejoicing because of Job's confirmation of Yahweh's trust in him. Instead, we
learn of a second assembly of the celestial beings and of the adversary's presence again. Everything up to a point is déjà vu. The new twist in the
conversation between the provocateur and Yahweh is the statement that "Job
has held tightly to his integrity although you incited me to swallow him
without cause," an obvious echo of the key word in the adversary's initial
question about disinterested righteousness. Unpersuaded, he raises the stakes
even higher using what seems to be a proverbial saying about bartering:
"Skin for skin; a man will give all he has for his life" (2:4). In short, afflict
him with grievous pain and see if he won't curse you to your face. Again
Yahweh agrees to the test and again with one condition: "Only watch over

his life." The text is heavy with irony, a term for providential care being attributed to the one who is bent on destroying Job.

The second, third, and fourth scenes begin with the verb *wayehi* ("Now it was"); the fifth (2:7-10) opens with *wayyeṣeʾ* ("Now he went forth"). The haste with which the adversary strikes Job's body with loathsome sores from his head to the soles of the feet is remarkable. In his misery, Job sits on an ash heap and scrapes the sores with a broken shard. His wife chides him, partially quoting Yahweh. "Are you still holding on to your integrity? Curse Elohim and die" (2:9). The ambiguity of the verb *barak* in this instance makes it impossible to determine the intent. Bless Elohim and die victoriously, or curse Elohim and get relief through death. Job's response shows that he interpreted her words as wholly misplaced. "You're speaking like one of the foolish women. Shall we receive good from Elohim and not receive harm?" (2:10a). As if to soften the stinging remark, the narrator returns to repeat the judgment he had given in 1:22, only this time with a minor change. "In all this Job did not sin with his lips." Later rabbinic interpreters will not miss this chance to question Job's integrity, noting that his lips may have remained pure but not his heart.

With these five scenes, the stage has been set for yet another confrontation, this time a philosophical debate among friends. The transition to this new exploration of issues already brought to focus in the divine assembly is quite brief (2:11-13). It introduces three friends (*reʿim*) who learn about Job's troubles (*raʿah*) and come to console him. The two infinitives, *lanud ulenaḥamo* ("to console and comfort him") indicate rocking back and forth and easing another's grief respectively. On seeing him from afar, they could not recognize him, causing them to weep loudly. Tearing their robes and throwing dust heavenward, they sit with him in silence for seven days and seven nights, the specified period of mourning (Shiva) in Genesis 50:10 and 1 Samuel 31:13.

Who were Job's friends? The noun *reʿa* indicates an intimate, a companion from whom one accepts advice. The name of the first mentioned, Eliphaz, means "My god is fine gold." A certain Eliphaz is mentioned in Genesis 36:9, 10, 12, 15; he was Esau's oldest son, and Teman was his son (Gen 36:11, 15). Job's friend is said to have come from Teman, "the south land," in northern Edom. The second friend is Bildad ("Son of Hadad") from Shuah, a region in southern Transjordan associated with Dedan and Sheba (cf. Gen 25:2 for Shuah as the name of one born to Abraham by his concubine Keturah). Zophar, the name of the third friend, means "young bird." He hailed from Naamah, also familiar as a personal name for a female descendant of Cain (Gen 4:22) and an Ammonite princess whom Solomon married (1 Kgs 14:21). These three friends are said to have made a long and difficult journey for the purpose of bringing comfort to an anguished Job. Their behavior, although partly strange—throwing dust on their heads heavenward, perhaps as a magical protection of themselves—is proof of fidelity to a friend. Will they, like Job's god, prove unfaithful in the end?

On the surface, this simple folktale introduces us to a fictional character who believes he lives in a safe world governed by a benevolent ruler who oversees reward and retribution. This naïve view is demonstrably false, as we soon learn (Clines 1985). Yahweh is easily manipulated and seemingly lacks the wisdom to comprehend the consequences of entering into a game to determine who is the better judge of character, Yahweh or the provocateur. Both Job and Yahweh illustrate the difficulty between two generations, the one anxious lest his children sin inadvertently and the other blissfully unaware of division within offspring ("the sons of Elohim, *bene 'elohim*").

Even the narrator of this drama that takes place in two realms presents a picture of the hero that is just as ambiguous as the choice of the verb *barak*. Conceivably, all seven uses of this verb can have its usual meaning, "to bless." Even the hypothetical remarks by the adversary may be sarcastic ("if he won't *bless* you openly"), and the desperate advice by Job's wife may have been completely misunderstood by her distraught husband ("Bless Elohim, and die" *in peace*). In his second summation of events thus far, has the narrator undergone a change of heart, no longer believing in Job's integrity as before? The addition of "with his lips" makes us wonder.

The First Cycle of Debate

Job Curses the Day of his Birth (3:1-26)

What has happened in the seven days and seven nights while Job's three friends sit with him in silence, something that could change him from devout worshiper to defiant critic of his creator? The text of chapter 3 does not provide the slightest clue that would help readers understand the radical transformation signaled by his first spoken word after their arrival. That word, in English, "perish" or more graphically "damn," contrasts vividly with his earlier use of "blessed" with reference to the divine name (Fishbane).

We can speculate. Did Job's second thoughts about his sharp rebuke of his wife that placed her, in his opinion, alongside foolish women later strike him as both harsh and uncalled for, the unfortunate result of his failure to grasp the deep affection lying behind her suggestion of a way to find relief from suffering? And did self-loathing follow this reassessment of her advice and his response? Alternatively, did the absence of Job's relatives and local intimates begin to grate on him as he pondered the difficulties his fellow mourners must have endured during their long journey to the land of Uz from faraway places? Could his brothers and sisters not spare the time to console one who had become an outcast by dint of extreme misery mistakenly viewed as punishment for wrongdoing?

Perhaps the speculation thus far has been too limited, focusing on psychological and sociological factors, when the real source of Job's strident attack on his creator is religious (complaint against the gods was common in the ancient Near East; see Sitzler). Does Job not have a just cause for complaint—faithful service rewarded by total loss? Surely Job has the right to expect loyalty from God in return for exemplary worship. It may be, then, that Job has undergone a deep theological adjustment that will require him to rethink his understanding of religion itself. In chapter 3 Job begins this reorientation, one brought about by a disorientation that renders him unrecognizable to all who know him from the prose narrative in the first two chapters of the book. He will not complete this adjustment of his view about the relationship between morality and well-being until he has provoked a response from Yahweh, who will remain silent for what seems to Job an eternity.

At first blush, Job's outburst sounds remarkably similar to the laments giving the book of Psalms the "down-to-earth" character that appeals to countless Jews and Christians. With a single exception, Psalm 88, these complaints take a surprising turn, leaving the impression that God has heard the prayer of the supplicant and brought relief from whatever had troubled the speakers. No such shift occurs for the poet who composed the eighty-eighth psalm. Abandoned among the dead, afflicted by Yahweh, rejected by friends and neighbors, this psalmist cries out for relief but is met by divine fury. No wonder the poet inquires, "Why do you reject me, Yahweh; why hide your face from me?" (Ps 88:15).

Still, this psalm, for all its kinship with Job's initial outburst, lacks the distinctive feature of the third chapter in the book of Job. What is that? A death wish. But not the kind of desire expressed by a blind Samson condemned to do the work of animals, or even that joining Tobit and his relative Sarah who could no longer endure the shame they felt so acutely.

How did Job's wish differ from theirs? Precisely in this way: he wished never to have been born. There was an answer for the dejection that overwhelmed Samson, Tobit, and Sarah, one that the former availed himself of and the other two merely entertained. That answer was suicide. Job could not, by taking his own life, undo what had taken place years earlier. That is, he could not alter the past so as to blot out his own existence. His wish was therefore unfulfillable.

If chapter 3 is neither a lament nor an ordinary death wish, what is it? Nothing short of a plea that the creator reconfigure the original result of the primeval utterance, "Let there be . . ." so that the night Job was conceived and the day of his birth are forever missing. His reason is simple; had those two temporal possibilities not existed, there would have been no Job to experience the suffering that has made his life so vile. And, coincidentally, we readers would be robbed of a profound testimony to the power of honesty in all relationships, human and divine.

What form does Job's wish take? It consists of two parts, the second concluding with a brief description of the unenviable position he finds himself in because his wish cannot be granted. Part 1 has ten verses (3:1-10), and part 2 comprises sixteen verses (3:11-26). Verses 1-2 are an introduction in prose, and the last three verses make up Job's closing comment. The first and last words, *yo'bad* ("perish") and *rogez* ("turmoil"), establish the emotional tone of Job's complaint. He may not actually curse the deity to his face, to quote the exact language of the adversary, but Job comes perilously close to doing just that. His reason: a lingering fear that underneath all his prosperity there lurked its opposite, a dreaded calamity waiting to happen. A single word announces that he was right to fear a fundamental shaking of his being, a *rogez*.

The initiating word "perish" is punctiliar, amounting to "one and done" like defeated basketball teams in the NCAA tournament, whereas the final "trembling" in the participial form, from which the noun derives, indicates continuation, like time itself. Part 1 closes with the clause "And hide toilsome misery (*'amal*) from my eyes." Here the favorite noun in Ecclesiastes for loathsome existence functions as a surrogate for *rogez*, both nouns emphasizing cursed toil and agitation, the human condition according to Genesis 3.

How does Job reinforce the high emotional pitch of these words? By stressing darkness, like the mood it conveys. A pall hangs over part 1, with the light merely serving as contrast. In part 2, light is understood as an unwanted gift, one bestowed on people who are searching for the grave, or it is a quality denied stillbirths. This second section substitutes death for darkness, contrasting with the earlier allusions to birth. The themes, light and death, are associated with the verbs of anticipation in vv. 9 and 21 ("who hope for light in vain," 3:9ab; "those who await death in vain," 3:21a). This twofold use of the Hebrew particle denoting nonexistence, translated here with the English words "in vain," is ironic, for non-being is exactly what Job wants.

Job takes advantage of a rich vocabulary to indicate darkness. The words practically leap off his tongue, in English: "night," "darkness," "deep darkness," "cloudy pall," "blacken"(?), "gloom," possibly "hidden" and "grave," at least by inference. Neither the "twilight stars" nor "dawn's glimmering" of v. 9 offset the overwhelming sensation resulting from the verbal barrage of vocabulary for darkness.

Part 1 (3:1-10)

With vv. 1-2 the narrator reappears, but what he says suggests a change of heart since thrice insisting on Job's integrity and even attributing the same opinion to Yahweh. Breaking his seven-day silence, Job curses his day of birth, but not with the verb *barak* that does double duty in the previous chapters. Instead of using that verb to soften the shock, he opts for *qalal*, surprisingly so, for his emotional state would have been better served by a stronger verb for curse such as *'arur*. Why the verb *qalal*? Perhaps to indicate the lowest possible esteem, a lightness bordering on nothingness. Job wants the day of his birth to vanish, floating into the desert like air itself.

With the words "his day" the narrator announces the theme of the first major section. The poet realizes that conception occurred months earlier, making Job's birth possible, and therefore the curse falls on it as well as on the birth day. "Perish the day on which I was born and the night someone said, 'A boy has been conceived'" (1:3). Is the indefinite "someone" (masculine) a reference to his father? After all, no one but father and mother would know that on a given night they had intercourse. No one, that is, except night, here personified. Or do the demands of parallelism explain the introduction of "night" into Job's curse? The three references to night and four to day add up to seven, a perfect number, according to ancient reckoning. The poet thus has Job curse his conception and birth as fully as if he had used an acrostic, an alphabetic poem amounting to our "From A to Z." These questions may be unanswerable, but the announcement that a boy has been conceived reflects the ancient sociological environment in which boys were preferred to girls, even if in this instance the mention of a girl's having been conceived would not fit the situation.

The poet's imagination reaches farther back into Canaanite tradition when recalling professionals who cast spells on Yam and Leviathan (v. 8). These mythic monsters, Sea and Twisting Serpent, symbolized chaos, the uncontrollable elements of creation that had to be contained for an orderly society to exist. When referring to the mighty Yam, Job actually uses the Hebrew verb ʾarar in its participial form, reinforcing it with another verb for cursing, qabab.

For whose ears were Job's strong words intended? Whom did he expect to carry out his curse? Only once does he mention the deity in this initial damning of day and night: "May Eloah not search for it from above" (v. 4). The preferred names for the divine in the prose frame of the entire book are Yahweh and the generic Elohim (one time only, 2:10). Curiously, the divine name Yahweh occurs only once in the poetic sections of Job 3–42:6 ("Among all these, who hasn't known that Yahweh's hand has done this?" (12:9).

Why the shift in nomenclature? The reluctance to place the sacred name YHWH in the mouths of non-Israelites elsewhere in the Hebrew Bible may be the reason Job uses Eloah, for he is apparently considered an Edomite, but it cannot explain Elihu's avoidance of the Tetragrammaton in chapters 32–37, for his lineage places him in the camp of the chosen people who believed the name Yahweh had been disclosed to them alone. The author of the poetic sections of the book of Job appears to have belonged to a group of sages who preferred the generic El and Elohim, as demonstrated in Proverbs 10–31 and Ecclesiastes. To these common designations for deity in the ancient Near East they added Shaddai and Eloah. Presumably, their use of general designations for deity, or deities, derived from wisdom's internationalism.

Why is Job so eager to damn his birthday? He answers this question in v. 10: "For it didn't shut the doors of my womb and hide misery from my eyes." He has done more than claim his mother's womb as his own; he has doomed her to perpetual pregnancy, permanently closing her womb, should his curse become effective. This gross idea also finds expression in a curse placed on the lips of the prophet Jeremiah. He, too, cursed (ʾarur) the day he was born, along with the man who brought the glad news to his father that a boy (ben zakar) was born (Jer 20:14-15). Jeremiah's fury is directed toward the messenger, but for the bizarre reason that the man did not murder him in the womb, transforming Jeremiah's mother into his grave, a permanently full womb (Jer 20:17).

Here, too, the Hebrew noun ʿamal ("misery") characterizes the emotional state of the one expressing such a terrible idea, but two additional nouns, "woe" and "shame," mark Jeremiah's days. In a culture where honor and shame determine one's standing in society, Jeremiah's closing assessment of his life as bošet ("shame") corresponds to Job's rogez ("trembling"), for both nouns indicate a shaking of the foundation equivalent to an earthquake.

The two curses, Job's and Jeremiah's, are similar in ways other than shared vocabulary. How so? Jeremiah also reaches back into mythic lore to articulate his animosity toward the well-intentioned conveyor of news about a successful birth. The fate of the doomed cities of Sodom and Gomorrah is wished upon this messenger, and, as if certain destruction is insufficient punishment, Jeremiah condemns him to hear the terrifying shout of battle in the mornings and also at midday. The prophet's use of Yahweh in connection with the doomed cities instead of the usual Elohim draws attention to the negated verb for compassion (*naham*) that occurs in v. 16 (cf. Amos 4:11 where Yahweh as speaker and destroyer attributes the destruction of Sodom and Gomorrah to Elohim).

Part 2 (3:11-26)

The second strophe of Job's initial curse consists of two sections, each introduced by the interrogative particle *lamah* ("Why?"), and a concluding rationale for his emotional outburst (vv. 11-19, 20-23, 24-26). Both of these interrogative units are linked with the causal clause with which the first major section, 3:1-10, ends ("Because you didn't close the doors of my womb, didn't conceal toilsome trouble from my eyes"). The first "Why" asks the fundamental question; how did I emerge from the womb alive? (v. 11). The formulation, however, stresses Job's wish that he had died at that precise moment. In the second section, vv. 20-24, the interrogative "why" of v. 20 picks up the reference to toilsome trouble in v. 10 while v. 23 repeats the verb "to hide" (*satar*) from v. 10. In this way, the poet conveys continuity despite Job's shift from the imagery concerning day and night to focus on the opposites, birth and death.

The theme of the section beginning with v. 11 is rest, a repose from which one does not rise. Job complains that he wasn't fortunate enough to die at birth or to have been a stillbirth. Instead, knees awaited him, as a temporary bed, and breasts supplied nourishment. Here the image of utmost intimacy is transformed into something undesirable, and the thought about an infant nursing at the mother's breast leads smoothly to a rest that was believed to have been, with a rare exception, undisturbed. I refer to the long slumber in Sheol, from which in biblical tradition Samuel alone was awakened, in this case by a woman from Endor. Verse 13 heaps up verbs for sleeping: "For then I would have lain down, would be quiet; I would sleep, then have rest."

Having described in this way his condition if he had actually expired at birth or earlier, Job now concentrates on the elite company he would be keeping in Sheol: kings and the land's counselors, princes also. Moreover, these companions have made a name for themselves by rebuilding ruins and by accumulating a fortune in gold and silver. How differently Job views residence in Sheol from the psalmist who complains about the absence of adoration for Yahweh in that shadowy land.

With v. 16 Job hazards a second possibility. "Why wasn't I a stillbirth, an infant who never looked on light?" Perhaps the remarks about vast wealth triggered in his imagination the necessity to hide silver and gold from potential thieves, and this momentary image reminded him of something else that was quickly hidden, an aborted birth. This departure from his reflection about Sheol derails him only seconds, for his thoughts quickly rush back to the place he thinks would offer repose to the one who has departed this world.

How does he conceive of that land once he moves beyond the elitism of vv. 14-15? Now Job emphasizes Sheol's universality by rhetorical merisms: the wicked and the oppressed, small and great, servant and master. Here, however, there is a decisive difference from reality on earth. The wicked cease generating turmoil (*rogez*), those whose energy is spent, the bone tired, find rest, prisoners can no longer hear an authoritative command, and servants are emancipated.

In the second unit that is inaugurated by the interrogative "why?" Job turns against the deity for bestowing life on those whom circumstances have made bitter. To such persons, light is not sweet, as in Ecclesiastes; neither is life. Their only source of joy comes when they discover death, for which they have searched diligently, digging for it in the same way one hunts for treasure. Job's association of the grave and hidden treasure makes sense in the larger cultural environment where kings were entombed along with vast hoards of wealth. Even curses aimed at robbers of graves and written prominently on tombstones failed to prevent unwanted disturbance of resting places and theft of their contents. Such warnings went largely unheeded because few people could read, especially in Egypt and Mesopotamia where the scripts required years to master.

The expression of utter perplexity with which Job terminates his imaginative flight into Sheol and contemplation of its inhabitants gives way to a pained description of a lost soul who must eat his food while being consumed by grief. What has set into motion his present state? A hidden fear that something terrible might happen to him: "For I dreaded a dread and it came upon me" (v. 25a). Has Job harbored a fear in such a way that it negated his trust in divine solicitude?

When one looks at the development in vv. 11-19 and 20-23, the shift from Job as center of attention to the deity, who is called Eloah, stands out. It is as if Job has finally gathered enough courage to blame the actual source of his misery. Even in the second section introduced by "why?" (vv. 20-23), Job seems reluctant to place the blame where he thinks it belongs, for he leaves the subject of the verb "to give" in v. 20 unspecified. ("Why does he give . . . ?") That does not change until v. 23, when Job finally identifies God as the one whose conduct is under indictment. Having done so, however, Job does not tarry with thoughts about Eloah but remains the center of attention in the concluding verses where he emphasizes the physical effects of his misery.

This attention to corporeality marks the entire curse (see the brilliant analysis of imagery for the body by Koosed). Job's extreme pain reaches beyond the physical, penetrating into the depths of his psyche. His language therefore accentuates this reality by focusing on various parts of the body. He mentions knees, breasts, eyes, belly, womb, and eyelids (in a metaphorical sense indicating dawn's first glimmerings). In addition, he uses language about sounds produced by the body such as harsh commands barked out by slave owners and groanings resulting from misery. Job also refers to bitterness and to tears that are so abundant they resemble water, as well as the opposite emotion, singing and rejoicing. Even hope, planted somewhere deep within the psyche, does not escape his interest, although Job thinks it unfounded. Instead of finding rest and quiet, the body only experiences turmoil.

How does Job conclude his curse? He picks up two verbs expressing quiet rest in v. 13 and adds a third, negating all three. The comforting image of an infant nursing at its mother's breast, which Job has emptied of its beauty, ultimately gives way to the absence of rest. In the end, turmoil (*rogez*) prevails, as its final position implies.

Links with the Prose Narrative

Is there anything besides the Janus-like "afterwards" in the prosaic introduction to Job's curse that links his powerful curse to the story in chapters 1–2? One can answer on two different levels, one semantic, the other thematic. First, we turn to semantic affinities. In the folktale, the adversary accuses Yahweh of building a protective wall around his servant Job, hedging him in so that no harm can come his way. One thinks of the rabbinic concept of building a fence around Torah, a wall that protects both the divine word and the interpreter of that revelation. In short, by adding prescriptions at crucial junctures, redactors have made it more difficult to violate a given prohibition. For instance, Eve's addition of "You must not touch it" to God's prohibition against eating fruit from the tree in the midst of the garden of Eden amounts to a hedge planted around Torah.

For Job, however, the deity has barricaded a miserable hero (*geber*) who is groping to find a hidden way. Use of the same noun for "a male" that the messenger employs when announcing Job's conception links him with the vagabonds in Sheol described in vv. 20-23. Hence the natural shift in the next three verses to Job's personal time has made a difference; bread, not breast milk, is his food. The verb for enclosing occurs in 1:10 and 3:23, although in the later text Job does not view Eloah's hedge around a man as an indication of favor. Instead, he places this idea of a hedge in parallelism with someone's path being hidden.

Another connection between the prose framework and chapter 3 is the adverb *šam*, "there." Job's response to the first blow wielded by the adversary evokes the pious expression of trust: "Naked I came from my mother's womb and naked I shall return there; blessed be Yahweh's name" (1:21). This notion has nothing to do with a Freudian understanding of the womb but derives from the ancient euphemism for the grave. Rather than explicitly mentioning the underworld, one could simply refer to it as "*there*." Job's use of *beten* ("womb") in 1:21 anticipates its occurrence in 3:11, where it is parallel to another word for womb, *reḥem*.

Job's curse is aimed at his birthday (*yomo*). The story informs readers that his seven sons threw parties, each on his day (*yomo*). While it is possible to understand the noun to indicate an unending round of festivity, the restricted sense in 3:1, which is required by the specific reference to the day of Job's birth, seems to favor a similar interpretation in 1:4. On this reading, the brothers gave seven birthday parties in a year, to which they invited their sisters in a magnanimous act.

What about a continuity of ideas? In the story, Job is troubled by the possibility that his children may have sinned in the exact way the adversary thinks Job will go astray, that is, by cursing Yahweh. Just in case they have erred, even in ignorance, Job offers a regular sacrifice. In doing so, he behaves in a priestly manner before the levitical system was put into place. This secret fear is not unlike the hidden dread that Job thinks has materialized in 3:25.

Job has begun the debate with his friends in the form of a monologue. He will end it the same way, for he eventually becomes convinced that they have nothing worthwhile to say. Whereas his first monologue was about his birth, the last one contrasts his previous happiness with his present misery (chs. 29–30). Abandoned by his friends and God, Job has become a loner, "naked" in body and spirit. If his famous oath of innocence (ch. 31) inaugurates dialogue once more, now between Job and God, Job has risen above his earlier monologue and is ready for the struggle of his life. For now, however, he will argue with his three friends.

Eliphaz's Initial Speech (4:1–5:27)

Job's friend Eliphaz has difficulty hiding his shock over the tenor of the curse on the lips of one he takes to be undergoing divine chastisement. His earlier dismay at the extent of Job's misery is now matched by his surprise at the bitterness of his friend's outburst. Eliphaz therefore tries to combat emotion with cold reason, a sharp contrast with the profound empathy both he and his two friends exhibited for seven days and seven nights, according to the narrator. Their journey from afar had a single goal: to comfort Job in his distress. His vehemence underscores their failure; silence on their part gave Job time to become more and more agitated. From now until the friends disappear from the story line, speech will prevail.

But what kind of speech? Dialogue or debate? If the former, one expects the individuals engaged in dialogue to respond to one another and to advance toward further insight on the basis of commonly shared views. That is not what happens in the exchanges between Job and his three friends, for they often talk past one another, ignoring fundamental arguments and remaining silent about controversial claims. Once Eliphaz and his two friends are reduced to silence, a series of three monologues follows. The first is by Job, the second by a new figure called Elihu, and the third by Yahweh. Both Elihu and Yahweh invite Job to answer, but at best he manages a few words in response to the deity while refusing to dignify Elihu's remarks by responding.

If the speeches make up a debate, we look for sustained argument supporting a particular view, presumably marshalling evidence that carries persuasive force. That happens to some degree. The three friends argue that the world is under providential rule, hence virtue is rewarded and sin punished. Job naturally rejects their understanding of things, for it indicts him as guilty of major transgressions. Elihu's perspective resembles that of the three friends, while Yahweh's perception of reality removes human beings from the central position in the universe, making the issue of undeserved suffering of little consequence.

It seems better, therefore, to call the exchanges between Job and others a dispute, perhaps even a philosophical disputation. The disputants discuss matters on which reasonable people disagree, appealing to warrants they believe to be valid. What exactly do they debate? Scholars have answered this question in three ways: (1) the correct way to talk about God; (2) the existence of innocent suffering; and (3) the possibility that someone will serve God without thinking about either a reward for faithful devotion or punishment for its opposite.

Perhaps the participants in the debate understand the topic under discussion differently. Yahweh's reprimand of Job's three friends identifies the problem as the correct way of speaking about deity, while the adversary in the prologue introduces the contested issue as one of disinterested righteousness, and the three friends think what divides them from Job is whether or not innocent suffering occurs. Because of these fundamental differences, the disputants never come to a meeting of minds.

Eliphaz's initial speech, the longest of the friends' remarks, gives the main arguments in defense of divine justice that will be repeated in all of the friends' speeches. In short, no human being is righteous, the principle of retribution is operative in society, and the exalted God rescues repentant sinners from harm. Eliphaz, not Job, first raises the issue of theodicy. In his view, God's justice cannot be faulted, even if that viewpoint condemns Job as a heinous sinner.

For convenience, Eliphaz's speech can be divided into seven units: (1) 4:1-6; (2) 4:7-11; (3) 4:12-17; (4) 4:18-21; (5) 5:1-7; (6) 5:8-16; and (7) 5:17-27. It has been argued that 4:6 and 5:8 are nodal sentences, the first referencing Job's piety as his basis for hope and the second urging him to seek El in order to argue his case directly (Clines 1992). The two, one a rhetorical question, the other a suggestion, are at odds with one another. If Job is genuinely religious, which is the real sense of the expression "fear of God," and a person of integrity, implied by the adjective *tam* in the parallel stich, he should not be under such duress, according to Eliphaz's concept of divine justice. Either his confidence, grounded in hope, is misplaced or he is guilty of hypocrisy. The latter of these two is the conclusion to which Eliphaz will soon come. In such a state, seeking El as a supreme liturgical act will bring no relief. For that desired result, genuine repentance is necessary.

Words Aimed at Comforting Job (4:1-6)

The narrator's introduction of Eliphaz's first speech implies that Job's curse has launched the debate. In his dispute with the three friends, Job has the first and last words, to some degree leveling the odds created by pitting three against one. The central theme of this brief unit is "falling," a metaphor for Job's precarious situation. One who has previously enjoyed a position of strength now finds himself in need of assistance. Hence the tentative manner in which Eliphaz opens his remarks, the testing of a proper response that will not weary Job even more. Still, Eliphaz admits that he cannot restrain himself, even if the effect is disturbing to his friend.

Job's track record as comforter has left a positive impression on Eliphaz, who reminds Job that his words have prevented the frail from stumbling. The rhetorical ABA'B' structure of Eliphaz's praise in vv. 3 and 4 isolates four acts of kindness. Job's words have instructed the aged, or many, which is another meaning of *rabbim*, and they have lifted those who were falling. In addition, he has strengthened weak hands and braced unsteady knees. The rare *millah* (*milleka*, "your words") accurately reflects the distancing of the language of the book from ordinary usage, where *dabar* is preferred. Of the thirty-eight occurrences of *millah* in the Hebrew Bible, thirty-four are in the book of Job.

Finding himself in the situation of the weak, Job is exhausted and frightened. Why should that surprise Eliphaz? Has he been protected from all adversity, never having the threat of extreme sickness that turns one inward and isolates the hurting individual because of its potential to kill (see Crenshaw 1993)?

In describing Job's present condition, Eliphaz does not specify what has touched Job, which he conceals in the indefinite "it" ("But now it comes to you and you're weary; it touches you, and you're scared," v. 5). This extraordinary reticence on Eliphaz's part will be shared by Bildad and Zophar. None of them will ever give incontrovertible evidence that they know about the death of Job's children, unless Bildad's remark in 8:4 is not a hypothetical set piece about sin and its inevitable consequences ("If your sons sinned against him, he dispatched them into the power of their rebellion").

The Short Life of the Wicked (4:7-11)

The theme word perish (*'bd*) punctuates this whole unit. Its three occurrences in vv. 7, 9, and 11 are reinforced by verbs indicating destruction and dispersal. Eliphaz begins by trying to get Job to accept the axiom that justice always prevails, a point he can concede only by admitting his own guilt. Eliphaz appeals to Job's repository of knowledge acquired through experience. That is the function of the imperative "Remember." Job is asked to combine his experience with that of Eliphaz and to confirm the comforting proverb, at least to some, that "we reap what we sow." In this world of fantasy, which Eliphaz believes accords with what he has seen, innocent people don't perish. One can read this observation as moderately encouraging to Job. In a word, it could mean that adversity may strike, but in the end the sufferer will emerge safely. The two illustrations from agriculture and the animal kingdom suggest a different interpretation of what Eliphaz has said.

The first argument employs a proverb that mixes the literal with the metaphorical: "As I have seen, those who plow iniquity and sow trouble harvest it" (v. 8). Everyone was familiar with the activity referred to by the participles, but the usual objects of plowing and sowing are field and seed. Eliphaz replaces them with nouns indicating waywardness and strife. The second of these, *'amal*, is the word Job used with reference to trouble that should have been hidden from his sight (3:10). For Job, this word has the nuance of misery, like the stronger *rogez* that concludes his curse.

Eliphaz's use of the axiom from agriculture to demonstrate the misfortune that befalls sinners indicates a measure of cruelty, if he knows how Job's children died. The anthropomorphic language, or better zoomorphic, describes Eloah as a furious deity whose breath has the capacity of a dragon's fire, killing those who have angered him. The reader knows that the reference to a destructive wind in this context of punishing sinners indicts Job's dead children and serves as a warning to him.

When Eliphaz moves to discuss the realm of wild beasts, images of negated power prevail. He reasons that a lion may roar but its teeth will be broken, rendering it incapable of catching prey. The inevitable result will be death for the lion and the scattering of its young. If the object lesson is applied to Job's situation, it has things reversed, for Job has survived so far but his offspring are dead.

A Disturbing Dream (4:12-17)

In defense of his interpretation of reality, Eliphaz has already shown himself to be a learned sage by appealing to personal experience and to the natural order of things. Now he dons the mantel of prophet and reports that he has received a private message from a ghostlike visitor during the night. This extraordinary narrative combines vision and audition, and everything leads up to a moment of revelation. The entire episode, filled with mystery and dread, is replete with the language of the numinous: stolen, whisper, troubled visions during the night, deep sleep, dread, trembling bones, a breeze across the face, shivering flesh or bristling hair, an unrecognizable form at rest, and an eerie silence followed by a voice.

The revelatory word matches the mysterious buildup: "Can a person be more righteous than Eloah; can a man be purer than his maker?" This translation is the usual way of rendering a verb that is followed by the preposition *min* ("from"). Such an expression has a comparative sense "more than," which some modern interpreters reject as unsuitable to the context. It is the preferred reading in the King James Version and in the New International Version. In my view, it states precisely the problem that will soon rise to prominence, forcing Job and his friends to make extreme claims and ultimately prompting Yahweh to rebuke Job for exalting himself at the deity's expense.

The choice of the verb "stolen" suggests that Eliphaz recognizes his argument for what it is. He lets revelation enter sapiential discourse through a back door. Remarkably, he admits to hearing only a tiny sliver, a hint, of the revelatory word, just as the prophetic or priestly oracular formula *ne'um* YHWH originally denoted a message secretly conveyed like a divine whisper. Part of his problem derives from the context, a dream oracle, for which parallels exist in the ancient Near East. Eliphaz has been overcome by deep sleep, a stupor resulting from disturbing thoughts. The noun *tardemah* refers to heavy sleep such as that overtaking Adam before the divine surgical procedure that yielded Eve in the mythical account of the first couple, and the patriarch Abraham prior to the mysterious ceremony of covenant making that is recounted in Genesis 15:7-21. Its use in Proverbs 19:15 for sleep brought on by laziness removes the word from exclusively numinous contexts. Use of the verb *rdm* in the story about Jonah's undisturbed sleep during a horrific storm at sea may be understood either way but probably comes closer to the examples from Genesis than the one from Proverbs.

If *tardemah* seems to preserve an echo of the primeval history and patriarchal narrative, the words *marehu* ("its appearance") and *temunah* ("form") have a vague similarity with the description of Moses' unique relationship with Yahweh in Numbers 12:8, and *demama* recalls the silence that followed the mighty wind, earthquake, and fire in the theophany to Elijah recorded in 1 Kings 19:11-12. The language is too common, however, to imply that the poet wished to show that the Temanite knew biblical tradition. The essential point is that Eliphaz failed to recognize this nocturnal visitor even when it stood before him. In this experience, hearing is more important than seeing. Yet when Job finally confronts Yahweh face to face in 42:5, sight either reinforces or contradicts sound. The ambiguity of the *waw* particle makes it impossible to choose one reading over the other, "and" or "but."

What does the revelation convey to Eliphaz? If the language is forensic, the issue is innocence in a court of law. That is the judicial sense of the verb *ṣdq*; its opposite is *rš'* ("guilty"). If the verbal use of *ṣdq* refers to morality, the emphasis is rather on comparative virtue. In this oracle the parallel term comes from the area of ritual and carries the meaning of purity. Using the two terms *'enoš* and *geber*, the message contrasts mortals with Eloah, their maker. The reference to humans is general; Eliphaz must apply it to a specific case. Its principle leads him and his two friends to a view of mortals as loathsome when compared to the deity.

Was Eliphaz's dream the result of incubation, the intentional sleeping at a holy place with a dream oracle in mind? Nothing in the report indicates that he took the initiative. The initial position of the personal reference *we'elai* ("and to me") and the noun *dabar* ("a word") before the verb *yegunnab*, a passive form of "to steal," emphasizes its personal nature. The use of *lqḥ*, a verb for the acquisition of knowledge, stresses his receptivity.

The Meaning of the Dream (4:18-21)

The actual extent of the revelatory word is unclear; these four verses may continue it, offering the visitor's explanatory comment on the rhetorical question. Alternatively, they may be Eliphaz's interpretation of what he has heard. Either way, the contrast between God and not God is stark. Eliphaz seems not to recognize the delicious irony of the first "if clause." "If he cannot trust his servants" assumes new light when one thinks of the adversary in the prologue, whose loyalty is questionable. The second half of this clause is complicated because of the rare word *taholah*, but context seems to require something like "guilt." Even divine messengers are culpable in God's eyes, it seems to say. The reasoning is from the greater to the lesser. If divine appointees are flawed, how much more clay houses with foundations of dust are crushed before moths. The image, although striking, is ambiguous. Does it stress the unstable condition of mortals who in mythic lore were shaped from dust, or does it refer to the destructive work of moths on the peculiar mix from which houses in ancient Israel were constructed?

Fashioned by their creator in one day between evening and morning, these creatures are crushed in the same span of time, perishing unnoticed. The concluding rhetorical question functions as a statement: "Their tent cord is pulled up, and they die without wisdom." The theme word "perish" in vv. 7-11 returns here with considerable force, but now it applies to everyone, not just to the guilty. The final *welo' beḥokmah* ("and not by wisdom") emphasizes its universality. Is the irrational quality of human mortality the point? Or does this rhetorical question, which matches the revelatory disclosure in v. 17, emphasize the human incapacity to discover either the time of or the reason for death?

Is the Oracle a Misplaced Speech by Job?

It has been argued that the dream oracle originally concluded Job's curse of his birthday in chapter 3 (Greenstein). In this view, the shaking of Job's inner being led to a special disclosure from above. This theory of textual dislocation is not supported by any manuscript and rests largely on three things: (1) the dissonance between the content of the revelatory discourse and the remainder of Eliphaz's speeches; (2) Job's accusation in 7:14 that God scares him with dreams and visions, and the friends' attribution of its main views to Job; and (3) Eliphaz's failure to appeal to the authority of revelation when it would presumably have been a stronger argument than the appeal to ancestral teaching that he chose to use.

If Eliphaz were consistent in what he said throughout his three speeches, the argument from dissonance would carry more force. The difficulty of determining actual quotations in ancient texts that employ few indicators for such use of others' words makes that argument tenuous at best. The appeal to ancestral teaching as the ultimate source of authority may imply that claims to private revelation did not carry as much weight as the accumulated wisdom of the past.

The history of prophecy in ancient Israel illustrates the difficulty inherent to this mode of revelation (Crenshaw 1971). It was always impossible to judge the authenticity of a prophetic word, for opposing claims in the name of the same deity, as illustrated by the confrontation between Jeremiah and Hananiah, left the people without a means of choosing one over the other. The various attempts to offer criteria for distinguishing true from false prophecy failed in the end. This flaw in the prophetic phenomenon may have been a significant factor contributing to the demise of prophecy. The sages who represented a quite different approach to knowledge would have been aware of this weakness in every appeal to revelation. That suspicion may explain Eliphaz's choice of ancestral teaching as his final authority.

Life Has Its Problems (5:1-7)

Still, it does seem that the oracle and its interpretation interrupt the natural flow of Eliphaz's speech. The illustration of arrogance being brought low leads easily to the description of the unhappy existence into which mortals are born. Exasperated at Job's extreme language, Eliphaz rebukes him sternly: "Call now; will anyone answer you? To whom among the holy ones will you turn?" In his thinking, Job has endangered his chance for a favorable appeal to the heavenly patron. The underlying notion here is that individuals had a patron deity among the lower hierarchy of gods who would intercede on behalf of them. Angering these intermediaries therefore lessened the likelihood of recovery from sickness or distress of any kind (Jacobsen).

To support his assessment of Job's peril, Eliphaz quotes what seems to be a proverb: "For vexation kills a fool and zeal slays a simpleton." Job has strayed far from the sages' ideal of emotional tranquility, having lost self-control and given in to rash speech. The angry outburst on Job's part has convinced Eliphaz that Job has abandoned the camp of the wise and moved dangerously close to that of fools.

The following three verses comprise traditional teaching about the destiny of sinners. As in the case of his citation of a proverb from agriculture in 4:8, Eliphaz again adds his weight to a traditional saying. He claims to have witnessed an instance of a sinner taking root in apparent defiance of what is supposed to happen, prompting in Eliphaz an abrupt curse of the wrongdoer's dwelling. The rest of the scene goes according to expectation. His children, far from safety, are crushed in the gate without anyone to rescue them, the hungry devour their harvest, carrying it off in baskets, and the thirsty deplete their wealth. The extra stich in v. 5 about the mode of conveying the harvest may be an editorial addition.

Once again, if Eliphaz knows about Job's children, the remarks are grossly insensitive as well as inaccurate. The location of their trouble is the city gate, which could either refer to a judicial decision that resulted in execution or to military conquest. In the latter case, the noun "gate" functions as a general term for wholesale slaughter by invading soldiers. The haunting expression "with none to deliver" is a set phrase for hopelessness. A variant, "with none to help her," occurs in Lamentations 1:7, and "with none to comfort them" is in Ecclesiastes 4:1 two times. "With none to comfort her" is used in Lamentations 1:2, 9, and 17.

In vv. 6 and 7, Eliphaz's fondness for aphorisms produces a memorable description of the source of evil. "For evil doesn't go forth from the dust nor does trouble sprout in the ground, but a mortal is born to trouble and Reseph's children fly upward." The two words in v. 6, *'awen* ("iniquity") and *'amal* ("trouble, toil"), are precisely those used by Eliphaz in the agricultural proverb about plowing and sowing (4:8). His point seems to be that iniquity and trouble do not come from the natural world but are generated by humans, indeed belong to the essence of humankind. Reseph, the Canaanite god of pestilence and plague, is used here as an illustration of inevitability. Sparks fly upward, according to their nature. People are born to trouble, for that is the human condition. There is a subtle difference here from the account in Genesis, which implies that a sinful condition is the consequence of choice and not the natural state. The word for a person is *ʾadam* rather than *ʾenoš* or *geber* as in the revelatory message of 4:17. The cluster of words in vv. 6 and 7 recalls their use in Genesis 3:17-19, where *ʾadam, ʾapar, ṣemaḥ,* and *ʾadamah* also occur.

God Is the Solution (5:8-16)

Trouble may well be the human condition, but what should Job do? Grin and bear it? That is not what Eliphaz recommends, for he thinks an escape mechanism has been provided. One can turn to God for relief from the misery that has come to plague existence. Therefore Eliphaz urges Job to seek this remedy. "But for me, I would seek El and make my case before Elohim." In only one other place in the book of Job do El and Elohim occur in parallel stichs, and that is in Zophar's concluding statement concerning the fate of a wicked person in 20:29 ("This is the portion of a wicked man [*ʾadam rašaʿ*] from Elohim, his inheritance ordained by El"). It is not clear whether Eliphaz encourages Job to enter into a lawsuit with Elohim or to confess his sins as a repentant, but given what follows the latter is more likely.

In vv. 9-16 we find the first of several hymns. It praises Elohim for the extraordinary works that exceed the grasp of the intellect (5:9-16). The opening verse sets the tone: "Who does great things, unsearchable, wonders beyond numbering." This dispenser of wonders too mysterious to comprehend is active both in nature and in society; he gives rain in fields and streets, but also controls human destinies in other ways than supplying essential water. This majestic deity maintains order in society, exalting those who have despaired, frustrating the schemes of the clever, trapping them in their conceit, so their advice quickly goes awry. For them, daytime is dark, and at noon they feel around as at night. The needy, however, he delivers from the sword and from the power of the strong. The object of divine solicitude appears last in the verse: *ʿebyon* ("the needy"). As a result of Elohim's assistance, the poor have hope and the one seeking to harm them is stopped in his tracks.

The variation in the participles within the hymn is noteworthy. Beginning with the usual participle in such texts (*ʿośeh*, "the one who does"), the hymn quickly shifts to an articular participle (*hannoten*, "*the* one who gives") in parallelism with a participle without an article (*šoleaḥ*, "one sending"), then it substitutes an infinitive (*laśum*, "to set") followed by two participles without articles (*meper*, "one frustrating"; *loked*, "one taking"). Such variety in grammatical forms matches the richness of the deeds ascribed to God. The verse that paves the way for the hymn is equally striking; eight of its nine words begin with the Hebrew letter *'alep*.

Divine Favor (5:17-27)

Having established an appropriate context for Job's expected repentance, Eliphaz now paints a rosy picture of the state of one who accepts divine correction, as in Proverbs 3:11-12 and Psalm 38 (cf. Heb 12:5-11). The operative word is *'ašre*, "happy" ("See, happy is the man whom Eloah instructs; don't reject Shaddai's discipline," v. 17). The divine name Shaddai occurs nearly twice as many times in the book of Job as elsewhere in the entire Hebrew Bible (31 times in Job, 17 times elsewhere). Eliphaz appeals to traditional understanding of the deity as both afflicter and healer as stated in Deuteronomy 22:39 and Isaiah 45:7, but in doing so he employs a numerical saying that departs from reality if applied to Job. The one who wounds and heals has definitely not kept harm from Job ("He'll rescue you from six adversities, and in seven harm won't touch you," v. 19). It seems that the poet uses a standard observation about divine protection and does not change it to fit the situation. Numerical sayings served to emphasize the whole scope of something; sometimes the items enumerated match the numbers, but at other times they do not (contrast Prov 30:18-20 with Amos 1:3, 6, 9, 11, 13; 2:1, 4, 6). Precisely how many dangers are mentioned in this instance is a matter of debate. Death (during famine), the sword (in battle), slander, calamity, starvation, wild beasts, and fear itself will have no power over him, according to Eliphaz's positive spin.

In this idyllic world, the curse of Genesis 3:17b-18 has been revoked, at least for the one basking in divine favor. Even wild animals pose no threat, and the rocks are in league with the repentant one. At peace in his tent, Job will visit his wife, who will successfully bear offspring like the grass. The reference to grass probably suggests vigor and growth. In divine promises to Abraham, the images of sand on the seashore and stars in the sky symbolize the vast number of descendants the patriarch will have. Content with children around him, Job will come to his grave at the appropriate time, like grain at harvest.

This utopian vision rivals those preserved in Leviticus 26:3-13 and Deuteronomy 28:1-14, but also biblical prophecy that envisions a world where war no longer exists and nature freely pours out its bounty for God's people who dwell securely under their vine and fig tree. (The articles in Ben Zvi cover a wide range of topics related to grand visions of a different world from the present one.) In Eliphaz's vision of a better day, there is no mention of a messiah, unlike the hope expressed by Isaiah and endorsed later at Qumran and in the New Testament.

Eliphaz concludes his opening address with an attempt to draw his two companions into the testimonial about the accuracy of what he has already said. He claims that they have thoroughly investigated the matter (*haqer-nuha*, "We've searched it out") and determined its veracity (*ken hi*ʾ, "It is true"). That being so, he adds, you must accept it as reliable. Such an argument leaves Job no wiggle room. He must, according to Eliphaz, either acknowledge the truth of what he has heard from his friend, or he can deny what the three friends have found to be accurate, if Eliphaz has correctly reported the opinions of the two friends who have to this point remained silent.

Job's Response to Eliphaz (6:1–7:21)

Stung by remarks that he takes to be personal attacks, Job responds in highly emotional language and disconnected images resembling stream of consciousness. The abrupt shift from one image to another matches his rolling and tossing during the night. His loss of equanimity appears to confirm the friends' growing suspicion that he is hardly the good person they thought he was. It seems advisable, therefore, to leave his presence.

Recognizing their intention, Job begs them to stay and look him in the face. Although they stick around, Job begins to address the deity directly, for the first time raising the issue of justice but also pressing beyond justice to forgiveness. Job argues that he is inconsequential in the grand scheme of things and will soon disappear like a cloud. Why then, he asks, not pardon me of any unintentional offenses? In his mind, willful sins are out of the question; he has committed none.

The Scope of Job's Misery (6:1-7)

The pressing weight of Job's misery gets him to thinking about scales. In an ironic play on the Egyptian belief that at death a person's soul is placed in a pan on one side of scales balanced by a single bar in the middle, with a feather representing *ma'at*, the god of justice (see Lichtheim 1992), in the other pan, Job claims that his vexation would outweigh something as immeasurable as the sand of the sea. Ordinarily, sand in biblical contexts is a positive image and represents that which cannot be counted, like Abraham's progeny. In Job's mind, his pain and loss have become identical with his *nepeš*, his troubled inner being. That being the case, Job suggests, his rash language is justified. The choice of *ka'aś* ("vexation") to indicate his suffering is a response to Eliphaz's insistence that vexation slays the fool. Think again, Job implies, for fools are not the only ones slain by *ka'aś*.

Shifting from mercantile imagery of weights, Job introduces military language, but the attacker is not human. Job accuses Shaddai of shooting poisoned arrows at him and lining up terrors, as it were, on a table prepared with food for Job to ingest. This is the only mention of poisoned arrows in the Bible, despite their use in ancient warfare. Two rhetorical questions press the image of nurture even further. Does a wild ass bray when feasting? Or a wild ox when fodder is plentiful? His point: both free and domesticated animals cease from complaining while feeding. Poison, Job's fare, demands a different reaction. Some types of food require an additional ingredient to make them palatable, Job observes, or they will be refused. His food, suffering, has no taste. Therefore he rejects it. Actually the misery he endures has left a bitter taste, so the proverb is not exactly apropos.

Job Restates his Wish to Die (6:8-13)

Unable to believe Eliphaz's affirmation that God both wounds and heals (cf. Isa 45:7), Job looks on death as relief from his pain. He directs his wish to God: "Oh that you'd give me what I've asked for, and Eloah would grant my hope" (v. 8). How differently Job views hope from Eliphaz's use of the word in 4:6 as Job's basis of confidence. For him, hope has turned violent, provoking the desire to be thoroughly crushed with a death blow that cuts him off from the living. He is tired of the "cat and mouse game" that only prolongs his misery. Will his death accomplish anything other than relief from suffering? Yes. Job is convinced that it will prove his innocence, because God will have answered his prayer.

Job does not apologize for such strong language. Indeed, he draws comfort (*nhm*) from the certainty that he has not concealed the truth about God, even while writhing in pain. The epithet, "the holy one," occurs only this once in the book, and like the reference to arranging terrors in v. 4, it makes the line longer than the other twenty-eight in the chapter. If the clause is not a later addition, the genitive *'imre qadoš* is objective, "words against the holy one."

Facing imminent death, Job has nothing to lose. Contrasting his weakened state with bronze and stone, symbols of strength in his world, Job sees no reason to prolong life, for he has no help (*'ezer bi*, "internal resource") and is deprived of effectiveness (*tušiyyah*, "practical success"). According to Genesis 2:18, Yahweh considered the lack of a helper to be "not good," and that is exactly Job's situation. In a weakened state and confronted by the divine "warrior," an epithet ascribed to Yahweh in Exodus 15:3, Job is helpless.

Unreliable Friends (6:14-30)

His precarious situation is similar to that of caravans attempting to cross a desert whose only source of water sometimes threatens drowning and at other times becomes the burial site of those who die from thirst. Job compares his friends to wadis, stream beds that in good seasons supply adequate water but in sweltering heat dry up entirely, dismaying travelers who have counted on finding sufficient liquid to replenish their empty water skins. The description of desperate travelers from northwestern and southwestern Arabia as ashamed because they trusted in something that did not materialize seems strange. Modern readers would view it as a stroke of misfortune that in no way reflects negatively on the character of the unfortunates. Job's observation demonstrates the power of honor and shame in the ancient world where natural calamities were thought to have been brought on by human guilt and therefore to have given rise to shame. That is why the book of Joel describes farmers as overcome by shame when the combined onslaught of a locust infestation and drought threatened livestock and humans alike.

Job's use of "brothers" when referring to his friends, and the mention of *hesed* ("loyalty"), suggest that he thinks the four of them are bound by a covenant. For this reason, his accusation of unfaithfulness carries considerable weight. In his eyes, they have either refused loyalty or let it melt away into despair, the two possibilities of the adjective *lammas* in v. 14. Regardless of which choice an interpreter makes, the parallel stich adds a theological component ("They have forsaken the fear of Shaddai"). In Job's eyes, loyalty toward one's "brothers" was a religious obligation, yet when he stands before them like a thirsty traveler in the desert, they refuse to give him water. Their response is surprising, since the metaphor of wadis credits them with lavish generosity as long as Job had plenty.

Verse 21 suggests that Job thinks his misery poses a threat to his friends, presumably that calamity could happen to them. Fear in the presence of disease can be a devastating force, as modern reactions to the AIDS virus and to "Swine Flu" (H1N1) attest. Job therefore tries to allay their anxiety by means of rhetorical questions. Basically, he asks if he has requested either money or physical assistance from them. In this way he assures them that their loyalty has cost nothing, that their friendship has entailed no risk on their part.

In vv. 22-23, Job's language carries legal overtones for the first time, specifically the images of bribing a judge and of offering a ransom for someone in jeopardy. Forensic vocabulary peaks in v. 25, where Job accuses his friends of indicting him rather than instructing him of his error. The latter approach, gentle instruction, would silence him, according to v. 24. Confronted with the friends' assumption of his guilt, Job reminds them that his innocence is at stake (ṣidqi-bah).

At this point Job realizes that his rash words can be used against him, but he presses recklessly forward. "You'd cast lots over a person of integrity and barter over your friend" (v. 27). This translation divides 'al yatom ("over the fatherless") into 'ali tam ("over one of integrity") and supplies the missing "lots" that the verb implies. The judicial image from the gates of a village gives way to the crowded market place where one haggles over the cost of an item, an image Yahweh will use later in answering Job (40:30).

The frontal assault stirs the friends to action, but not the kind of movement Job seeks. They rise as if to take leave of the one who has shown ingratitude for their attempts to comfort a friend. In their view, nothing they have done deserves such personal questioning of their morals. A desperate Job pleads with his companions to return, appealing to their knowledge of him from the past. "Show a willingness to face me; could I lie to your face?" (v. 28). Long before Emmanuel Levinas turned the notion of "face" into a powerful ethical imperative, the biblical poet has Job implore his friends to recognize the demand placed on them by his face. He may be suffering from the effect of poisonous arrows, but his tongue and palate can still distinguish between innocence and guilt, prosperity and disaster. That is the force of the double rhetorical question in v. 30.

The Human Condition (7:1-10)

Although the friends decide to remain with him, Job addresses God for the first time in the poetry. In doing so, he draws general conclusions about the human condition from his own suffering. Job's two requests of God in this and the following section appear to be contradictory: "Remember that my life is wind; my eyes won't see pleasure again" (v. 7) and "Leave me alone, for my days are empty" (v. 16). The inability to look on good things (tob) drives him to request divine absence, for presence has emptied his life of value. Job uses the word hebel to signify lightness akin to a vapor.

His existence may be empty, but so is that of everyone else. Life is no more than that of a conscripted soldier or a hired worker, a slave who longs for a moment in the shade or a hireling who eagerly hopes to be paid for his labor (vv. 1-2). In a reversal of its customary use, Job thinks he has "inherited" nothingness and grinding toil (*'amal*). Unable to sleep and restless throughout the night, he suffers from a physical condition that encrusts skin infested by worms. The later "Testament of Job" describes him as so devout that he picks up a worm that has fallen to the ground and replaces it on his sore flesh.

Not only is the human condition unpleasant; it is also brief. One could argue, as did a later Ben Sira, that transience is a blessing when life is miserable, but Job does not do that. Instead, he employs a vivid image of the speed with which an individual moves from birth to death. "My days are swifter than a weaver's shuttle; they reach the end without hope." The word translated "hope" is similar to one indicating a thread, which would yield the image of thread on a loom running out. Having worked in a cotton mill as a weaver during my years as a junior and senior in high school, I can appreciate Job's image about a hireling and a shuttle. On either reading, Job's image describes an exquisite picture of life's cessation.

At this point Job appeals to divine pity and self-interest. If his own eyes will never again look on good, that may also be true of God. Job's descent into Sheol will make him invisible to God, whose eyes will search in vain for a good servant. Like Enoch, who in sacred tradition is said to have walked with God and was not, Job too will not be. Like a cloud that suddenly dissipates, Job will vanish in Sheol, never to come back from what the people of Mesopotamia called "the land of no return." Even if he were to pay a surprise visit to his old place of residence, Job insists, it would not recognize him.

Job Wants to Be Left Alone (7:11-16)

He may not have many days left, but Job will use them well, letting his complaint ring out. The cohortatives expressing determination in v. 11 make that clear. He cannot understand why someone as light as a cloud can be viewed by God as sufficient threat that he must be watched constantly. Reaching back into a mythic tradition about primordial conflict between the creator gods and chaos, Job asks another rhetorical question: "Am I Yamm or Tannin that you place a guard over me?" (v. 11; cf. Ps 74:13). In Egypt the god Re engaged in daily battle with Apophis, just as Baal fought Mot and Yamm in Phoenecia, and Marduk had to conquer Tiamat in Mesopotamia. A conflict between Yahweh and a monster of chaos is mentioned in several places within the Bible, mainly in Psalms, Isaiah, and Job. The monster bears the names Rahab, Leviathan, Behemoth, and Tannin. These representatives of chaos were formidable foes; in some instances they are said to have been killed, while in others they were subjected to divine decree (Levenson). Does God consider Job a threat equal to theirs? In due time, Job will learn that Yahweh does think of him as worthy competition, like Enkidu the noble savage in the Gilgamesh Epic.

For most people, hours of sleep restore the spirit, but Job gets little rest. A certain irony clings to the verbalized thought that his bed will offer comfort. Was that not the stated purpose of his friends' journey? Yet they have failed to bring any consolation during the daylight hours. What about the night? Job says God frightens him with dreams and visions like the one that so deeply disturbed Eliphaz. Unable to find any rest, Job prefers death to his pitiful state.

Lest there be any doubt about his preference, Job announces his renunciation in the exact language he will later use in his final response to Yahweh: *ma'asti* ("I reject"). Although he omits the direct object, the sequel leaves no doubt that it is "life" ("I would not live into the ages [*le'olam*, traditionally translated as "forever"]; leave me alone, for my days are empty [*hebel*, v. 16]). Tired of being the object of divine surveillance, he simply wants to be left alone to die. That is the basis for his plea to be abandoned.

A Parody of Psalm 8 (7:17-21)

Job concludes his speech with a satirical rendering of the assessment of mortals in Psalm 8, adding a reversal of the traditional concept of divine providence, an audacious request, an unthinkable idea, a suggestion that God let mercy triumph, and a reminder that a time will come when God searches for him in vain.

His question, "What are mortals (*'enos*) that you exalt them and set your mind on them?" echoes the lofty praise of humans (*'adam*) in Psalm 8, which places them only slightly lower than Elohim. But Job's emphasis falls on the way God constantly tests individuals. This thought leads Job to request that God leave him alone so he can swallow his spit (v. 19). At least one psalmist felt the same way Job did while meditating on life's brevity and harshness (Ps 39:14).

In a single stroke, Job jettisons the connection between sin and God while infusing a divine epithet with a negative connotation. "If I sin, what have I done to you, watcher of mortals" (*noser ha'adam*, v. 20)? Apparently, Job does not mean that sin, even hypothetical as here, only affects humans. Instead, he probably implies that divine majesty easily shakes off the effect of transgression. If that is true, his next words belie it. "Why have you made me your mark so I've become a burden for you" (v. 20b)? The depiction of God chafing under a heavy load like a slave was so disturbing to later interpreters that it was changed to put the burden on Job (ʿaleyka ["on you"] became ʿalay ["on me"]). Job's implication is that hitting him from dawn to dusk has wearied God. This idea is hardly less shocking than Job's changing the positive notion of God's watchful eye into a wholly negative concept.

Job's parting shot inquires as to why God doesn't pardon him of any offense so he can then lie down in the dust, where God will be unable to find him despite initiating a search (v. 21). Lest he be thought of as taking sin lightly, Job uses three different words that cover the entire range of possible offenses (ḥaṭaʾ "missing the mark," pešaʿ "rebellion," and ʿawon "iniquity"). The speech ends with a missing Job ("I'd not be"). The decisive difference between Job's description of his nonexistence and that of Enoch in sacred lore is the lack of the comforting "For God took him" (Gen 5:24b).

Bildad's First Speech (8:1-22)

Because divine justice lies at the heart of Bildad's theology, he begins with a rhetorical question that from his perspective can only be answered with an emphatic "No." "Does El pervert justice or Shaddai pervert the right" (v. 3)? Bildad then defends this theological conviction by offering proof, first from tradition and then from nature. He concludes, however, with an encouraging word for Job provided that he begins an earnest search for God. This condition is a reversal of Job's remark that the deity will search for him but he won't be (7:21d). Bildad picks up on the nonexistence of Job and applies the negative particle to the wicked.

A Defense of God's Justice (8:1-7)

The shortened particle ʾan ("how long?") in v. 2, like the images from nature in vv. 11-19, may indicate agitation rather than a vernacular aberration. Bildad considers Job's entire speech a mighty wind issuing from the mouth rather than the mind. Such nonsense has gone on too long, he thinks, especially Job's questioning of God's justice. The rhetorical question in v. 3 repeats the verb ʿawah ("to bend; pervert") in both stichs, at the same time breaking up the epithet El Shaddai to accommodate both halves of the verse.

Three "if" clauses follow. The first of these may not be hypothetical, for Bildad's blunt sincerity leads him to emphasize the implication of believing that God cannot bend the scales of justice. Because that is true, he thinks, Job's children were wicked and God handed them over to their rebellion for punishment. By this logic, Job has also sinned but his less severe punishment is a sign of divine compassion. The other two "if" clauses relate to Job rather than to his children. "If you will search for El and implore Shaddai" (v. 5) and "If you are pure and upright, surely then he will rouse on your behalf and reward your righteous dwelling" (v. 6). Indeed, Bildad says, your future prosperity will dwarf your past good fortune (v. 8), a verse that apparently links the poetry to the prologue and epilogue, even if by means of a hint of a happy ending.

<u>Proof from Tradition and Nature (8:8-19)</u>

In vv. 8-10, Bildad presses the concept of former times even further by advising Job to seek counsel from previous generations. The reason is obvious. Our lives are brief, we're ignorant, and our days are a lengthening shadow. We can, however, learn from the wisdom of our ancestors, who will communicate from their hearts, unlike Job's "mouthy talk." Bildad assumes that tradition is fundamentally positive, the few examples of injustice like Abel's death at the hands of his brother Cain having been sloughed off as anomalies in an otherwise just universe.

He discerns a similar lesson in nature, although the examples he gives are not exactly transparent (vv. 11-19). Beginning with a proverb in the form of a rhetorical question ("Does papyrus grow apart from a marsh or do reeds flourish without water?"), he draws a conclusion and applies it to reprobates. In short, take away water and the plants that are most dependent on it wither and die; abandon El, and perish. Bildad's reference to hope as a perishing thing alludes to Job's use of *tiqwah* ("hope"), but the two employ the word in opposite ways. Job hopes to die (3:3; 6:8), whereas punishment for sin in Bildad's thought is the death of hope. In his enthusiasm, Bildad mixes images badly. Dry paths are welcome to travelers, but here they are "tracts of fate" (Hartley, 161, who quotes Edouard Dhorme as follows: "The paths are the tracts of fate, already marked out by God and inevitably followed by man").

Next, Bildad chooses the image of a spider's web to illustrate the fragility of Job's confidence. Because of its nature as the most fragile of things, anyone who trusts in a spider's web is doomed. He reaches for it but it offers no resilience; he tries to strengthen it but it won't stand up. The whole image is an ironic illustration of the disparity between expectation and reality.

The second example from nature may be read two ways. According to one reading, a plant flourishes initially and sends shoots that attach themselves to a pile of rocks, only in the end to be uprooted and to die. The other way of understanding the imagery is to think of a vigorous plant that withstands every effort to dislodge it. The use of *gal* to mean "pool" in Song of

Songs 4:12 makes sense if the "house of stones" refers to a rock wall enclosing a spring. In this case, the shoots reach for water and thrive. Bildad's application of the image of a plant is an ironic oxymoron: "Surely its way is a (cause for) joy, and others sprout from dust" (v. 19). The thought of a sprout rising from dust approaches the paradoxical.

El's Faithfulness (8:20-22)

Irony abounds in the conclusion to Bildad's speech. He was not privy to the narrator's affirmation of Job's integrity, which was confirmed by Yahweh, but readers are familiar with the picture of a virtuous Job. Bildad's confidence that "El will surely not reject the person of integrity (*tam*), nor strengthen the hand of the wicked" (v. 20) is predicated on the assumption that Job will repent. In Bildad's mind, only then will things turn around. He assures Job to his face, "Your mouth will be full of joy (as opposed to wind), and a shout of victory will fill your lips. Your enemies will be clothed with shame, and the tent of the wicked (rather than Job) will be no more." By the end of his speech, Bildad has partially atoned for his earlier insensitivity. He now shows Job the way to recovery without, however, conceding that his friend is innocent and God is guilty of wrongdoing.

Job's Response to Bildad (9:1–10:22)

Bildad's unwillingness to consider the possibility that El Shaddai could bend justice leaves Job little choice. He can either indict his dead children and himself by accepting Bildad's view of things, or he can challenge the deity's conduct. Job chooses the latter option. God, he says, possesses knowledge and power, but he uses both without any regard for justice. When ruthless power is combined with wickedness, the stability of the earth itself is threatened. That is precisely the situation in which Job finds himself. He cannot trust God to do the right thing.

What, then, can Job do? Purification rites will be only temporarily effectual, he thinks, for God will toss him back into filth. With nothing to lose, he decides to enter into litigation with God, who has wronged him, although he realizes that his opponent will act as both prosecuting attorney and judge. Even if the odds were not stacked against him, and he somehow came out on top, no one would be able to enforce the sentence against God. That impasse leads Job to complain that there is no arbitrator who has the strength to make God amend his ways. He will return to this idea more than once.

In his mounting anger, Job vacillates between outright attack and an indirect plea for compassion. He accuses God of mocking victims of injustice, but Job also describes his own birth in terms of God's careful attention to every intimate detail (Mettinger). "How can you," Job inquires, "turn around and destroy what you have painstakingly created?" Having no qualms about hastening that process of destruction, Job repeats the wish to die that he first expressed in chapter 3.

An Awesome Opponent (9:1-10)

Bildad's remarks are met with sarcasm: "Truly I know this is so: and how can a mortal (*'enoš*) be innocent before El?" (v. 1). The second half of the verse echoes the oracle to Eliphaz in 4:17a, but there is a significant difference. Whereas Eliphaz understands the question as one of morality, Job thinks in terms of legality. Continuing the forensic language of innocence inherent to the verb *yiṣdaq*, Job conjectures that even if he desired to go to court (*larib*) against El he would not answer one in a thousand questions. The pronouns are unclear here, so the second "he" can refer either to God or to the one who contends with the deity. In the first case, God would simply refuse to respond to charges; in the second case, a mortal would be unable to answer a single question thrown at him during a trial.

The snippets from the tradition of theophany in vv. 4-10 favor the former interpretation: "He" refers to El, the awesome creator whose dominance over nature bespeaks sheer power. El overturns mountains, shakes the earth with devastating quakes, exercises complete control over sun, stars, and constellations, and conquers the chaos monster Yamm. The exact identity of the constellations mentioned in v. 9 is a matter of debate, but they probably are Aldebaran, Orion, Pleiades, and the "Chambers of the South." The rare word for the sun (*ḥeres*) as in Judges 14:18 and the language of combat ("treading on the back of Yamm") mark this hymn with a semblance of antiquity, to which may be compared doxological fragments in Amos 4:13, 5:8-9, and 9:5-6 (Crenshaw 1975). Job concludes this accusatory use of the hymnic tradition with the exact words of Eliphaz in 5:9, except for the adverb *'ad*. "Who does great things, unsearchable, wonders beyond number." In Job's mouth, praise has become a taunt. The actions described here are those carried out by monsters of chaos.

A Mismatch (9:1-19)

Although the contest is a mismatch regardless of how it is defined, whether as one of justice or of power, Job presses forward. He imagines that if he were as fortunate as Moses, or even Eliphaz, to experience a theophany, like them he would be blind to the one passing by. Indeed, were the divine appearance a gangster's act of seizing a victim, nobody could do anything about it. The two hypothetical cases in vv. 11-12 indicate the nature of the opposition. Justice is out of the question, as the verb *yahtop* ("to seize") indicates. An angry Eloah does not relent.

Before such fury, even Rahab's helpers bow in submission. The irony is subtle. Whereas Job found himself entirely without a helper, Rahab, the West Semitic variant of the Mesopotamian monster of chaos who is named Tiamat, is surrounded by helpers. Nevertheless, they are useless against Eloah's wrath. (Cf. 26:12, where God is said to have split Rahab open just as Marduk in Enuma Elish divided Tiamat and from her two halves made heaven and earth. This ancient myth is recalled in Ps 89:11; Isa 51:9, to which may be compared Ps 87:4 and Isa 30:7.)

Undaunted, Job determines to defend himself before ruthless power, even though, being innocent, he must plead for justice. Moreover, Job does not believe God will hear him even if he can articulate his just cause. Job sees no evidence that the one who wounds also heals, as Eliphaz has claimed in 5:18. Job's experience is that God increases his misery, starting with a tempest and then multiplying the wounds for no reason (v. 17). The word for a tempest, *se'arah*, is different from the *ruah gedolah* ("mighty wind") in 1:19 that killed Job's children, but it is the same word used for the storm wind in which Yahweh later appears (38:1).

When Job accuses God of multiplying his wounds, he uses *hinnam*, echoing the language of the adversary in 1:9 when questioning the motive behind Job's morality, a term that the Lord used in 2:3 to describe his own swallowing of Job "for no reason." The reader must suspect that the adversary's question was wrongly put. It is God's behavior that should be subjected to the question: "Is it *hinnam*?" Sated with bitterness from Eloah, Job ponders the dilemma in which he finds himself. Regardless of the issue, power or justice, he is no match for God.

An Absence of Justice (9:20-24)

Both the narrator and the Lord attributed integrity to Job in the prologue, but so far an afflicted Job has refrained from making such a claim. That reluctance vanishes as he twice defends himself with *'ani tam* ("I'm innocent," vv. 20-21). He begins by asserting his hypothetical innocence in a court of law but complains that he would be forced to deny it. "If I'm innocent," he blurts out, "he declares me perverse." Not satisfied, he repeats, "I'm innocent," but this second time the matter is not hypothetical. Job goes on to admit that he doesn't recognize himself and even rejects life (v. 21). If Job is innocent, then God must be perverse. That is the conclusion Job reaches in a high state of emotional unrest. No stronger indictment of God is imaginable than vv. 22-24. In short, God destroys both the innocent and the guilty. It is as if Job answers Abraham's question in Genesis 18:25 with a resounding "No." God does not act justly, and what is more, like the most loathsome of fools in the book of Proverbs, he mocks helpless victims. Having abdicated his responsibility as guardian of justice, God hands over the earth into the power of the wicked and aids them by covering judges' faces.

Job is not thinking of impartial justice as we do when representing personified justice as blind; instead, he describes judges who are blind to the cause of the defenseless. He can think of no other explanation for evil's dominance. "If not he, then who?"

At this point Job has come up against the inevitable result of believing in a single deity. There's no one else to blame for cosmic wickedness of the kind he is witnessing. Job does not enjoy the modicum of comfort that is available to readers who know about the adversary's role as the instigator of Job's misery, but even they realize that the ultimate responsibility for the murder of his children and for his sickness lies with God, whom Job has served faithfully.

A Missing Arbitrator (9:25-35)

Job's rapid deterioration, both physically and psychologically, conjures up images of speed. He ponders the possible effect of positive thinking but abandons the idea because God is bent on destroying him, going so far as to hurl a freshly washed Job into muck. If only, he thinks, God were a mortal, then the two of them could compete on even terms. Regrettably, he laments, there's no arbiter who could make God play fairly.

Two of the three images of speed in vv. 25-26 refer obliquely to Bildad's remark about reeds and to Yahweh's speech from the storm wind. Job pictures the swift boats that were built from reeds, whose fast movement on the surface of the water compares favorably with the rapid descent of an eagle, or a vulture, to devour prey below (cf. 39:27-30). When Job thinks of a runner, he brings readers into the semantic range of the messengers who brought bad news in the prologue, although there the language is about escape. Job thinks time passes with speed equal to that of runners, boats, and eagles.

Aware that his meditation (*siaḥ*) has been overwhelmingly morose, Job considers putting a positive spin on things and managing a smile, but he is afraid suffering will prevail. Nearly despondent, he resents being considered a sinner; by whom, he does not say, but he probably thinks of his friends and of God. Job questions the effort he has put into being moral, for it has been in vain. Why participate in purification rites when God will only hurl him back into filth, making his clothes a stench?

In v. 32 Job turns away momentarily from directly addressing the deity and states a truism ("For he's not a man like me—I could answer him; we could come together in judgment"). Hence the need for an arbiter (*mokiah*). Alas, no such creature exists (v. 33). The contradictory particles together, *lo' yeš* ("not" and "there is"), are unique, and some interpreters follow the Greek and Syriac in reading *lu yeš* ("Oh that there were") as in Job 16:4 and Numbers 22:29. A similar phenomenon to *lo' yeš* occurs in Psalm 35:17, where one finds *'en yeš*. The text need not be emended. The missing arbiter does not dissuade Job from risking everything. His determination (*'adaberah*) immediately leads to an expression of fearlessness (v. 35).

Destroying What One Has Made (10:1-12)

It occurs to Job that one who takes pride in the work of his hands would not reject it, as God is doing now. Life for Job has become loathsome enough to make him wish to exit it, but the one who made him is under no such duress. Why, then, does God reject the product of his own creativity? Even craftsmen, artisans, and smiths took such pride in their work that their adoration of the finished product was one of three explanations for idolatry put forth in Wisdom of Solomon. The beauty of the finely carved and gilded idol functioned as a symbol for invisible deities, but this practice was so misunderstood that it was widely ridiculed in the Bible and the Apocrypha. The worshiped object has eyes but cannot see, ears but cannot hear, feet but cannot move, and so on. Idols were called "nothing, non-entities" and were mocked for their inability to save themselves from theft, fire, and the proverbial pigeon dung.

Job does not think along these lines. Instead, he uses rhetorical questions to emphasize the difference between mortals and God. The focus is on sight and lifespan. Because God has perfect vision, he should recognize Job's integrity and celebrate it rather than crushing it along with Job. Because God's existence is not limited, he should have compassion for one whose days are rapidly coming to an end. Job's determination to declare his objection to God, reiterated in v. 1 from 9:35, is matched by God's will to search out every one of Job's sins so as to prove his guilt. Job closes this sub-unit with an awful reality: "According to your own knowledge, I am not guilty, but I have no deliverer from your grasp" (v. 7).

Verse 8 shows that Job has not abandoned outright attack, for he accuses God of swallowing him completely. According to 2:3, Yahweh blamed the adversary for enticing him to swallow Job for no reason (*ḥinnam*). In v. 9 Job reminds God that he was made from clay and will return to dust, an obvious allusion to Genesis 2. Yet what follows is an exquisite picture of divine solicitude, albeit in an ironic mode. Job thinks God was intimately involved in the mixing of semen with the female vital fluids as well as the gestation period of the fetus. The practice of cheese making lies behind this image. For the formation of the body, the combination of flesh, sinews, and bone, he thinks about the sewing of intricate fabric, describing his own development as something fashioned by divine hands just the way a garment comes together. Moreover, Job ascribes life, loyalty, and providence to the creator, who is determined to swallow him (v. 12).

No Hiding Place (10:13-17)

His existence threatened by his maker, Job thinks God has hidden deep within his heart the memory of creative work. Alternatively, "these things" anticipate what Job is about to say, namely that God ignores fundamental reality in Job's case. Twice he presents his own guilt as a hypothetical possibility, the closest he comes to admitting wrongdoing. "If I sin, you watch me; you won't pronounce me cleared from any of my guilt" (v. 14). "If I'm wicked, woe is me; I'm not guilty but cannot raise my head, full of shame, humbled" (v. 15).

Recalling earlier allusions to a lion, Job still possesses enough courage to compare himself to the king of beasts, but he envisions God as a hunter whose arrows inject additional pain in him. Returning to the legal metaphor that has come to dominate his thinking, Job says God renews witnesses against him, but the image changes abruptly to attacking soldiers (v. 17).

A Renewed Death Wish (10:18-22)

God's not the only one who is capable of renewing things. Burdened with the threat posed by a relentless warrior, Job renews his death wish from chapter 3. "Why did you bring me forth from the womb? I wish I had died so you couldn't see me" (v. 18). He thinks of nonexistence as desirable, a life's journey from womb to tomb. As it is, Job believes his days are numbered, so he asks God to look away so he can smile a little. The duplicated *me'at* ("a little") in this request emphasizes how minimal Job's existence has become. In 9:27 Job entertained the possibility of putting a better face on his suffering, even smiling; now, however, he actually implores God to make that a reality, even if momentarily (v. 20). Earlier, it may be recalled, he asked God to look away so he could swallow his spit (7:19).

Job has no illusion about his final destiny. He knows what death holds for him, if traditional descriptions of Sheol are accurate. He awaits an imminent journey to that dark land of no return, a chaotic region that shines like gloom. With this oxymoron that corresponds to the present structure of the universe, Job ends his response to Bildad.

Zophar's First Speech (11:1-20)

Zophar wastes no time in getting straight to the point. He indicts Job, contrasts human ignorance with divine intelligence, and urges Job to repent or suffer the consequences. The logic of the doctrine of individual retribution that Eliphaz and Bildad have championed leads to the inevitable conclusion that either Job is guilty of wrongdoing or God is unjust. Zophar chooses to accuse Job and exonerate the deity. To what authority does he appeal? Whereas Eliphaz based his teaching on revelation and Bildad relied on ancestral tradition, Zophar argued from sheer logic. He failed to recognize the irony of his position when praising Eloah at the expense of clueless mortals. If human beings are by nature "clueless," and Zophar is human, then he too is devoid of knowledge.

Job's Errors (11:2-4)

Bildad's concise presentation, as measured by the number of verses attributed to him, entitles him to accuse Job of excessive talk, which according to Proverbs 10:19 and Ecclesiastes 5:2 opens the flood gates of sin. The interrogative covers four rhetorical questions: (1) Should a talkative person not be answered? (2) Should a mouthy individual be declared innocent? (3) Should your presence silence the weak? (4) Should you mock without rebuke? The idiom, "man of lips," concentrates Job's essence in a single image, a garrulous person. That image corresponds to its parallel in 2a, "a multitude of words," which Zophar equates with babble, that is, utter nonsense. The forensic background suggests that Zophar thinks Job's testimony requires a response that does not permit him to receive a favorable verdict.

If the goal of a trial in the world of this writer was to silence accusers, Zophar thinks those individuals whose social standing carries less weight than Job (cf. 11:11) should not be rendered speechless. The last of the four questions may pick up on Job's remark in 9:23 that God mocks at the suffering of innocents. Instead of the deity's mocking, it is Job who engages in such loathsome conduct, according to Zophar.

To establish the veracity of the charge against Job, Zophar quotes what he has heard Job say. Unfortunately, Zophar has been either inattentive or he is guilty of false attribution. Job has nowhere said that he is without a moral flaw, although he has insisted on his integrity. The closest he has come to saying "My teaching is spotless and I have been pure before you" (v. 4) is the assertion of integrity in 9:21 (*tam-'ani*). Zophar has changed the metaphor to connote purity, like the shine given off by polished metal. Furthermore, in the expression "my teaching" he has emphasized what Job has been taught, and the singular "your" with reference to eyes shifts the direction of Job's supposed boast from his friends to the deity. Perhaps Zophar has recognized the subtle move in Job's speech away from the friends.

The Contrast Between Eloah and Humans (11:5-11)

Zophar wishes that Eloah would break the silence and convey something of the divine mystery to Job, who already is experiencing special forgiveness. That is the brunt of vv. 5-6. Zophar does not hesitate to refer to Eloah's lips, for divine speech will be intelligible as opposed to Job's prattle. The preposition *'immak* implies more than "with you." It has an adversative sense, "against you." The irony is hidden from Zophar, for when God does speak wrath extends to the three friends, according to the Epilogue.

What does Zophar want Eloah to disclose? Two things: (1) the hidden aspects of divine wisdom and (2) the two-sided nature of sagacity. By this obscure word, Zophar probably means what is manifest in creation and still other undivulged mystery of divine essence. The root *'lm* conveys the notion of impenetrable darkness, and the dual form with reference to inner resourcefulness probably indicates comprehensiveness.

Zophar seems to need no divine communication to settle the issue of guilt and innocence where Job is concerned. He already knows that Job is guilty. Deducing from the fact that Job is suffering at Eloah's hands, Zophar pronounces his friend guilty. His language does not equivocate: "But know that Eloah has forgotten some of your iniquity" (v. 6c). This translation takes the verb *yaššeh* as a form of *nšh* ("to forget"), and the preposition *min* as partitive ("some of"). In short, Zophar says, you can thank your lucky stars that Eloah, whom you wrongly accuse of mocking the innocent, has shown compassion to the guilty.

The next five verses praise Eloah's majesty and underscore human ignorance about the scope of transcendence. They refer to the four geographical points (height, depth, length, and breadth) as in Psalm 139:8, which mentions sky, Sheol, and the far reaches of the ocean. Zophar inquires whether Job can find what Eloah has researched or Shaddai's limits.

Curiously, the verb *timṣa'* ("find") occurs in both halves of v. 7, and the nominal form of *ḥqr* ("to investigate") is associated with the deity instead of Job. The obvious answer is "no," for no one can discover the scope of transcendence.

What are the implications of divine hiddenness? Zophar applies them to Job. "The height of heaven, what can you do? Deeper than Sheol, what can you know?" (v. 8). Faced with the inability to fathom God's ways, Job can do nothing to alter them. Possessing only human knowledge, how can he charge the deity with wrongdoing? If Zophar is right, Job must abandon his quest to enter into litigation with God. How can anyone's vision cover the entire earth and the sea's expanse, much less the skies and the deep? Yet God's activity stretches from one end to the other.

In vv. 10-11 Zophar again applies these insights to Job's situation. Both Eliphaz and Job have spoken of the deity's gliding past them (4:15 and 9:11), so Zophar chooses the same verb (*ḥlp*) to indicate divine power at Job's expense. "Even if God glided past, confined you, and convoked (an assembly), who could undo it?" (v. 10). God has indeed imprisoned Job in painful sickness and assembled the friends, and no one can do anything to revoke that action. Surely this account of divine activity is not new information for Job. Zophar goes on to state that God observes human nothingness and sees iniquity but does not take it into consideration. Either Zophar is guilty of a colossal lapse in reasoning or the negative particle *lo'* should be construed as a *lu'* emphatica, meaning "he certainly considers it." The contrast between Job's ignorance in v. 8 and God's knowledge in v. 11 is striking, as is the emphatic pronoun "he" with reference to God.

Repent and Rest Securely (11:12-20)

The third section of Zophar's speech opens with a proverbial saying, replete with assonance and alliteration: "A stupid man (*'iš*) will become intelligent when a wild ass's colt is born a man (*'adam*)." Like many ancient proverbs that no longer betray their original setting, this one is ambiguous. Does the second half affirm or negate the first half? It is possibly a play on Genesis 16:12, where Ishmael is identified as a "wild ass of a man." If *'adam* was added later to make that association, the two halves of the original verse match perfectly. The meaning would then be that just as a person devoid of the ability to learn will never become intelligent, a wild ass will never become tame. If the final verb *yiwwaled* is changed to *yimmaled* ("born" to "taught"), this alternative interpretation is compelling. It singles out two distinct types of people and donkeys.

If the proverb is meant to describe Job, it fails badly. Zophar's additional remarks assume that Job can change and that repentance will make a decisive difference in his life. Perhaps Zophar's point is that Job's failure is moral rather than intellectual. Just as animals are dumber than humans, so people are stupider than God.

That is why Zophar urges Job to correct his intellect and to couple that achievement with humble supplication (v. 13). The personal pronoun "you" (*'attah*) emphasizes the need for immediate action. Zophar pictures a complete adjustment in Job's thinking plus contrition in the place of arrogance. The image of palms open before God to expose any blemish on those hands is one of petition.

Verse 14 shows that Zophar believes Job is guilty of something, although he does not say what. He begins hypothetically: "If there is iniquity in your hands, thrust it far away, and do not let evil dwell in your tents" (v. 14). In other words, clean up your own life and that of your associates. "Then indeed you will lift up your face without blemish (cf. Sir 11:31), be stamped (from a mold) and not fear" (v. 15). Apparently, from Zophar's perspective, Job is presently marred by a dirty spot, but he can be firmly established if he repents.

The next four verses promise that sinners who change their ways will experience a complete turnaround. The personal pronoun "you" occurs once more. "For you will forget misery (*'amal*), you'll remember it like water that has flowed by" (v. 16). In modern idiom, Job's suffering will be water under a bridge. As frequently happens, happiness conjures up images of light. Accordingly, Zophar assures Job that his life span will be as bright as noon, and evening darkness will be like morning. Is this a play on the oxymoron that ends Job's previous speech (chaos shining like gloom)? In v. 18 the language of hope occurs again. It weaves in and out of the debate like a drunk driver moving from one lane to another in heavy traffic. Zophar combines the word "hope" with trust, then shifts to the image of sheep lying down safely. Repeating the image of resting securely, Zophar then thinks of the restoration of Job's honor. Now the great, or many, another meaning of *rabbim*, will openly seek his favor. What more can Job ask, at least from Zophar's perspective.

The verdict is not in, and Zophar pointedly reminds Job that failure to change his ways will bring serious consequences. "The eyes of the wicked will be dim, flight will perish from them (that is, the wicked), and their dying gasp will be their hope" (v. 20). In this way Zophar corrects Job's remark in 9:22 that God slays both good and evil. "No," Zophar insists, "it is the wicked person who loses sight, refuge, and hope." Zophar's parting shot combines two themes we have often encountered: "hope" and "perish."

The Second Cycle of Debate

In the longest of Job's dialogues except for the concluding remarks in chapters 29–31, he rejects the friends' not-so-subtle urging to repent as a means of returning to God's good graces. Job chooses instead to plead his case before the deity, even if it costs his life to do so. Job is convinced by now that power, not justice, best characterizes God's conduct regarding human activity. Chaos reigns in the world, and mortals are even more vulnerable than nature itself. Perhaps Job's awareness of his mortality energizes his sharp rebuke of the friends as well as his bold assault on the creator.

Job's Lament (12:1–14:22)

The three chapters can be divided into two large units (12:1–13:12; 13:20–14:22) and a brief transitional section (13:13-19). Alternatively, they can be broken down into a number of smaller units. The latter approach will be taken here.

Job has Become a Joke (12:1-5)

One can cut the sarcasm of v. 2 with a dull knife. The initial adverb "For sure" serves as an appropriate introduction to an alliterative jab at Zophar and his two friends (*'attem*, "you" plural), one that has nine m's and five gutturals (see the complex system of rhetoric proposed by Lugt). "For sure you are the people with whom wisdom will die." A tinge of elitism may rest in the word *'am* (people), as if mockingly conceding Zophar's clever denigration of a stupid man.

The next verse includes Job's bold assertion that he is just as intelligent as they, although the concluding question, "Who isn't like these?" is obscure. It could refer to Zophar's views. The unusual expression, "I am not falling more than you," which denies intellectual inferiority, occurs again in 13:2 and nowhere else. Job insists that he is not stupid (cf. 11:12). In fact, he is like Noah, both just (*saddiq*, cf. Gen 6:9; Ezek 14:14, 20) and a person of integrity (*tamim*, cf. 1:1), although his friends have turned him into an object of contempt, a living joke. One who once called on Eloah and was answered is now a joke. The word for joke ("one being laughed at," *śeḥoq*) occurs twice in the verse, the second time alongside his actual status as "just" and "blameless." Worse still, a torch of contempt exposes him to idle onlookers, making him a fixed point for unstable feet (cf. Prov 6:13).

Proverbial Wisdom (12:6-12)

Job next directs his friends' attention to lessons to be learned from nature. He begins with a radical assertion that those who enjoy security are ruthless slanderers, not moral people. What is more, they openly mock Eloah, either by deifying their sword or by carrying small idols with them. The plural of intensity, expressing security, and the singular "in his hand," may suggest a different translation of the final clause in v. 6 ("whom Eloah brings in his hand"). The deity, that is, lies behind their acts of villainy.

The next two verses demonstrate the poet's familiarity with traditional pairings (beasts, birds, creeping things, and fish), although "earth" replaces the third member of this group, possibly through ellipsis. Moreover, the plural word for beasts, Behemoth, anticipates the powerful creature who will appear in the divine speeches at 40:15-20. The twofold use of the verb for teaching with non-human instructors in vv. 7-8 is telling. Job advises his friends to ask some questions of their own, unlike his rhetorical ones. Zophar has emphasized the inscrutability of divine ways, a point with which Job would agree, but Job insists that there is much that can be known if those who search for insights from nature use the principle of analogy, as sages were wont to do.

Verse 9 appears to continue the thought about four types of creatures from whom lessons can be learned, but it alone in the entire poetic dispute uses the divine name Yahweh. Moreover, the second half of the verse is also found in Isaiah 41:20 ("That the hand of Yahweh has done this"). There it is part of a comforting promise to an exiled people, whereas Job employs the clause to bolster his argument that even non-humans recognize the exercise of divine power. Job's suffering while in the adversary's grasp and indirectly in God's hand has taught him something very different from the solace felt by the unknown psalmist who wrote the moving words in Psalm 73:23 ("I was always with you; you held me by my right hand; by your counsel you led me and you will later take me [to] glory"). Not everyone considered the prospect of being held by the divine hand comforting; for example, the author of Ecclesiastes observed that it is impossible to discover whether God's intentions while holding humans in his hand are favorable or unfavorable (Eccl 9:1).

Job continues to draw upon conventional wisdom when introducing another rhetorical question: "Doesn't the ear test words and the palate taste food?" (v. 11). Just as the palate discriminates between good and bad food, the ear distinguishes between truth and falsehood. The importance of accurate listening in an oral culture can hardly be emphasized enough

(Crenshaw 1997). In 34:3 Elihu uses the same argument about the discriminating capacity of the ear and palate when trying to refute Job's claim to be innocent.

Verse 12 gives voice to the widely shared view that wisdom increases with age, a view that will eventually be challenged by a young Elihu. The unusual word translated as "old age" (*yešišim*) occurs only in Job (cf. 15:10; 29:8; 32:6) and Sirach (8:6; 25:4-6). Given the close relationship between this verse and the following one, which can be confirmed by their reference to four words brought together in Isa 11:2 ("wisdom," "understanding," "power," and "counsel"), it is possible to interpret the two words for longevity as divine epithets: "The Aged" and "The Long-lived One." The point would then be that wisdom and understanding reside in God. If read this way, v. 12 provides a fitting transition to the hymnic material that follows and an antecedent for the personal pronoun "him" in v. 13.

Thus far Job has drawn a huge question mark over the friends' claim that God doles out justice for one and all. "Tell that to the plunderers," Job might say, "and listen to their raucous laughter." He will reinforce his negative assessment of things in the parody of a doxology, God's so-called wisdom (Janzen 1985, 102–105).

Hymnic praise usually emphasizes the deity's beneficial works such as establishing order and acting on behalf of good people, but vv. 13-25 describe the chaos that ensues when power usurps the place of wisdom. The one who sat for this portrait was no benign deity but a ruthless tyrant bent on destabilizing society. This God no longer balances weal and woe, dispensing favors to the just and punishing the unjust. Instead, he resembles a divine monster occasionally portrayed in Mesopotamian myth, although without the focus on creating hideous creatures.

In Job's mind, God has turned into a despotic ruler who lacks the customary good qualities of a sovereign. The shift from intelligent rule to corrupting power is signaled in vv. 14 and 16, whose syntactic structure is exactly the same.

"With him, wisdom and power; his, counsel and understanding" (v. 14). "With him, strength and perspicacity; his, erring and leading astray" (v. 16).

This tyrant's actions are irreversible, whether they disturb nature's rhythms or society's balance. This God demolishes so completely that the very thought of rebuilding is futile. He imprisons, and no power on earth can affect release (a point Zophar made in 11:10). He withholds rain and people die of thirst; he sends torrents that drown indiscriminately. The verb *hapak*, "to overthrow," in v. 15 echoes the language memorialized in the story of the destruction of Sodom and Gomorrah (cf. Amos 4:11 as well as 5:8 for water's role in destruction).

With vv. 17-25 the deity's corrupting influence comes to the fore. Even nobility is not spared in this litany of dubious praise. Intellectual leaders are turned into madmen, no longer able to give sound political advice or to render just decisions in the gates where the powerless hope for judicial fairness. Royalty is robbed of its power; in exploits requiring strength kings resemble defeated wrestlers. Religious leaders, like counselors, become madmen lacking intellectual acumen adequate for the task. Similarly, ordinary people who have demonstrated their worth in society through remarkable achievements are made useless, unable to think clearly or speak persuasively. Suddenly, the great and highly respected find themselves objects of loathing. In some ways, this description reminds one of Isaiah 44:25, in which Yahweh boasts about frustrating diviners and turning sages into fools.

In Job's troubling account of the deity's destabilizing activity, v. 22 seems out of place. It states that God exposes the deep things residing in darkness and brings obscure things to the light of day. The belief that God will ultimately bring hidden things to light functions in Ecclesiastes 12:14 as a warning to those who think they can hide something from their creator. For Job, the revelation of mysteries inherent to the depths seems to suggest that God has extracted evil from its hiding places and given it free reign despite its new visibility.

The logical implication of ineffective leaders is national disaster. Verses 23-25 therefore state the obvious. They do so, however, with robust images of a nation's most esteemed citizens wandering where deserts conceal any sign of a path and stumbling in the dark like drunks. A cruel deity first exalts a nation then destroys it; one could add, "Like flies to wanton boys." In Job's mind, the original chaos of Genesis 1:2 is matched by the situation in which he finds himself, and God is its source. Job even uses the word *tohu* ("waste") in v. 24; in addition, he makes a play on words between the verb *ta'am* ("to taste") in v. 11 and *wayyat'em* ("he makes them stumble," from *ta'ah*) in vv. 24 and 25, as if to indicate that God has destroyed the human capacity to discriminate (cf. v. 20). The statement in v. 24b also occurs in Psalm 107:40 and may be a stock phrase about wandering aimlessly in the desert.

Bildad's rhetorical question in 8:3, "Will El pervert justice or Shaddai pervert the right?" has been answered in a way Job's friend could not have imagined. Although in the thematic sixteenth verse Job chose different verbs for leading astray, *šagag* and *šagah* rather than *'awah*, the charge that God champions falsehood and wanton behavior underlies the entire doxology of terror (Perdue 1991, 153–56).

Job's suffering has led him to a new understanding of God, one that approaches the demonic. He comes close to universalizing the corrupting influence of the creator. Job accomplishes this comprehensiveness by referring to nine categories of leaders and to three qualities that are juxtaposed, namely wisdom, power, and darkness. When intelligence competes with power and darkness, it quickly meets its match.

Job's Self-Defense (13:1-3)

A literal reading of Job's description of the deity would suggest that the divine corrupting influence renders null and void everyone's ability to reason accurately. He does not draw this conclusion with respect to his own thinking but insists that his powers of observation and his capacity for listening are just as keen as those of his friends. Emphasizing personal pronouns, he claims to have seen and heard all this, and he repeats that his discriminating ability is not inferior to theirs (cf. 12:3). This assertion also means that he knows as much as they do, which leads him to a bold decision to argue with Shaddai. The unusual position of an infinitive absolute as direct object before the subject and verb puts the stress on his argument, one that is capped by the verb *'ehpaṣ* ("to delight in"). This desire to face God in a court of law dominates much of Job's discourse in the ensuing chapters, for deep down he cannot surrender the idea that against all odds he will eventually encounter a just deity.

Job Accuses his Friends of Distorting his Image (13:14-16)

Unable to recognize himself in the picture his friends have painted, Job turns away from them and confronts God directly, but not before asking that divine majesty be held in check so that Job can speak freely. Even under this condition, he imagines that such boldness can cost him dearly. The surprising thing is that Job wants to enter into litigation with one who clearly has shown disdain for simple justice by overthrowing those who give compassionate judicial decisions.

What wrongs have the friends committed that upset him so much and make him call them quacks? Job accuses them of showing partiality for God. That is the meaning of the idiom, "lifting the face," most notably by a bribe. The friends have, as it were, strengthened a dejected and embattled deity rather than allowing justice to proceed to its logical end. They have been guilty of making Job into something he was not, "plastering" him with lies.

Men who were supposed to bring healing have proven to be ineffective physicians.

Given the ancient belief that sickness was punishment for sin, it is understandable that physicians were shown little respect in the Bible. The New Testament anecdote about someone who had squandered her entire assets in search of healing but was still no better speaks volumes. Even Ben Sira's attempt to justify the medical profession on the grounds that God created the ingredients that were used as medicine and that doctors added prayer to their prescribed treatment fails (38:1-15), for Ben Sira still clings to the notion that sin and sickness are somehow connected.

When two people have completely different understandings of reality, it is convenient to introduce the category of deceit (Crenshaw 2006a). Thus a conflict between two prophets with differing views about the deity's will naturally evoked the accusation of falsehood. For example, the prophet Jeremiah thinks Hananiah is guilty of lies, and Hananiah is equally certain Jeremiah speaks falsehood. In such circumstances, charges of lying abound and onlookers have no means of distinguishing who proclaims the truth. Job's friends have let their imaginations conjure up lies as convenient explanations for his misery. Silence, he thinks, would be preferable to speech. According to proverbial lore, in some situations silence demonstrates genuine wisdom (Prov 17:28). Job therefore wishes his friends would be quiet and by this means demonstrate their intellectual grasp of the situation.

Their silence will enable Job to present his case before the court of justice. The language becomes more and more legal as Job directs his attention heavenward. "Hear my teaching" is clarified by the parallel stich, "Listen to my lawsuit" (*ribot*). Job's friends are said to be pleading God's lawsuit (the verb in v. 8 is a form of *rib*). Even worse, they are lying on God's behalf, at least as Job sees things. He asks, "Will you speak perversely (*'awlah*) for God or declare deceit (*remiyyah*) on his behalf?" (v. 7). In a word, will you tilt the scales of justice in God's favor?

Job has previously denied that *'awlah* has found a resting place on his tongue. Indeed, he considered his friends' premature abandonment an instance of *'awlah* (6:29-30). They, not he, are acting perversely. In Job's mind such behavior, even in God's defense, will surely bring censure. Therefore he asks them, "Will it go well when he examines you, or can you dupe him as one fools a man?" (v. 9). The idea that one can mock God with impunity is almost as arresting as the internal irony concerning how the friends will fare when the episode about Job's test approaches its resolution.

In v. 10 Job seems to accuse his friends of hiding their true feelings: "He will surely rebuke you if you lift his face in secret." There is nothing hidden in their speeches thus far, for they have almost single-mindedly defended God at Job's expense. Here as elsewhere, especially in hymnic praise, stock phrases make it difficult to apply what is said in the dialogues to the actual situation involving Job and his friends.

Appearing before the Holy One always carried with it an element of fear—*mysterium tremendum et fascinans*, in the language of Rudolph Otto—and guilt increased that trepidation greatly. So Job reminds his friends that they will eventually experience terror in divine presence. Facing God, their recollection will amount to no more than dust, their defensive shield becoming brittle clay. Although Job sits on a pile of ashes, the friends' collective memory is said to be no more substantial than his dwelling place.

Job, too, experiences awe when confronting God, but that dread does not deter him. "Be quiet," he commands his friends, "and I'll speak, come what may" (v. 13). Here Job's ego asserts itself: "I myself." Aware that he is risking everything, Job takes his life in his hands, expecting to be killed. The image is that of a wild animal with its prey in its teeth. Two different textual traditions have been preserved in this case, the one written and the other to be read aloud. The former has Job declare, "He may slay me; I have no hope." The latter reads, "Though he slay me, I trust in him" (v. 15a). The second stich is less controversial: "Surely I'll defend my way to his face." The attenuation of Job's bold assertion (the Ketib, "what is written in the Hebrew text") that has been preserved in the Qere' ("what is read aloud") suggests that a later editor considered Job's temerity ill advised.

Job's boldness, however, rests on the confidence that a profane person, a reprobate, cannot stand before God (v. 16). That certainty constitutes Job's safety, for he knows that he is innocent (*ṣaddiq*). Therefore he proclaims, "This will be my salvation (*yešu'ah*), for a reprobate will not come before him." Without knowing it, Job has successfully anticipated the outcome of his terrible ordeal. He knows that he will be vindicated, even though it seems that God has become unreliable. Job's irregular syntax emphasizes openness, first in the verb *lo' 'ayaḥel* ("I won't wait" or "I have no hope") and then in the unusual *lepanaw* ("before him") between the verb of coming (*yabo'*) and its negation. Does Job expect to be killed? "He will kill me; I cannot wait." Time is running out on him, so he must set forth his case now.

Job Demands Quiet before He Is Silenced in Death (13:17-19)

Confident in his own innocence but fearing his demise at God's hand, Job directs a strong imperative to his friends. "Hear my defense; I'll speak in your hearing" (v. 17). There's nothing hidden here, and Job insists that his friends listen to what he has to say in his defense. He points out that he has carefully prepared his case (*mišpaṭ*) in full knowledge of his innocence. The verb *ʿarakti* has the sense of arranging things in order; elsewhere it is used with reference to laying out items to be sacrificed, lining up soldiers in preparation for battle, and setting a table. In Job's case, the verb indicates an argument that has been painstakingly prepared to meet every possible objection his opponent might raise. Above all, however, he insists on his innocence: "I know that I'm innocent (*ʾani ʾeṣdaq*). The personal pronoun is emphatic. Job throws down the gauntlet before his opponent, daring God to pick it up.

His audacity is followed by a sober realization of the gravity of his situation. Nevertheless he presses his luck even further by asking, "Who is he who would enter into litigation with me" (v. 19a). Should the unimaginable happen, Job concedes, it would bring my death ("For then I'd be quiet and die," v. 19b). His reasoning seems to be that if God, who knows that Job is not guilty, does not drop the case, then all hope is lost. Justice will not be handed out; instead, Job will be found guilty.

Job Flirts with the Language of Prayer (13:20-27)

The power differential between Job and his opponent gives the advantage to God, so Job appeals to a divine sense of fair play. "Two things don't do to me; then I won't be hidden from your face" (v. 20). Because the ancients believed that God withdrew his face from those whose sins incurred divine wrath, Job thought he was hidden from God's face. Ironically, he also felt the harsh hand of God every waking moment. Therefore he asks God to remove that crushing blow, making it distant (*rahaq*) and to minimize the dread accompanying every experience of the divine. In essence, Job petitions for healing and a return to favored status.

Job's request that God not do two things is syntactically curious, for the negation applies to just one of the things mentioned. A similar disparity occurs in the only prayer that has been preserved in the book of Proverbs. Here a certain foreigner named Agur requests that two things not be withheld before he dies but mentions three: "Empty, lying words keep far from me; give me neither poverty nor riches, and tear off my allotted bread for me" (Prov 30:7-8). Agur goes on to give the reason for his prayer: "Lest, sated, I lie and say, 'Who is YHWH?' or being impoverished, I steal and sully the name of my God" (Prov 30:9).

Assuming that God actually hears his prayer and acts accordingly, Job shows his willingness to let God go first in presenting the case against him. If

God prefers to go last, however, Job volunteers to initiate the discussion, marshalling his case before witnesses. He moves immediately to the heart of the case, requesting that God inform him of his offenses. Job covers his bases thoroughly by varying his language to embrace all types of wrongdoing (*'awonot, ḥaṭṭa'ot, peš'a*, v. 23).

In v. 24 Job accuses God of linguistic reversal. His name, *'iyyob*, has been transformed into *'oyeb*, inveterate foe. The friend of God has become the enemy, and it is God's doing. Job wonders why God has hidden the divine face (Balentine 1983). Here Job finds himself in the same situation as count-less others through the centuries who have pondered the reasons for divine hiddenness precisely when help is most needed (see the Barthian interpreta-tion of divine hiddenness in Miskotte).

Now Job begins to reflect on his own misery as illustrative of the human situation. It seems that he is a mere leaf, nothing more substantial than chaff, and God pursues him relentlessly until the tempest blows him into oblivion. Job does not claim to be sinless, for he has committed youthful indiscretions like everyone else. What he cannot understand is why God writes bitter things about him, presumably trumped up charges, and harbors rancor, forcing him to inherit peccadilloes of long ago. The belief that deities could write was common in the ancient Near East. The language of inheritance has been explained as a commercial term, a medicinal one, and a family bequest. The latter is more likely, given the sociological context of the book.

Job thinks he has been reduced to a slave; so he uses images of bondage. He is imprisoned, made immobile by wooden stocks on his ankles, and marked on the bottom of his feet for easy tracking should he manage to escape the watchful eye of his captor. The knowledge that God keeps an eye on the possible paths to freedom is a deterrent to every attempt to escape.

The Human Condition (13:28–14:22)

Death's nearness prompts Job to think about the human condition in general. He does so by comparing mortals with nature itself, probably because in popular tradition men and women were thought to have been fashioned from the earth, *'adam* from *'adamah*. Job's images shift from fragile garments and flowers and fleeting shadows to a stately tree and substantial streams, moving finally to more durable mountains, rocks, and the earth. All this, Job insists, is subject to decay, just like people.

The opening section, 13:28–14:6, treats the brevity of life and its unwel-come limits. The initial description of mortals as decaying matter and moth-eaten garments implicates God as the agent of destruction, at least in

Job's case. It follows that everyone is of short duration and full of trouble (*rogez*). Job's use of *'adam yelud 'iššah* ("a mortal born of woman") is merely a way of being inclusive; the reference to birth has no pejorative connotations. An individual emerges as a thing of beauty, like a delicate flower, but fades and withers away, or quickly (*barah*) lengthens like a shadow into an unrecognizable blur.

Job was not alone in comparing life's brevity to a flower. The poetic author of Isaiah 40:6-8 links grass with flowers and considers all flesh to be no more substantial than these elements that are subject to the sun's relentless heat. In his view, grass withers and flowers fade when the divine breath blasts away, in contrast to the lasting quality of God's word. Another writer, the author of Ecclesiastes, joins Job in likening human existence to a shadow.

God's attentive gaze on such frailty puzzles Job, as does the personal litigation expressed with "me" in an emphatic position. (I follow the Masoretic Text in v. 3b; the Greek, Syriac, and Latin versions have a third person object, "You bring him into judgment.") The difficulty comes from Job's movement back and forth between his own situation and the human condition. That vacillation complicates the interpretation of v. 4, which asks who can transform the unclean into something pure, answering, "Nobody." Does Job refer to humanity as corrupt, or does he ironically indict God who sees him as unclean when he really is pure?

The next two verses apply universally, although they accurately describe Job's present circumstances. God imposes limits on human life spans, mandating (*hoq*), the duration of life on earth. Given the short time mortals are allotted, it seems that God should at least grant some privacy. Accordingly, Job asks that God look away and cease (*weyehdal*), like a kind taskmaster who leaves workers unattended (cf. 7:19 for a similar request that God focus on someone or something else). The jussive "let him cease" offers a smooth transition to the next unit, 14:7-12, which discusses nature's dormancy and resuscitation as a grand backdrop for human decay.

Unlike mortals, a tree has hope. Job freely exaggerates to make his point that even when cut down its stump responds to the mere scent of water, new sprouts appear and endure (*lo' tehdal*; cf. Janzen 2009). There is strong irony in the notion of a tree of life and a family tree, both of which were thought to represent or promise longevity to mortals. Job recognizes that like humans, trees also grow old and face oblivion when their roots die in the ground. Here Job echoes his previous remarks about his own condition resembling that of a slave with marks stamped into the "roots" of his feet (13:27). Although water works magic on an old stump, it has no power to rejuvenate humans. People die and are prostrate; mortals expire, and where are they? Great bodies of water dry up and so do rivers, but the fate of humans is worse. They lie down and don't get up until the heavens are no more, never awakening (v. 12).

In vv. 13-17, Job flees for a moment into the realm of fantasy, imagining that God places him in a protective bubble until the divine anger has abated. Suddenly, the language of hiding and imposed limits takes on a positive resonance and even Sheol becomes a place of temporary refuge. Memory, too, functions to mitigate supposed wrongs, for now God recalls his servant Job. In this changed circumstance, Job asks the question that has troubled human beings for millennia: "If individuals die, will they live again?" The Septuagint omits the interrogative particle and at the same time removes any possible theological offense to later readers who come to believe in resurrection (Crenshaw 1999).

Within his newly created imaginary world, Job thinks comforting thoughts. The expression, "like a warrior or a weary laborer (ṣeba'i)," places the spotlight on Job. Longing for the work of his hands, God would number Job's steps, watch over his errors, sealing them in a bag and covering them out of pure grace. The verb *ḥatum* signifies a wax seal, the ancient means of making official documents tamper-proof.

The last two verses of this unit can be understood as the result of cold water being thrown in Job's face, bringing him back to reality. In this reading of vv. 16-17, God counts every misstep, watches every sin, and seals it in a bag, which is then glued shut until the day of reckoning. The adverb *ki 'attah*, "but now," is susceptible to this interpretation, although the Hebrew can also be translated "For then." In this case, it supports the favorable reading above.

In the final section, vv. 18-22, reality returns with a vengeance. Now it is no fragile flower or fleeting shadow that quickly comes to naught. Rather, Job turns to consider natural elements that give the illusion of permanence: mountains, rocks, the earth. Even these three cannot withstand the constant force of water, which moves mountains, displaces rocks, wears away boulders, erodes soil. Just so, God destroys mortals' hope and forcefully dispatches them far from the divine presence. Meanwhile, children of the unfortunate victim of divine wrath either enjoy public esteem or fall into disgrace and their dead parent knows nothing, feeling only the pain of a miserable state. Throughout this description of destructive activity, Job points an accusing finger by means of indicators for "you" (cf. especially vv. 19b-20).

If one assumes that Eliphaz begins the debate rather than Job, the first round of debate comes to an end with Job's description of universal human misery that he has exemplified in his own pitiful state. His friends have tried to comfort him, but their patience has worn thin because of his refusal to admit what was obvious to them, given their worldview. That is, sickness indicates a broken relationship with God, who rightly punishes wrongdoing in this manner. Their dogma and Job's persistence produce increased rancor. Job insists that he is innocent, and the friends contend that no one is pure in God's sight.

Seemingly abandoned by his friends, Job begins to look heavenward, but not as a repentant. Instead, he challenges God to face him in a court of law. Wistfully, Job longs for a mediator but gives that up, in the same way his hope for a kinder deity fades away. Increasingly, he wages battle on two fronts, using strong language against his friends and God. Job reasons that he has nothing to lose by such audacity.

Eliphaz's Second Speech (15:1-35)

As in his first speech, Elpihaz opens with a barrage of rhetorical questions interspersed with personal affirmations. His aim here is to demonstrate Job's folly and thus to prove the accuracy of his own assessment of things, which he thinks is the result of the dream described in 4:12-17. He then launches into a traditional description of the destiny of sinners that confirms for him the law of retribution.

Job's Abysmal Ignorance (15:1-16)

The first six verses accuse Job of being a windbag, a foolish person filled with hot air. Such nonsense, Eliphaz thinks, makes a mockery of religion (*yir'ah*) and its outer manifestation, meditation (*śihah*). Unlike the opinion expressed in 4:6, Eliphaz no longer views Job's religion as a source of comfort. The personal pronoun *'attah* ("you") and the emphatic particle *'ap* ("surely") amount to a strong indictment of Job like the rhetorical question that demands a negative answer, "Will a wise person respond with windy knowledge?" To emphasize the perversity of Job's language, Eliphaz uses a rare verb that appears elsewhere only in Psalm 144:13 and means "to multiply a thousand fold." The parallel half verse accuses him of choosing a clever tongue, perhaps an allusion to the serpent's natural characteristic in Genesis 3:1. Job has said that although he is innocent, his own words will condemn him; Eliphaz intones the identical thing but refuses to accept Job's claim to be *tam*, beyond repute. Therefore Eliphaz feels no obligation to refute him but points out that "Your words, not I, will indict you." In other words, the primary witness at Job's trial will condemn himself.

In the ancient Mediterranean world, wisdom was associated with seven celestial primal figures, and that idea was carried over to some degree in society below, particularly in the attribution of understanding to the aged. Eliphaz sarcastically asks Job if he were primal man, either Adam of biblical myth or possibly the heavenly prototype for mortals. In doing so, Eliphaz goes beyond Bildad's suggestion in 8:8-10 that Job should consult past generations, for in 12:7-10 Job has appealed to creation. Alternatively, Eliphaz inquires into the source of Job's knowledge: "Did you listen to the divine council?" Mockingly, Eliphaz asks whether Job monopolizes knowledge. Readers will recall that this same Eliphaz has claimed to be the recipient of a divine revelation that set him apart from the others.

The argument from seniority gives the edge to Job's friends, according to vv. 9-10. "What do you know that we don't?" is followed by a reminder that one of them is older than Job's father. The statement is wholly unexpected and may simply be exaggeration for emphasis. Alternatively, he may fail to adjust standard rhetoric to fit the situation. It is even possible that he refers to listeners who have gathered to hear the debate. Verse 11 alludes to El's gentle comfort on Job's behalf, perhaps picking up on Zophar's claim in 11:6 that Job's punishment is less than he deserves. Is Eliphaz completely insensitive to his friend's suffering, or is he merely oblivious to reality?

After momentarily returning to the image of windy speech, Eliphaz tries to get more mileage out of the nocturnal vision that was the highlight of his opening address. Now he emphasizes mortals' innate impurity and extends it to the heavens and its inhabitants. That leads him to an argument from the greater to the lesser, from the holy ones to human beings "who drink iniquity like water, being abominable and corrupt" (vv. 14-16). Eliphaz seems to think that being different from God necessarily implies impurity (Good, 243, thinks Eliphaz's statement comes close to the Christian notion of total depravity).

The Downfall of the Wicked (15:17-35)

Having condemned the entire human race, Eliphaz fails to recognize that this extraordinary view of reality destroys his principal argument that everyone gets what is deserved, the virtuous receiving a blessing and sinners a curse. If human depravity is real, all are subject to ruin; however, Eliphaz proceeds on the assumption that only reprobates endure punishment from above and that Job belongs in this camp.

He begins by appealing to Job for attentive listening and defends his right to hand out wisdom. Essentially, he appeals to his own experience and to tradition, that is, to information that has been transmitted from parents to children over the generations. The curious statement that "the land was given to the fathers and no stranger passed in their midst" is out of place in a body of literature that prides itself for universalism. The sages borrowed freely from international wisdom on the premise that the human intellect, whether belonging to an Israelite, Egyptian, or Mesopotamian, was capable of discovering truth on its own.

The rest of the chapter consists of stock phrases from traditional descriptions of troubles besetting the wicked. The images shift from passive victimage (vv. 20-24) to active aggression (vv. 25-27), then return to passive suffering once more (vv. 28-30). The wicked's entire existence is described by a single image, that of birth pangs (*mitholel*), every waking moment filled with imagined terror and devoid of safety. The merism of full and empty at the same time is striking. Unable to turn away from darkness, the reprobate's destiny is death by a sword. Wandering about in search of food, the hapless one either asks, "Where is it?" or becomes prey for vultures. Surrounded by adversity, he is no match for an attack like that wielded by a king trained to hunt, a popular sport in both Egypt and Mesopotamia.

The picture of aggression is actually one of futility. Aiming a fist at Shaddai, running toward him with neck poised for maximum effect, equipped with a strong shield, and covered with grease as camouflage, he suffers the fate of all who challenge God. Suddenly, the picture shifts to nature and rubble (vv. 28-35). For a second time, Eliphaz says that the wicked person cannot turn away from darkness (vv. 22a and 30a). Interestingly, Eliphaz varies the language, using different verbs for turning, *šub* (in the infinitive) and *sur*, as well as an additional verb in v. 22 (*'aman*, "to trust, rely on"). The same verb occurs in v. 31, which states that "he shouldn't trust in unreliable vanity, for his reward will be vanity." The problem, it seems, is that of the sterility of premature ripening, like grapes that fall off the vine before fully ripening, or blossoms of an olive tree that drop off in alternate years. Eliphaz counters this thought with one of fertility, but hardly what the pregnant mother anticipates. Here the conception and birth are already said to be barren. In this context, Eliphaz's final words are haunting: "Conceiving toil and giving birth to sorrow, their belly establishes deceit." In his view, Job faces even more trouble than he has experienced thus far.

Job's Response (16:1–17:16)

After briefly discussing talk itself, Job describes the deity's aggressive attack on him that drives him to an emotional outburst about a powerful friend who will take his side against the deity. His excitement quickly subsides, and depression sets in while he ponders a dark and dismal fate as an intimate of Sheol and worms. All hope, briefly renewed, is now a thing of the past.

Only a few links with previous dialogues are discernible. Eliphaz's words, not Job's, are windy; instead of Job's words bearing witness against him, his emaciated state will do so; it is not Job who runs to attack God but precisely the reverse; Job's prayer is pure despite Eliphaz's insistence that no mortal can be pure; and Job's vanishing hope seems to confirm Zophar's comment in 11:20, although Job would disagree.

The shifting subjects from singular to plural create difficulty, for the singular "you" does not always refer to God. It appears that Job has nearly given up on the deity, for he rarely addresses him from here on in the speeches until commanded to do so in 40:4-5 and 42:2-6. Furthermore, legal language plays only a minor role in this speech.

The central issue in vv. 2-6 is the nature of discourse. Job claims to be familiar with what they say, for he has heard many similar things. That being so, he derives no consolation from them. Therefore, he uses the adjective *'amal* that indicates hard labor to call them toilsome comforters, friends who only weary him, the equivalent of ineffective healers in 13:4. He wonders if their windy observations can be explained as arising from pain. Naturally, he thinks he would react differently if the friends were suffering and he were the comforter. The image of shaking his head over them can be understood either as a sympathetic gesture or a sign of disapproval, but the context favors the first of these options. Unlike the friends, he would speak to ease their misery; unfortunately, Job is the sufferer and his speech fails to relieve his own pain. If he stops, he asks, how much leaves him? In short, he has nothing to lose from speaking plainly.

The friends' talk has exhausted Job, who has been robbed of all support through the death of his children ("my whole group"). Forced by circumstances to testify against himself, he imagines being the victim of relentless pursuit by an adversary who tears him apart and sharpens his teeth on him. Knaves attack him verbally, and El hands him over to these vicious adversaries. Under these conditions, Job cannot identify his real attackers, so he mentions both El and his troops as active in splitting him open and pouring out his gall on the ground. These images combine features of wild animals seizing prey and military assault.

So far this second section, 16:7-17, has concentrated for the most part on the foe. With vv. 15-17, a significant shift takes place in Job's direction. He describes his defensive maneuver of sewing sackcloth on his skin, transforming his very body into an emblem of grief. Just as a defeated beast plunges its horns into the ground, Job lets his brow drop in submission. Weeping has reddened his face and darkened his eyes, although his prayer is pure and his palms are free of violence. This claim of innocence is a defiant rejection of the friends' interpretation of the facts.

The third section, 16:18-21, introduces the theme of a heavenly witness who, like the earlier arbitrator, has sufficient power to make Eloah act justly. Job begins by appealing to the earth, which he asks to leave his blood uncovered and to refuse to provide a place for his outcry to rest. In ancient oaths, the earth was often personified and summoned as a witness. The belief that unrequited murder left a vocal witness that could be heard by God, as in the story about Cain's slaying of Abel, lies behind this plea (cf. Ezek 24:7-8 for a similar idea). The request anticipates Job's death, which he thinks is imminent. Job now looks to the sky for added help. He thinks of this assistance as present reality ("Even now, look, my witness is in heaven, my advocate's on high, my go-between, my friend").

The emotional pitch that has seized Job affects the clarity of his language, especially in v. 21, but also in the last half of the previous verse. Job seems to think that his eyes drip to Eloah or that they can get no sleep, and he believes that his witness will adjudicate between a hero, presumably Job, and Eloah. The additional phrase "and between Adam and his friend" can be understood several ways. It may envision Job as the primal man and Eliphaz as his opponent, or 'adam represents humankind and the friend is Job. A third possibility is that both Job and the human race are covered by the Hebrew 'adam and the friend is the deity, Job's opponent (Good, 248–51).

Verse 22 serves as a somber conclusion to Job's outburst and an introduction to the next section, 16:22–17:16. He realizes that his days are numbered, and he contemplates a journey on a road of no return. The Hebrew verb 'ehelok ("I shall walk") is occasionally used for going to the place of one's ancestors, here designated "a path I won't return." Only a few gods were thought to have returned from this lonely journey, as described in the "Descent of Inanna" (ANET, 52–57) and the "Descent of Ishtar" (ANET, 106–109). Most surprisingly, Job mentions the passing of years rather than days, whereas his description of suffering suggests that death is near. He therefore acknowledges that his spirit is broken, his days extinguished, the grave his.

How quickly he has forgotten the emotional high point of this speech. In v. 3, he asks. "Who will strike a bargain with me?" The certain guarantee seems to have vanished into thin air as Job once more returns to a description of his misery and its causes. He has been made into a popular proverb, his face becoming the target for spit. Alternatively, he is appalling in the same way the valley of Topeth had come to be—a site where people sacrificed their children by burning. Good people are shocked by this treatment of Job, who is reduced to a shadow, and conflict grows between the just and the unjust, but no true wisdom can be found in all those whom the friends bring to the place of arbitration ("and I will not find wisdom [or a wise person] among you," v. 10b). Even the usual distinction between day and night ebbs and Job anticipates death.

Verses 13-16 return to the idea expressed in v. 1 that Job has already taken possession of the grave. He describes his hope for what it truly is, emptiness. "If I hope for Sheol as my dwelling, lay out my bed in darkness, I've called corruption 'my father,' the worm, 'my mother and sister,' where then is my hope? Will they go down with me to Sheol, or will we descend together to the dust?"

Bildad's Second Speech (18:1-21)

Infuriated by Job's reference to the friends' consolations as ineffective and windy, Bildad vents his anger on his pitiful friend (vv. 2-4) and intensifies Job's pain by a blow-by-blow account of the downfall of the wicked (vv. 5-21). Fury may explain the inconsistent grammar and syntax, which leave the impression of a rift among Job's three friends. The similarities in their arguments lend no support to any division among them, but the plural verbs and second person pronouns (v. 4 is an exception) are odd if Job is the one being addressed.

Even when overcome by anger, Bildad exhibits a remarkable understanding of the art of trapping small birds and wild animals. His elaborate conceit of this practice uses six different Hebrew terms to cover all types of devices used in catching wary creatures. He mentions a net that was spread over a pit, webbing formed by branches strewn over a pit, snares made from a rope and tied to form a noose, and traps made from sticks. All these made it difficult for birds and beasts to pass unharmed, an apt image for the destiny of a sinner. Neither his offspring (*'ono*) nor his wife (*ṣal'o*, "rib," cf. Gen 2:22) endures.

Bildad also displays familiarity with some tropes and mythopoetic commonplaces. He describes the impending darkness in Job's life by recalling proverbs about a sheikh's lamp going out and leaving his tent in total darkness, and he imagines his unrepentant friend being devoured by the firstborn of Mot, the king of the underworld. Mot figures prominently in Canaanite literature, but a firstborn is limited to UT 67:I:19-20. Much more may have been known to ancient Canaanites, just as the biblical allusions to a chaos monster named Rahab suggest that a myth about it has either been suppressed or was so well known that specifics were not needed to render the allusion intelligible.

Scattered allusions to Job's earlier speech indicate that Bildad has been listening even if not agreeing with his friend. Two links with Job's comments stand out. First, Job has claimed that even durable rocks are slowly worn away by flowing water, but Bildad sarcastically quotes Job, rearranging the position of the verb to its normal order ("A rock disintegrates from its place") and accuses him of expecting the earth to accommodate his own needs. Second, Job has insisted that, contrary to mortals, a tree can live again if sufficient water reaches its stump, but Bildad says that decaying roots indicate a dead tree, even if at the moment its branches appear to be alive. One wonders why he didn't inform Job that a stump that sends out shoots was never dead.

Why is Bildad so angry? He objects to Job's labeling his friends "cattle," at least by implication. Job has said that he would be unable to find an intelligent person among his friends, so Bildad has rightly perceived Job's low estimate of their intellect. That disagreement is the main theme of vv. 2-4, which open in the manner of a traditional lament ("How long?"). Bildad quickly cuts to the chase and uses a rare verb for hunting (*qanaṣ*) that anticipates the images of trapping in the next section. Here, however, the search is for words, and Job is told to gain some understanding so that the friends can later respond. Bildad pictures Job tearing himself angrily, which contests Job's observation in 16:9 that God's anger tears him. Bildad also accuses Job of expecting earth to favor him, and in that he is partly correct. Job did ask the earth not to cover his blood, but he did not request a rock to crumble for him. Does Bildad use rock as a metaphor for Job, whose supposed self-importance has given the friends the impression that he thinks he is primal man?

With vv. 5-21, Bildad paints a dismal picture of the downfall of the wicked, among whom he counts Job. A pall of darkness falls on the wicked in accord with proverbial thinking (Prov 13:9), and his death is believed to be the result of his own wrong choices. In the eyes of many, sinners may flourish briefly, symbolized by a vigorous beginning ("strong strides"), but their steps are soon shortened when adjusting to external constraints. That slowed pace leads naturally into images of various traps hidden along the path. A clever pun within verbs of being hurled headlong into disaster (*šlḥ* and *škḥ*) mingles with elements of surprise and capture. Central to them all is the concentration on walking and feet. The evil one stumbles, shivers because of ever-present terrors, and is marched off from his empty tent, his destiny that of a slave to the king of terrors. Images of limbs being devoured echo the belief that Sheol's maw is never satisfied. In this scenario, Mot's firstborn nibbles away at unfortunate sinners. The syntax of v. 13 is unusual, like the concept it conveys; the verb *yo'kal* ("It devours") occurs in each half of the verse and the subject *bekor mawet* ("Death's first-born") is withheld until the very end.

Bildad thinks the destruction is hardly piecemeal, for he pictures the wicked as land that has been purified with sulphur in warfare to make it unsuitable for habitation (cf. *Odyssey* 22. 480–81, 492–94 and Judg 9:45; Deut 29:22). Using a different image and heavy alliteration, he describes the death of a majestic tree, an obvious rejection of Job's momentary optimism. Worse still, Bildad insists that the wicked are completely forgotten and there-fore denied any future existence, for in the time of the book the only hope for a future life consisted of being remembered by those left behind. Small wonder the themes of utter darkness and fleeing from pursuers return at the end of Bildad's speech. Robbed of any surviving kin, the wicked individual faces a day of judgment that sends a chill over his successors and predecessors (or westerners and easterners, literally those behind and in front). The Israelites indicated directions by facing east, so behind them was the west. The emphatic particle *'ak* ("certainly") indicates Bildad's confidence in his own interpretation of reality. He thinks Job belongs to these doomed people who don't know El.

Job's Fifth Response (19:1-29)

"Failure" is the theme of Job's response to Bildad. Not only have his three friends failed to bring comfort (vv. 2-5), but the deity has compounded his problem (vv. 6-12), leading to social ostracism (vv. 13-19) and physical misery (vv. 20-22) so extreme that Job wishes for a permanent witness to such injustice (vv. 23-27), even if posthumous. After lingering momentarily over the conviction that a vindicator will come to his aid, although too late, Job returns to reality and warns his friends that they won't escape judgment (vv. 28-29).

Job's sense of having been abandoned by family, friends, and associates, as well as by the deity he has served faithfully, leaves him aware of the distance separating him from them. Ironically, he speaks of an uninvited guest, an unintentional error, lodging within his own psyche. Eloah's net has enclosed him just as Bildad predicted, but Job insists that he has been wrongly condemned.

Sarcastically, Job imitates Bildad's opening interrogative particle, "How long?" (cf. 8:2 and 18:2) to inform him that his talk is harmful, both annoying and crushing. Exaggerating for effect, he accuses Bildad of humiliating him "ten" times. A similar use of the figure ten occurs elsewhere in the Bible (Gen 31:7; Num 14:22; 1 Sam 1:8; Lev 26:26). In vv. 4 and 5, Job uses the adverb "truly" to urge his friend to sort out fact from fiction. In a word, if I have actually veered from the correct path, then my error affects me most personally by becoming a permanent houseguest. Moreover, if you really exalt yourself over me, then by using my reproach to instruct me you are guilty of doing something I would not do. The distorted syntax in v. 5 testifies to Job's exasperation, the accusative of the verbs in both lines appearing only at the end.

Rather than waiting to receive instruction, Job hands some out. "Know then that Eloah has wronged me (*'wt*," "to twist") and enclosed his net over me," in spite of Bildad's assertion in 8:3 that God would not distort things. Job does what is expected of victims; he shouts *ḥamas*! ("Violence!") but no one responds. The same complaint was raised by the prophets Jeremiah and Habakkuk (Jer 20:8; Hab 1:2; cf. Lam 3:7-9). In these instances, anticipated justice fails to occur, leaving the deity open to the charge of dozing at a crucial hour.

Not only has Eloah failed to respond to a cry for help, but he has also become an enemy denying mobility to Job and attacking his tent with all the force normally mustered against a city. Stripped of honor and crown, Job watches as his hope is uprooted like a tree, the opposite of the fate of a good person promised in Psalm 8:6. The image of Job as royalty will return in 29:25 and 31:36, but now he thinks of himself as a captive slave. Hope, present or missing, has been a constant motif, as has darkness, now enveloping his trail. He understands where this path leads, so he uses the verb *halak* ("to walk"), a euphemism for death (v. 10).

Abandoned by the god he once knew, Job discovers that all his human contemporaries have turned away too. That includes his wife, to whom he has become odious, his children (or siblings), his acquaintances, and his slaves. The mention of children ("children of my womb") is a literary convention, synecdoche for Job's clan, an instance of failing to adjust the dialogue/debate to the prose narrative, or a case where Job refers to his mother's womb as his own, hence siblings. The parallelism (wife/children of my womb) favors the first option. Job was not above adopting a proprietary attitude toward his wife's womb.

Even guests consider Job a foreigner; visitors no longer drop by, and slaves have the audacity to require him to beg them for service. Respect for him no longer exists, and boys dare to insult a person much older than they. In short, the norms of society have ceased to apply for Job. His psychic distress is summed up in these poignant words: "All my closest friends despise me; the ones I've loved turn against me" (v. 19).

One thing has clung to Job: his frail frame, now emaciated. So he claims to have escaped by the skin of his teeth, an expression that is not entirely transparent. Interpreters usually think it implies teeth lacking anything to chew, thus something very close to nothing. In such a condition, he thinks he deserves pity. Hence the twofold appeal: "Pity me. Pity me. You're my friends" (v. 21a). True friends don't pursue someone like an angry El. Why, then, he asks, are you chasing me as if not satisfied with my flesh? The image of a wild beast in pursuit of prey applies to El and to the friends. Animals hot in chase are immune to pleas for mercy, and Job knows it. Therefore, he seeks help from another place (cf. Esth 4:14).

Suddenly, Job introduces a daring thought. An avenger of blood stands ready to act on his behalf, taking the place of his relatives who have forsaken him. Unlike the arbiter of 9:33, who was only a figment of Job's imagination, a third figure enters Job's thoughts, one who is in some ways much like the witness mentioned in 16:19. This time Job leaves no doubt about the reality of the avenger: "But I know my vindicator is alive" (v. 25a). This triumphant declaration was at home in the Canaanite ritual about the dying/rising Baal. In Job's outburst, the confession is set in a context of permanence, not the wavering circumstances relating to the lord of the storm.

Job wishes for a lasting witness to his innocence. He begins with something written, which is more permanent than the spoken word. Some writing, however, is easily erased or soon becomes illegible, such as that on scrolls, papyrus, leather, or a wooden tablet. Therefore Job does not stop with the mention of a scroll. Instead, he thinks of an inscription incised in stone with lead filling that will glisten in sunlight, a monument like the Behistun Rock on which the accomplishments of the Persian king Darius were inscribed. Job wants the inscription to be both permanent and public, visible from afar. A similar thought is attributed to the deity in Habakkuk 2:2 who mandates a written oracle that can be read even as the herald runs to spread its message abroad.

This much of Job's wish is as certain as his emphatic *wa'ani yada'ti* ("But I know"). The rest is either defaced or incomprehensible. Every attempt to understand it labors under the illusion that it must make sense. Translating the Hebrew *go'ali hay* as "my redeemer is alive" carries the heavy weight of Handel's *Messiah*, Isaiah's identification of Yahweh as Redeemer, and the Christian interpretation of Jesus' role in redeeming sinners. The *go'el* in v. 25 is the redeemer of blood, a close kinsman who avenges a wronged member of the family (Num 35:19; Deut 19:6, 12). Job no longer believes that God will act justly toward him, so he thinks an avenger will vindicate him against God's scandalous conduct. He wants revenge now. He does not, in my judgment, appeal to God against God but counts on help from someone like the witness who has the power to make God submit. Obviously, a polytheistic background must be assumed, but that is also true of the prologue with its council of heavenly beings. It has recently become clear that monotheism was slow in coming to Israel.

What does the temporal adverb "afterwards" suggest? Flayed skin implies death, and after that has occurred, the avenger will stand up and Job will see this dramatic event from his disembodied state in Sheol. He insists that he, not someone else, will see Eloah, presumably joining him in death, if the image of blood revenge dominates to the end.

Others understand the words more positively. A living Redeemer, God as mercy, triumphs over the side of God demanding justice and intervenes on Job's behalf, either before death or by raising him from the grave. The alternative interpretations have been summed up as follows: (1) God will raise Job from the grave so he can see his vindication; (2) from the grave, Job, a bodiless spirit, will witness God's appearance to vindicate him; (3) the whole thing is conditional; and (4) God will intervene before Job's death (Hartley, 295–97). The problem with these explanations is that they ignore Job's true feelings and make nonsense of his arguments.

One thing is certain. Job's anger has not left him. So he repeats the charge that his friends are pursuing him; this time he omits "like El" and concentrates on their motive—to locate "the root of the matter in him." His closing observation reveals the lasting power of the concept of retribution, even in Job's chaotic world. It is precisely this sort of inconsistency that opens the door for the alternative interpretations above.

A pattern has evolved in the three emotional outbursts in which Job thinks of rivals to the god who has become a personal antagonist. The individual who might come to Job's aid brings only momentary relief, the brief euphoria that accompanies the conviction that all is not lost. Like a mirage that gives false hope to someone who is stranded in a desert, or a passing ship on the horizon that can be seen by those left on an island after a shipwreck in a tumultuous sea, Job's images of an arbiter, a witness, and an avenger promise more than they deliver. Ironically, the avenger of blood cannot come forth until blood has been spilled, which means that Job's vindication will not prevent his death. It seems that he has decided he will have to settle for revenge. No wonder his invective against Eloah extends to the friends.

Zophar's Second Speech (20:1-29)

In the second round of speeches the friends appear to have given up on Job because of what they take to be his obstinacy. Instead of anticipating his repentance and restoration, they seem thoroughly convinced of his flawed character. Accordingly, they take pains to describe the eventual destiny of evil people. They do not paint a pretty picture.

In his second speech, Zophar recognizes that the wicked may enjoy temporary prosperity, but he is convinced that their flourishing will be brief, making the final state all the more undesirable. To emphasize the woeful condition of reprobates, Zophar focuses on the corporal aspects of punishment. Because in popular tradition sin was associated with the serpent in the Garden of Eden, the image of a viper's poison has recognizable irony. The lethal effect on the victim's stomach and internal organs, together with the body's rejection of poison through vomiting, are conveniently summed up in a proverb: "Like wealth, its exchange." The meaning of this aphorism is not entirely transparent.

The image of eating dominates the entire speech. Zophar's irritation affects his rationality, giving the impression of inconsistency and a poorly thought out argument. He says there is plenty of food but the sinner cannot enjoy it, there is some food, and there is no food. He protests against the insults that Job hurls his way in 19:3, but it must be admitted that Job's accusations directed at his three friends pale in comparison to Zophar's attempt to provide a moral explanation for the punishment of the wicked, which he surely intends to apply to Job. In the following accusation, Zophar does not mince words: "For he crushed, abandoned the poor, stole a house he didn't build" (v. 19).

Whereas Eliphaz relied on external information—a revelation from a ghostlike visitor—for his interpretation of Job's situation, Zophar claims to speak from inner knowledge, a kind of conscience that constrains him to remain and to respond (v. 3). He admits to speaking without adequate preparation, surrendering to an inner haste that has resulted from disturbing thoughts, for which he uses a rare word (*śeʿippay*, v. 2; cf. 4:13). Nevertheless, he appeals to what he takes to be a self-evident truth from the beginning of human existence (*ʾadam*), specifically that the happiness of sinners is short lived. However successful they may be, like the building of the tower of Babel or like the growth of a mighty tree, as in Isaiah 14 and Ezekiel 28, their collapse is certain and total. No shred of evidence remains, and people ask in astonishment, "Where are they?"

No more than a vanishing dream, they leave an emptiness that places undue burdens on their offspring who must repay their parents' debts. Has

Zophar forgotten that Job's children are dead? What comes next suggests that
he has little if any interest in reality. Job's present condition can hardly be
described as full of vigor. His strength has long since fled and will not be
around to sleep with him in the dust, a pointed allusion to Job's own observation in 17:16 that he will descend to the dust.

Zophar rightly understands the powerful appeal of wickedness, which is
in his words "sweet to the mouth," and the natural desire to enjoy it fully by
hiding it under the tongue the way one savors candy. The author of Proverbs
9:17 attributes a similar insight to personified folly and has her say that
"Stolen water is sweet and bread eaten in secret is pleasant." No wonder the
sinner is reluctant to give up such sweetness. All in vain, Zophar insists, for a
remarkable transformation takes place in the stomach when the true nature
of evil manifests itself at El's command.

The attribution of this reversal of sweetness into bitterness to the deity
opens the way for military imagery. An angry God rains munitions on the
sinner so that there is no escape. Like the hypothetical person in Amos 5:19
who fled from a lion and met a bear, and on escaping it entered his house
and leaned his hand against a wall only to be bitten by a snake, the sinner in
Zophar's mind runs away from an iron weapon and is hit by a bronze-tipped
arrow. Zophar sloppily refers to a bronze bow instead of arrow, unless the
Hebrew is synecdoche for both bow and arrow. He surely knows that a
bronze bow has no usefulness in battle but is mainly for ritual or display,
hence aesthetic. The thought here does not linger on the source of the
sinner's downfall but zooms in on the arrow that has penetrated the gall and
protrudes from the victim's back. The image of burning competes with that
of total darkness as an apt description of his demise. A vacant and ruined
tent remains as a witness to his destruction, as if reinforcing Zophar's claim
that the sinner's place won't see him again (v. 9).

The closing observation indicates what Zophar thinks about Job's appeal
to the earth for assistance by refusing to cover his blood. In ancient treaties
Israel's neighbors called on heaven and earth as witnesses to agreements
between rulers seeking beneficial alliances. Zophar credits both heaven and
earth with exposing guilt by revealing the vanishing goods in a sinner's
house. Instead of inheriting the traditional rivers of oil, honey, and cream,
Job can expect to leave an empty tent when El determines his ultimate
destiny. The confusion of inheritance and of bequests further demonstrates
Zophar's illogical mind.

To sum up, Zophar's hasty and intemperate response, signaled by his
opening "therefore" and breathless pace through v. 5, slows to a crawl in
order to emphasize radical and sudden reversals. Joyful shouts are silenced,

the high becomes low, sweetness turns to bitter, and the visible becomes invisible. Zophar's sole purpose seems to be this: to replace Job's misguided hope for a redeemer with the sure knowledge of retribution. The entire speech lacks the faintest hint of hope for Job, who in Zophar's estimation deserves the ulcers in "his belly" (*biṭno*), a word that functions thematically in a speech so burdened with the language of eating (vv. 15, 20, 23).

Zophar's irritation and mistaken logic leave him open to charges of failing to question traditional attitudes toward good and evil. His admission that sinners may flourish for a time complicates the matter of distinguishing good people from bad. He thinks that misgotten wealth is "vomited" as in Proverbs 23:8 and the Egyptian Instruction of Amenemope (Lichtheim 1976, 146–63), and he reasons backwards from financial loss on Job's part to unlawful gain. In his first speech Zophar stated that Eloah had overlooked some of Job's offenses, but now he fully expects Job to suffer for every transgression. He no longer issues an invitation to pray for forgiveness. Instead, he thinks a prophetic day of judgment awaits the guilty Job.

The Third Cycle of Debate

Job's Refutation of the Friends' Worldview (21:1-34)
As he did at the beginning of the second round of speeches, Job emphatically asks to be heard (v. 2; cf. 13:17). Before proceeding to dismantle his friends' doctrine of retribution, he wants to make sure that they pay close attention to his argument. Ironically, he reminds them of their stated purpose in visiting him. Their failure means that instead of their comforting him, he must offer words of consolation to them. The irony of v. 2 turns into sarcasm in the next verse as he requests that they lift him up so he can address them. Either he introduces an element of the dramatic by implying that he is too weak to stand on his own, or the verb *naśa'* has an extended sense of "toleration." Clearly, Job does not expect a favorable response; otherwise he would not have added "and after my reply, you can mock."

To justify his self-defense, Job emphasizes his emaciated condition that terrifies him and leaves him nothing more solid to grasp than a shudder. No wonder his temper is quick and his meditative thoughts (*śiaḥ*) directed heavenward. Verse 5 reintroduces drama as Job tries to prevent his friends from walking away. "Turn to me," he says, "and be appalled; lay your hand over your mouth," either in awe or as a gesture of silence.

Having succeeded in capturing his friends' attention, Job quickly launches an attack on the fundamental premise of their view of things as safely under the control of a just creator. "Not so," Job insists, for the wicked live sheltered lives (vv. 7-16). Job's question, "Why do the wicked live, grow old even, and become strong?" was often heard in the ancient world (cf. Jer 12:1-3 and Ps 73:1-16). For unscrupulous people, everything goes as hoped; their children surround them, a point emphasized by the redundant "with them/before them," and their possessions multiply. The picture Job envisions is one of complete serenity: safe houses, an absence of punishment from Eloah, bulls that breed successfully, calves that are born healthy, children who dance and play musical instruments. Such idyllic existence is a far cry from what Job's friends think characterizes the lives of bad people.

Even worse, their success has made sinners both irreligious and pragmatic. They boldly order El to turn away from them, adding that they take no delight in discerning divine standards of conduct. Instead, their sole interest lies in profiting from any contacts they initiate. The internal irony can scarcely be missed, for the adversary of the folktale thinks everyone, including Job, serves the Lord for gain. By contrast, these sinners see no benefit in serving Shaddai, for their dwelling is secure from dread. The very idea of meeting the deity (*paga'*) issues in an aside remark: "Look, their well-being is not in their own hands; the reasoning of the wicked is far from me" (v. 16). Either Job wishes to distance himself categorically from their reasoning, or a later editor has introduced a cautionary word. In short, things aren't exactly as the wicked think.

The decisive argument, however, occurs in v. 13, although the two different readings in the Ketiv and Qere' (see above) complicate matters. Do the wicked wear out their days, as in the Ketiv, or end them, as in Qere'? The latter reading seems likely. The sinners spend their whole lives in the lap of luxury and then quickly descend to Sheol. The implication is that they never experience divine punishment, not even in the form of a slow, excruciating death. If the safety of such reprobates is not in their own hands, who then is responsible for watching over them? The gods themselves who are spurned for their effort.

Job realizes that the friends will counter by insisting that the offspring of the wicked are punished for their parents' transgressions, as stated in Exodus 20:5 and 34:7 and refuted in Ezekiel 18 with painstaking effort. Therefore, he challenges the traditional way of reinforcing a failed argument. Whereas in 18:5-6 Bildad thought the wicked person's lamp was often extinguished, Job claims that seldom happens. Rarely are they snatched up in the destructive windstorm like chaff. To the convenient answer that Eloah stores up punishment for offspring of the wicked, Job says, "Let him destroy the guilty so he knows" (v. 19b). For punishment to be effective, sinners must actually see the consequences of their action by drinking from the cup of divine wrath. Just as they took no delight in God while alive, in death they take no delight in what transpires on earth, for their passions have at last been stilled. In plain language, punish the guilty; that is what Job thinks a just deity should do.

At this point, Job states a brutal fact of life. Everyone shares a common destiny, whether saint or sinner (vv. 22-26). The opening salvo is ambiguous because of uncertainty about the identity of two pronouns indicating an active subject: "Will he instruct El—he who judges exalted ones?" (v. 22). The first "he" must refer to the sinner of the preceding verses, and the second "he" can also indicate this person, or it can refer to El, who judges celestial beings (cf. Ps 82 for a similar point about Eloah). The next four verses couldn't be plainer. They describe two types of people, those who thrive and those who don't. The language of prosperity echoes Zophar's remark about vigorous bones but extends the image to include either milk-filled breasts and bones full of soft marrow or testicles full of semen. The meaning of the hapax 'atinau in v. 24 is unknown, and one is left with no solid clue, except the curious attribution of milk to men on the first reading above. The other type of individual dies as he lived, overcome by bitterness. Together the two types lie in the dust, covered by worms.

Before Job's friends can object, he claims to know what they intend to say. His opinion of them surfaces in the way he characterizes their thought as intrigues that violate him (v. 27). To their hypothetical question, "Where's the aristocrat's house?" Job has a ready response: "Ask those who travel the highways and byways of life." Those who have vast knowledge acquired through travel know that disaster does not always strike the wicked (cf. Sir 39:4 for this topos about knowledge gained through travel). Frequently, their houses escape ruin when earthquakes occur, for natural calamity strikes randomly. No one dares confront the powerful and unscrupulous nobleman, who at death is given a grand funeral while countless admirers march by the side of his casket. Just as life was sweet for him, Sheol brings no essential difference (v. 33).

Job's closing remark reverts to his comment in v. 2 about the friends' failure to comfort him (cf. 15:11). Now he makes explicit what was only implicit earlier. "How empty is your comfort to me; your responses lack faithfulness" (v. 34). He considers their treacherous reassurances no weightier than a breath or a puff of wind (hebel).

What does Job's speech reveal? That he has entirely abandoned his old worldview, shared with his friends, to wit that retribution is a fact of life, doled out either directly on sinners or deferred for their progeny. He tells them that they should be appalled not by his weak frame but by the unsavory conduct of the deity. Instead of punishing the wicked, El rewards them lavishly. Job has taken a step beyond a few limited remarks to God. Now Job turns a barrage of criticism against the one he served faithfully in the prologue.

Eliphaz's Third Speech (22:1-30)

Eliphaz seems to accept Job's claim that wicked people prosper, at least until their sudden fall, but he undercuts its significance by emphasizing divine transcendence. In his lofty view of the deity, human conduct contributes nothing to enhance El and is actually a matter of indifference to God. No one, Eliphaz insists, is good enough to demand favor from the heavens. This elevated theology propels Eliphaz into outright cruelty as he concocts a fictional account of Job's sins. Then in a surprising move, he shows a more hospitable side and urges his friend to repent, promising a return to a life of bliss.

In his initial address, Eliphaz reinforced his persuasiveness by resorting to a revelatory oracle. Now in vv. 6-11 he introduces an accusatory speech typical of prophecy. Three components of prophetic accusations are recognizable: (1) a *ki* clause ("because") followed by (2) specific charges and (3) a concluding threat introduced by *'al ken* ("therefore," "for this reason"). The similarity with texts like Hosea 2:7-8 and Isaiah 8:6-7 explains why interpreters often identify elements of prophetic discourse in the book of Job. Eliphaz must have realized that such a tissue of lies as those fabricated here must stand on their own merit, so he resorted to the familiar language of prophetic threats that were believed to carry divine authority.

His entire speech falls conveniently into three parts: (1) an account of Job's supposed wrongdoing, (2) a description of the deity's loftiness, and (3) an unexpected warm invitation to repentance. In the end, Eliphaz reverts to his earlier sympathy for his friend, but not before condemning him for serious breaches of morality and common decency.

What is at work here? Apparently, Eliphaz is so wedded to his worldview that he refuses to entertain the possibility that it may be wrong. The general character of his discourse remains unchanged from his second speech. In fact, the similarity in vocabulary is striking, whether intentional or not. Eliphaz seems fixated on the following ideas: benefit, piety, instruction, and guilt.

In vv. 2-11, two things stand out. First, El takes no pleasure in human morality and intelligence, and second, Job's claim to be innocent is bogus, at least as Eliphaz views things. The idea that the gods depend on humans for food, a common rationale for an established priesthood and lavish sacrifices, finds no place in Eliphaz's understanding of things. The result is an exalted concept of a deity so removed from the activity of mortals that Job's hope of entering into a trial with God becomes ludicrous.

All the more ridiculous, therefore, are Eliphaz's trumped-up charges against his friend in vv. 5-11. If Shaddai is indifferent to morality, what is the purpose of tarring Job's reputation? The background for the list of specific sins reminds Job that it could go on ad infinitum. Instead of trying to be complete, Eliphaz chooses to mention only the most egregious sins. Not only has Job cheated his own family, but he has taken advantage of widows and orphans, the most vulnerable members of society. The traditional language in this tissue of invention suggests that Eliphaz has simply borrowed a set piece of moral discourse and used it without checking for accuracy when applied to Job.

The logic is impeccable. Job's suffering is grievous; therefore, his crimes must be heinous. What is worse than taking advantage of one's brothers "for no reason"? The thematic word *ḥinnam* from the prologue returns at this strategic place, suggesting that Job's behavior cannot even be justified either from necessity or from a desire for gain. Instead, Job acts out of sheer malice, refusing food to the starving and water to those dying of thirst. By stripping the naked of their clothes, he has moved beyond the violation of common decency to the breach of law (cf. Deut 24:12-13, which stipulates that clothes taken in pledge from the poor must be returned by nightfall to give them something to provide warmth during the night).

In Eliphaz's convoluted logic, were Job innocent of these sins, he would not be undergoing the punishment reserved for the wicked. That is what Eliphaz now makes explicit by picking up on Bildad's picture of snares and traps awaiting sinners (18:7-10). As if the panic and dread brought on by hidden traps were not sufficient punishment, Eliphaz adds the threat of darkness and raging waters reminiscent of the flood. Covered in sores, Job would welcome a merciful drowning, a foretaste of Sheol.

The contrast between Job as depicted in vv. 5-11 and the deity of vv. 10-20 is mind-boggling. Eliphaz's fondness for rhetorical questions returns in vv. 12-13, each demanding positive answers. "Isn't Eloah in high heaven . . . can he judge through thick clouds . . . and can you guard the hidden paths?" The pessimistic questioning of the deity's ability to see through the heavy clouds and the inference about the distance separating humans from the creator are here attributed to Job, despite the fact that he has never said, "What does El know?" The ancients believed that the earth was separated from the heavens by a rim that was a walkway for the deity, and sinners sometimes drew the conclusion that God couldn't observe them through thick clouds (cf. Lam 3:4).

Eliphaz links Job to hardened criminals who walked along concealed paths (v. 15, repointing ʿolam to ʿalum) but were unexpectedly subjected to rushing waters, like unfortunates in wadis suddenly filled by a cloudburst. He thinks they have told El to turn away (cf. 21:14a), believing that Shaddai lacked the power to punish them. The closest Job has come to such an audacious request is his plea that the deity look away so he can catch his breath momentarily. The second line of v. 18 reiterates Job's observation in 21:16 that his reasoning is not that of a wicked person. That may well be true of Eliphaz, but the logic of vv. 18-20 is difficult to unravel. Does he mean that El has freely bestowed good on defiant people who push him away? If so, why would the righteous express happiness over this serious breach of their concept of reward and retribution? Their own survival is only half of the equation. Recognizing this, Eliphaz has the righteous anticipate a fiery end for the sinners who are flourishing at the moment.

In vv. 21-30, Eliphaz urges his friend to amend his ways and promises him a serene ending to his present memory. Although he has argued that humans cannot benefit El, now he changes views and suggests that Job act so as to benefit El. Ironically, Eliphaz concentrates on the good things that repentance brings to Job. In a hidden play on the meaning of the name Eliphaz ("My El is gold") he suggests that if Job returns to El and makes the deity his prized "possession," more treasured than the finest gold of Ophir, and if he takes pleasure in Shaddai, blessings will come his way. Praying will enable him to fulfill his vows, speak with effectiveness, and assist those in need through a comforting word and intercessory prayer. The irony between this optimistic account and the actual restoration of Job in the epilogue is palpable. Not only is the picture that Eliphaz paints lovely to behold; it is also aesthetically pleasant to the ear because of puns between gold and dust, prize possession and wadi (v. 24, ʿapar/ʾopir; baṣer/beṣur). In this idyllic setting, light replaces darkness and "not-innocents," a rare word like the name Ikabod in 1 Samuel 4:21, escape because of Job's pure palms. The lowly need not fear this changed man. Ironically, Eliphaz himself will escape the consequences of divine wrath through Job's intercession.

What can the morally sensitive interpreter make of Eliphaz's final speech? Torn between the demands of friendship and theological accuracy, he attempts to sustain both. The problem, however, is that Job's miserable condition places too much of a strain on belief as Eliphaz understands it. To his credit, he adjusts that belief, but the distancing of the deity virtually removes every thought of a relationship between the lofty one and lowly humans. The final appeal to his friend indicates that Eliphaz sees the bank-ruptcy of his revised theology. Nevertheless, he is still caught up in the bind created by a strict concept of reward and retribution.

That is why he cannot imagine that Job is innocent of all wrongs. And here we are presented with the negative side of Eliphaz's character, his refusal to question dogma even when it flies in the face of what he knows to be true about his friend. Lest we be too hard on him, we should be reminded that turning against what one has been taught comes at a heavy cost. It means we are willing to say that our mentors were mistaken and that the accumulated wisdom of the past is untrustworthy. Eliphaz chose fidelity over innovation, and in this regard he was typical of his era.

How should readers understand such a character with conflicting senti-ments about mortals and the deity? Perhaps the same way they react to the presentation of the character Job, one equally torn between fidelity and rebellion. Whatever else Eliphaz represents, he surely stands for real human beings who try to reconcile belief with the actual circumstances of daily existence.

Job's Response to Eliphaz (23:1–24:25)

In chapter 21 Job insisted that God rewards human misconduct. Now he goes beyond that audacious claim and accuses the deity of actually causing criminal activity by withdrawing from the scene and withholding divine directives. Strangely, Job continues to wish for a judicial hearing at which time he can present his case and hear the verdict, "Not guilty." Why have the implications of his picture of God's disdain for simple justice not erased from Job's mind every thought of entering into litigation? The answer is unclear, but he seems to cling to the notion, earlier introduced, of an avenger who will champion his cause against El, although he does not make that assump-tion explicit here.

Chapter 24 poses even greater problems for understanding Job's thinking. The views expressed there appear at times to be at odds with the themes that have run through his comments thus far. That sudden change in perspective, the truncated nature of Bildad's next speech, and the missing response by Zophar have led interpreters to attribute portions, if not all, of the chapter to one or both of them. So far, no manuscript supports a reallo-cation of text, and every rearrangement of the material is speculative even if deriving from a valid intuition. To some extent, all interpretation of ancient texts depends on disciplined imagination, so such an effort to clarify the chapter is not wrong in principle.

The idea of a trial dominates vv. 2-7. The temporal marker "today," rare at least for the speeches, like the earlier "these ten times," sets Job's comments off as distinct from the others, and his description of his complaint (*siah*, "meditation") as bitter links past and present (cf. 15:4). An expression of wishful thinking (*mi-yitten*, "oh that") is followed by a verb indicating knowledge, but the object of that verb is missing. What does he hope to know? Quickly, he shifts to a verb of locating, and the attached personal pronoun leaves no doubt about whom Job wants to find. He adds, "I'd come to his established seat, arrange my case before him, and fill my mouth with arguments" (vv. 3b-4). Confident of his ability to present a strong case and to comprehend what the judge would say to him, Job thinks God would personally argue the case against him. There Job could count on a fair trial, he believes, because in such a place the upright are free to argue with the judge. That being so, Job expects to be exonerated of all charges. His affirmation leaves no doubt: "And I would be forever free from any case against me" (v. 7b).

The next section, vv. 8-12, exposes the flaws in such optimism by indicating the total hiddenness of the deity. Job covers the points of the compass in search of God but all in vain. He begins in the east facing the sun ("before") and turns 180 degrees to look behind him; then he faces north and finally south, where he thinks God hides. Despite his hiddenness, God knows Job's character, according to v. 10. Job is so sure of this theological statement that he thinks he will come forth as pure gold when tested. In this context, Job cannot resist the temptation to remind Eliphaz that he has already purified his values by esteeming the deity's words as more precious than food. Job thinks highly of himself and denies that he has ever veered from conduct that the deity has mandated.

The idea of divine testing is widely explored in the Bible. The patriarch Abraham is said to have been put to the test by being told to sacrifice his beloved son Isaac, the newly rescued Israelites were tested in the wilderness, King Ahaz was subjected to a test of his reliance on Yahweh by an Assyrian army, and so on. This motif appears prominently in the book of Psalms, always placed in the mouth of a devout worshiper who does not fear, indeed welcomes, a close scrutiny of mind and heart. The supreme example of divine testing is, of course, the story of Job. It is noteworthy that Job thinks God sees his every move even if he, Job, cannot see or grasp the one who chooses to remain in hiding.

The following section, vv. 13-17, presents an entirely different side of Job's mental outlook from the confident, self-congratulatory tone in vv. 10-12. At the present, and pending the divine test that proves Job's innocence, the deity acts unreflectively and frightens him. Job blurts out, "He's as one; who can reverse it? For he carries out what's decreed for me . . ." (vv. 13-14a). The echo of the Shema (Deut 6:4) is probably accidental; after all, Job is represented as a foreigner who would not be expected to know this creedal statement. In reality, monotheism leaves no other explanation for anomalies than to attribute them to the deity. No wonder Job complains that El has weakened his mind. Verse 17 is difficult, largely because of the two different references to darkness. Job seems to think the deity has preserved him from annihilation, somehow covering up the darkest threat. Alternatively, he may describe El's throne as gloom, but this reading requires a minor emendation (*mippanay kissah* to *mippene kisseh*).

In a properly governed society, those criminals who turn things upside down through force and deceit will eventually face a day of reckoning. The same should be true of those who lack moral standards of decency. That conviction leads Job to ask why Shaddai doesn't store up times (of judgment) and make them visible to devotees. In the absence of the threat of retribution, rogues plunder the weak and behave like wild asses. That is the picture Job paints in 24:1-12, which concludes with a scathing indictment of Eloah. The failure of cosmic rule couldn't be plainer than this: "From the city, the dying cry out, the throat of corpses screams, but Eloah attaches no blame" (v. 12). If the word translated by "blame" is pointed differently, so that *tiplah* becomes *tepilah*, the charge is even more damning, for it means that Eloah turns a deaf ear to prayer. The divine champion of widows and orphans dozes while they pray for help.

The description of malfeasance that falls between Job's question in v. 1 and accusation in v. 12 is marked by complex grammar, unspecified subjects, and uncertain antecedents. The activity appears to shift from that of criminals to the desperate attempts of marginalized citizens to survive. Job begins with the removal of boundary stones, a crime that is prohibited in legal codes from Mesopotamia and Israel (cf. Deut 27:17), while an Egyptian proverb preserved in the "Instruction of Amenemope" and in Proverbs 23:10 indicates its significance outside law codes. In addition to stealing land, criminals increase their flocks by taking advantage of orphans and widows. In biblical texts referring to the mistreatment of widows and orphans, two additional adjectives often occur. The addition of the poor and needy in v. 4 is therefore entirely traditional, even if the language is not (*'aniyye 'ares* for *dal* or simply *'ani*).

It seems that Job refers to the consequences of powerful predators on the weak in vv. 4, 6-8. They hide together, glean in unproductive fields, spend cold nights clinging to rocks; wet, they freeze from lack of adequate clothing.

Verses 9-11 make this relationship of act/consequence even clearer. Powerful men snatch orphans from their mother's breasts and take in pledge infants of the poor, later forcing them to work with flimsy covering but forbidding them to eat some of the wheat they are carrying or drink some wine while treading the press. People, that is, are treated worse than animals, for legislation permitted working beasts to sample the food they trod.

The twenty-fourth verse in the following section is so antithetic to anything Job has said that it has often convinced interpreters to attribute vv. 13-25 to someone other than him. In this verse, sinners are said to experience a brief season of prosperity and then are cut off like heads of grain. The prospect of a fixed judgment day throws a whole new light on the description of wrongdoing in this section. These rebels against light don't recognize God's way or adhere to it the way Job claims to have done.

Two types of people carry the brunt of the argument here. The murderer kills the poor and needy in broad daylight, then he becomes like a thief at night. The adulterer disguises himself and breaks into houses. Why would he risk discovery by breaking down structures rather than entering doors? Does he fear guardian spirits at thresholds more than being seen? He is said to be sealed inside during the day, experiencing something much more sinister than the light. These types of people are scum; cursed, they are shattered and go down to Sheol, where maggots are sweet.

Unlike the scoundrels whom Job described as receiving fine burials, these people are not even remembered. They may have taken advantage of the weak, but they are being watched by one who is far more powerful. After momentary success, they are cut off. The speech concludes with a challenge to disprove the assertion of a just retribution for sinners. Perhaps one could have imagined Job taunting his friends by exposing the shallowness of their responses, but the final verse makes that highly unlikely: "If this is not so, who can prove me a liar and make my words nothing?" (v. 25).

The missing antecedents for pronouns in this final section of the speech attributed to Job make it possible to view vv. 18-24 as a description of the deity's arbitrariness. In this scenario, he refers to God who feeds on the barren and fails to help widows but also drags away the strong and cuts him off after letting him prosper briefly. The defiant challenge in v. 25 would then refer to the arbitrary treatment of mortals by the deity. This interpretation would then place the last unit in line with the earlier questioning of divine days of judgment and the accusation of Eloah as indifferent to the desperate screams of widows, orphans, and others whose only hope in such a topsy-turvy society is celestial.

Bildad's Third Speech (25:1-6)

The brevity of Bildad's third speech is striking, even for someone known for sparse language. Perhaps he could be forgiven such a laconic final address if he had something new to say. He does not. In fact, he makes only two points, both of which have already been hammered home by Eliphaz (cf. 4:17-19 and 15:14-16). He emphasizes the deity's power and reduces human worth to the lowly status of worms.

The ideas expressed in his closing remarks are only tangentially related to Job's argument. Whereas in 21:9 Job has characterized the lives of evil-doers as secure (*šalom*) from dread (*paḥad*), Bildad attributes these two qualities to the deity. *Paḥad* ("dread") is attached to "dominion," both words functioning as one and meaning something like "awe-inspiring rule." The other word, *šalom* ("peace") appears in the parallel line ("He makes peace in the heights"). The allusion is probably to the primordial chaos of ancient myths, specifically to the chief god's defeat of the monster of chaos. Readers are aware of internal irony between Bildad's assertion and the presence of a heavenly adversary in the prologue. Apparently, peace has yet to be established on high despite Bildad's confidence in divine control of the heavens. It follows that his point in stressing the deity's rule above as proof of complete sway over what transpires below is flawed. Job's emotional outburst about a witness in the heavens (16:19) is therefore credible, and Bildad has failed to undercut his friend's only basis for hope.

Verse 3 may have been inspired by Job's comment about being attacked by the deity's troops (cf. 19:12). Bildad insists that their number is limitless, hence the unlikelihood that anyone could escape their assault. He fails to address the brunt of Job's remark: that the divine army is training its sights on an innocent victim. The second half of this verse unexplainably shifts to universal light issuing from the deity, unless the Septuagint *enedra par 'autou* ("his ambush") is accepted. The point would then be the impossibility of anyone resisting divine hosts. Retaining the Masoretic Text permits one to see Bildad's observation as a response to Job's self-description as not silenced (or annihilated) by darkness (23:17).

The central thesis of Bildad's view of human nature is found in the fourth verse. It takes the form of a double rhetorical question: "How can a person (*'enoš*) be innocent (*yiṣdaq*) before El; how can one born of woman (*yelud 'iššah*) be pure (*yizkeh*)?" Eliphaz has already stated this low opinion of mortals in 4:17 and 15:15b, but Job has linked himself with maggots in 7:5; 17:14; 21:16; and 24:20. Bildad's contribution is to take Job's exasperated remark about maggots (*rimmah*) being his mother and sister (17:14), applying the general sentiment to all mortals, and adding a reference to worms (*tole'ah*). Both words, maggots and worms, occur in parallelism in Isaiah 14:11. In v. 6, Bildad uses the parallel terms *'enoš* and *ben 'adam* rather than *'enoš* and *yelud 'iššah* as in v. 4.

Bildad's low view of humanity contrasts with his exalted view of deity. Moon and stars serve his purposes well, as the waxing and waning of the former illustrate instability and the twinkling of the latter suggests impermanence. Bildad repeats the language of purity that he applied negatively to mortals in v. 4. His failure to label the sun impure is later corrected by the eloquent contestant in 1 Esdras 3:1–4:41, who dismisses wine, king, and woman as strongest and subsequently calls the sun *adikos* ("impure"), leaving the God of Truth alone as righteous.

Job's Response to Bildad (?) (26:1–27:23)

The question mark in the heading of this long section indicates the difficulty presented by the closing unit, 27:11-23, which seems entirely inappropriate in Job's mouth. For this reason, many interpreters attribute it to Bildad or consider it a truncated version of the missing speech by Zophar. After Job has adamantly promised to maintain his integrity to the very end in 27:5-6, one hardly expects him to chronicle the activity of a just avenger of wrongs, and thus to abandon his belief that El has turned vicious.

The initial unit, 26:2-4, reeks with sarcasm, but at whom is it directed? The singular pronominal suffix "you" usually indicates deity. If that is true here, Job turns against God who has failed in two important ways. First, he has not championed the cause of those lacking strength, that is, has not lived up to what was expected from a high god in the ancient world. Second, he has not provided insight for individuals who breathe the divine enlivening that is mentioned in Genesis 2:7. The god in this brief unit has definitely not revealed directives for living, even indirectly like the oracle that made such an impression on Eliphaz.

If Job's sarcasm is aimed at Bildad, the last speaker, or even at all three friends, it blasts them for not providing encouragement in his weakened condition and for the bogus nature of their advice. Even more damning, he questions their presumption of divine inspiration, which the story about Micaiah ben Imlah in 1 Kings 22 puts in a negative light. That appears to be the purpose of the veiled allusion to the divine animating breath, *nešamah*. If Job intends to indicate himself as one devoid of wisdom, the expression "not-wisdom" is surely ironic, for he definitely believes he has tapped into a source of knowledge.

In 26:5-14, Job paints quite a different picture of the deity from that in vv. 2-4. The emphasis now falls on the ancient mythic tradition about a conflict between the embodiment of chaos and the creator. The purpose in returning to the theme of divine power may be to underscore the earlier point that the deity has not lent assistance to the weak. Failure, that is, was the result of a conscious choice and not necessity. The deity had sufficient power to dispense for good yet chose not to do so. According to Psalm 82, the penalty for such failure was death.

Job begins by declaring that the underworld was subject to divine surveillance: "Sheol is naked before him; Abaddon lacks covering" (v. 6). The latter term for the netherworld appears to derive from the verb 'abad, "to perish," an apt name for those who even in death are said to writhe beneath the waters. Job now turns to the other two realms in his worldview, heaven and earth. He says that the creator stretched Ṣapon over chaos and hung earth over nothing. In Ugaritic texts Saphon is the domain of the gods, like Olympus to the Greeks. As a geographical term, it refers to the north. This account of the suspension of heaven and earth in space is undoubtedly the most abstract one in the Bible. It assumes that heaven is separated from earth by a huge water bag, as it were, and that the earth is sunk in the waters below by giant pillars that shake periodically because of tumultuous waves.

Since life on earth depends on photosynthesis, the mention of light in this context is interesting. Job first refers to the moon, a minor source of illumination, which the deity intentionally shields from full view. Then he describes the delimitation of a path at the upper edge of the suspended waters, a circuit traversed by the gods. Here, too, is the outer limit of light and darkness. Curiously, there is no direct reference to the sun.

Attention now turns to the primordial conflict between order and chaos, light and darkness. The frightening announcement that "Heaven's pillars shook, terrified at his blast" sets the mood for what follows. The echo of the battle between Marduk, originally Enlil, and Tiamat is easily recognizable, even if the name of the opponent differs. Here the monster whose body is split to form heaven and earth is called Yamm, Baal's enemy in Ugaritic literature, and in the parallel line Rahab of biblical lore. Whereas in the Babylonian myth, Enlil/Marduk divided Tiamat's body with a mighty wind, here the wind both clears (?) heaven of all darkness and splits the fleeing serpent. The same expression, "fleeing serpent," occurs in Isaiah 27:1, a mythic application of the story to Yahweh's special relationship with Israelites. The additional act of Marduk, slaying Tiamat's companion Kingu and creating mortals from his divine blood, has not left any trace in the Bible.

The final verse of chapter 26 is an eloquent testimony to human ignorance about the divine. It identifies the mythic description in vv. 5-13 as nothing but the outer fringe of the deity's power (*darko*, reading the Ketib and understanding it as an indication of strength as in Ugaritic literature and a few biblical references). The Qere, on the other hand, implies that even astute readers know little about God's activity. The last two lines in the tercet (a line of poetry containing three units) contrast the faint whisper (cf. 4:12) that is apprehended by humans where God is concerned with the mighty crescendo (*ra'am*, "thunder") of his power that none can understand.

Until 27:1, the formula introducing each speaker has been consistent. It reads as follows: "Answering, x (plus a gentilic in the case of the three friends) said." The new formula, "Again Job took up his discourse (*mašal*) and said," also appears in 29:1, where it may have been inserted because of the disruptive nature of the poem in chapter 28. There is no reason for an introduction of Job in 27:1, for his speech has not been interrupted, unless, however, the hymnic material in 26:5-14 has been mistakenly attributed to him.

In vv. 2-6, Job swears that he will not relinquish his integrity as long as he lives. Thus the poetic debate has him confirm Yahweh's assessment of him as well as that grudgingly given by his wife, namely that he has maintained his integrity (*tummah*) in spite of everything (2:3, 9). He is convinced that El has turned away (*hesir*) Job's justice and Shaddai has embittered him, but even in the face of such cruelty he will not turn (*'asir*) his integrity from himself. To take an oath in the name of a deity was a serious act. Job compounds things by combining the oath with an accusation. In 19:25, Job has declared that his avenger is alive; unfortunately for him, so is El, his tormentor.

In 2:10, the narrator stated that "In all this Job didn't sin with his lips." Neither the loss of all he had acquired, including children, nor physical affliction had moved him to accuse Yahweh of doing something unworthy (*tiplah*, 1:22). Now even the friends' false accusations and his certainty of being mistreated by the deity have made no significant difference in how Job responds to difficulty. He takes an oath to be damned if he utters wickedness (*'awlah*) or deceit (*remiyyah*). In vv. 2-4, his language stresses the inner nature of resolve (soul/breath/wind/nostril/lips/tongue), and v. 5 specifies the consequences of the oath if Job dares to declare his friends to be justified in their beliefs. The verb *hazak* ("to strengthen") rather than merely holding (*'ahaz*) points to Job's resolve, one grounded in conscience. Emboldened, he curses his enemies but in doing so accepts the traditional view that El punishes sinners. He does vary this doctrine to include El's refusal to hear sinners' cry, presumably even pleas for forgiveness. Exasperated, Job tells his friends that he'll teach them about El's power. If 26:5-14 has been wrongly put in Job's mouth, 27:11-12 carries a sting. Job also knows something about El's might, perhaps even enough to justify his labeling their talk vapid, merely thin air (*hebel tehbalu,* v. 12b). The verb and cognate accusative underline the empty talk and Job's question: "Why?"

The description of punitive justice in 27:13-23, if taken literally, would be a reversal of Job's previous arguments and, as such, a betrayal of his integrity. Perhaps it can be salvaged by reading the sentiment as a parody full of cynicism and sarcasm, with Job seeing himself as the sinner in El's eyes who therefore thinks it right to punish him for gross wickedness. The description of a topsy-turvy world and a sadistic divine ruler in 24:1-12 leaves room for Job to stress divine arbitrariness. In short, the deity can punish evildoers just as he can bring disaster on good people. On this reading, El has been guilty of doing exactly what Job refused to do, declaring something the opposite of what it is. He has "declared" Job guilty, but Job did not "declare" his friends right.

The more likely interpretation of vv. 13-23 requires an adjustment of speaker. Many commentators therefore assign them either to Bildad or to Zophar. The views expressed are in line with their interpretation of reward and retribution. What is that? A sinner inherits nothing good from El. The sword devours his children; or they go hungry; his widows weep; his possessions disappear into the hands of the innocent; terrors abound; and a tempest hurls its awesome force against him without mercy. In this description of the woes that overtake the wicked, the mention of widows reminds modern readers that the book was composed in an age of polygyny even though the prologue and Job's speeches mention only one wife.

The contrast between Eliphaz's promise to Job, conditioned on his repentance in 22:24-25 and 27:16, is noteworthy. Both texts mention dust alongside wealth, but what a difference. If Job lays aside his gold in the dust and values the deity as his supreme treasure, he will do well, Shaddai amounting to silver piled up for him. The wicked, however, are said to gather silver like dust and clothing like clay, apparel being an indication of social status. Both items of personal wealth, however, will be lost to the righteous in this imaginary just universe.

The listing of three kinds of punishment in vv. 20-23 is solidly traditional. Whereas this text refers to terrors, a tempest, and an east wind, both Jeremiah and Ezekiel use a similar device when combining either three, or sometimes four, kinds of devastation (Jer 14:12; 15:12; Ezek 5:12; 6:12). According to the speaker of vv. 20-23, a personified east wind grabs the sinner and hisses at him, emitting an apt sound for his sorry fate.

Wisdom's Inaccessibility (28:1-28)

Both style and vocabulary set chapter 28 apart from what precedes and follows. It seems to have been composed later and inserted as a kind of interlude, its final verse forming an inclusion with the statement in 1:1 that Job was both religious and moral, that is, he feared Elohim and turned away from evil. The theme of the entire chapter is wisdom's inaccessibility to all but the deity despite almost superhuman searches for things of value by brave mortals.

Because the original meaning of *ḥokmah* indicated skill at various tasks such as weaving, metal working, sailing, and so forth, the use of mining as a paradigm for understanding is entirely appropriate. The first eleven verses give a poetic description of ancient mining for precious gems that result in the discovery of an assortment of valuable ores (van Wolde 2003b gives a detailed discussion of the techniques of ancient mining). The success of this endeavor is then contrasted with the total failure at locating wisdom.

The poem begins with an emphatic particle *ki*; otherwise the usual translation "for" suggests that something originally stood before the observation about a source for silver. It is best rendered as follows: "There's a sure source of silver, a place gold is refined." Not until both iron and copper are mentioned does one find any reference to those involved in the search for these ores, and even then it is only implied. Scholars debate the identity of the one or many who engage in such dangerous activity. For some, the missing subject is God who is said elsewhere to move mountains (cf. 9:5; Greenstein 2003, especially 267–72, thinks God is the subject of vv. 3-11 and that these verses were originally Elihu's concluding remarks). Others think of human daredevils who venture into earth's bowels and swing by ropes or hang in suspended baskets while digging for precious metals. If mortals are indeed the subjects of the verbs, their achievements are nearly divine, for they are said to control the flow of water, put an end to darkness, bring hidden things to light, and search the very limits, tasks more suited to deity. The verb forms are not decisive in this debate, for the singular masculine subject can be taken either as generic or as specific. Even if mortals are the intended subjects, their activity is paradigmatic for God's search for wisdom.

This description of mining is the only one in the Bible. Clearly, the author had exceptional knowledge of the difficult process of extracting precious metals from the earth beneath. There were three basic types of mining: (1) open cast mining on the earth's surface; (2) horizontal gallery mining; and (3) deep shaft mining. The dangerous and back-breaking work was carried out by slaves, many of whom were prisoners of war. The death toll on these workers was high because of the demands placed on them and the remote areas in which they toiled, regions far from adequate food. Some mining sites were known for specific treasures: Canaan for iron and copper, Edom for copper, Asia Minor for silver, Nubia and south Arabia for gold, and the coast surrounding the Sinai Peninsula for coral (Hartley, 380).

In their search for rare gems, men venture where no animal has been before; they go to places never seen by the keen-eyed falcon nor traversed by proud beasts (cf. 41:26) or dragon lizards. The comment that food comes from earth is curious, given the desolate areas where mining was carried out. More revealing is the remark about turning the earth over by fire, presumably causing hard rock to crack and making it brittle. The task of finding adequate materials to burn and bringing them to the scene must have been daunting.

In vv. 1-11, then, the poet has moved from something remote (vv. 3-4) to surprising discovery (vv. 5-6), from ignorance (vv. 7-8) to knowledge acquired through diligent effort (vv. 9-11). The whole literary unit emphasizes success as the result of hard work and native intelligence. Against this story of ringing success will be set a similar account of complete failure. Precious gold and lapis lazuli are found, much to the delight of those who will have ownership, but the search for wisdom ends in abysmal failure, with a single exception.

We will not learn about that exception until all others are said to be unable to locate wisdom, which is defined as altogether incommensurable with every other human value (vv. 12-19). A rhetorical question opens this discussion: "But wisdom, where can she be found; where's the place of understanding?" (v. 12). The first exclusion is *'enoš*, human beings; and the second is the underworld, here designated as the deep (*tehom*) and the sea (*yam*). Like wisdom herself, who bears the definite article to indicate a distinct entity, these two are personified. Each denies having her in its possession. That is quite a confession, given the aggressive nature of these cosmic powers in Canaanite mythology.

Wisdom's unique worth is the topic of vv. 15-19, which give a list of gems that are highly valued in society. In vv. 16 and 18, the precise identity of these precious ores is unclear. Moreover, four different words for gold occur in the space of six lines: *segor, ketem, zahab, paz*. The irony of comparing available gems with a quality that cannot be obtained is palpable. Further irony exists when one recalls that teachers invited prospective students to buy wisdom and promised them significant returns on their investment just as modern colleges and universities hawk their wares today.

The rhetorical question of v. 12 recurs in v. 20, only this time the verb is "come" rather than "find." ("But wisdom, where does she come from, and where's the place of understanding?") The emphasis now falls on wisdom's hiddenness, a quality otherwise attributed to deity (vv. 21-22). Once again mortals are joined to the underworld in ignorance, and this time the birds of the sky are also mentioned. Furthermore, the earlier Tehom and Yamm are here replaced by Abaddon and Mot (Death), who admit that they have heard a rumor of wisdom but have no direct knowledge of her. Yamm and Mot, sons of El in Canaanite myth, were antagonists of Baal. For the poet who composed this poem about wisdom, they are ignorant and inferior as in 26:12-13.

Knowledge replaces hiddenness as the theme of vv. 23-28. Suddenly, Elohim enters the picture as the lone exception to ignorance: "Elohim understands her way; he knows her place" (v. 23). The personal pronoun "he" is emphatic, pointing to the contrast with previously mentioned figures. His knowledge is both original and complete, unlike the derivative rumor that Abaddon and Death possess. Elohim is said to have put that knowledge to good use, establishing order in the universe and keeping the wind, lightning bolt, and dispersal of rain under a watchful eye.

In v. 27, four verbs that nicely describe the ancient intellectual process are attributed to Elohim. He observed (ra'ah), discussed (sapar), established (kun), and probed (ḥaqar). In short, on the basis of careful study, he formed theories, fixed them into discussable arguments, and examined the various aspects of insights that evolved (Crenshaw 1998a, 205–19 and 2006e). That accomplished, Elohim became a teacher. Then he said to Adam (or humans generally), "Look, the fear of Adonai, that is wisdom; turning from evil is understanding" (v. 28). With a single stroke, wisdom has become available to one and all.

This concluding statement is problematic for several reasons: the length of the verse, the prosaic introduction, the reference to Adonai, and the refutation of the central thesis that mortals have no access to wisdom. In place of "the fear of Elohim" in 1:1, we have *yirat 'adonay*. Not only is this the sole use in the book of the special name by which Israelites identified their deity, but it's the ordinary word for "sir" or "master." It eventually became the replacement for the Tetragrammaton YHWH whenever the Bible was read in worship.

The actual person to whom this information was communicated is debatable. Given the lines that precede it, one can legitimately conclude that the primordial setting calls for the first human to be the addressee. That being the case, it would still apply generically to all Adam's descendants.

Moreover, this disclosure links religion and morality, worship and ethics. Does the absence of the article on wisdom in Elohim's revelation distinguish it in some way from that described in vv. 12-27? If so, it would mean that practical wisdom is readily available to mortals whereas true understanding only comes as a revelation from the creator.

The Contrast between Job's Past and Present
(29:1–31:40)

The dialogue between Job and his three friends ends with chapter 27. The interlude focusing on wisdom relieves the tension that has built up during the debate, at least for readers whose thoughts shift from the issue of justice to one of understanding. In the interval, Job pauses to reflect on "then" and "now," contrasting a happy past (ch. 29) with his present misery (ch. 30). Then taking life in hand, he swears that he is innocent and dares the deity to prove otherwise (ch. 31).

Job's selective memory of his favored existence before calamity struck fails to mention his earlier anxiety over possible sins by his children (1:5). Moreover, his vocabulary leaves itself open to double meanings, suggesting that nostalgia has not completely eased his pain. For example, when recalling the days of shelter under divine surveillance, he has not forgotten that it is precisely that constant watching that permits him no relief. And when Job boasts of being eyes to the blind, feet to the lame, and a source of singing for widows, he claims to have done what Eloah has failed to do—look after the well-being of the weak in society who have no one to champion their cause.

A Nostalgic Past (29:1-25)

Chapter 29 can be viewed as a chiasm. Its structure can be seen from the following analysis: (A) previous blessing, vv. 2-6; (B) previous honor, vv. 7-10; (C) Job's implementation of justice, vv. 11-17; (B¹) expected blessing, vv. 18-20; and (A¹) previous honor, vv. 21-25. For the most part, the text is transparent, even while abounding in sensual images.

A wish introduces the description of bygone blessing, "oh that" (literally, "who will give?"), emphasizing the chasm between past and present. Job wants to return to the good old days when Eloah, the *šomer* ("Guardian") of the righteous, watched over him providentially. Job has deduced this solicitous concern on the deity's part from his prosperity just as its disappearance has convinced him of divine malfeasance. As irrefutable proof, he uses the image of a lamp (*ner*) shining on him to illuminate the darkness while he walked and Eloah's counsel in the intimacy of his tent. Elsewhere, Job is pictured as a city dweller, so the reference to his tent in v. 4 may be conventional, a kind of frozen term for one's place of abode. Readers will remember that Eliphaz asked Job whether he had listened in on Eloah's council (15:8).

Job recalls the days of his prime ("harvest season," *horep*) as pleasant, made all the more enjoyable by the presence of Shaddai and surrounded by his youngsters (*ne'arim*). This word for young people is the same one used in the prologue to refer to Job's children in 1:19 and also servants in 1:15, 16, 17. It occurs widely with reference to young boys and even soldiers; hence gives no clear indication of age. Although Job avoids the usual word for children, *banim* (or even *yeludim*), he probably means his sons and daughters. The additional comment reveals the power of traditional language; Job mentions steps, *halikay* (from *halak*, "to walk"), washed with cream and a rock that poured out pools of oil. The divine epithet *sur* ("Rock") probably lurks behind this idyllic image.

Job now thinks about his social status in earlier days (vv. 7-10). He implies that a seat was reserved for him at the gate of the city where justice was administered by its leading citizens. His mere presence brought awe to the aged and fear to the young who hid themselves. From the double verb, it appears that the old people dared not take their seat in his presence, for they rose up (*qamu*) and stood (*'amadu*). The verbs function as one, "they remained standing." Even nobility (*sarim*, "princes"; *negidim*, "nobles") were silenced in his presence, their speech being restricted (*'aseru*) from within as well as from covering their mouths with their hands. In v. 10a, Job uses the curious expression, "the collective voice of the nobility hid itself," while the second half of the verse indicates blocked speech, the organ of speech clinging to the palette. For some readers, "Methinks he doth protest too much" seems best to describe Job's self-understanding. Are the friends confronting the testimony of an arrogant man who is blithely unaware of his own arrogance?

Has Job done anything more than frighten the young and cow the old? He thinks he has. That is the brunt of vv. 11-17, which begin with an emphatic particle *ki* ("indeed"). Continuing the personification of parts of the body from v. 10, Job has the ear listen and bless him and the eye observe and testify on his behalf. Why? "Because I delivered the weak who cried out and the orphan who lacked help" (v. 12). The participle *mešwwe'a* plays on the similar sound of the verb *yaš'a* "to save," while the verb *'amallet?* ("to deliver") recalls its threefold use in the Qal (simple perfect or imperfect, "to escape") in chapter 1 (vv. 15, 16, 17). Even the word for blessing in 29:13 resembles that for "knee," while the reference to the widow's heart continues the catalog of body parts. "The blessing of the perishing (ʾobed) reached me; I made the widow's heart sing."

Verse 14 breaks away from the focus on parts of the body, but only barely. In it, Job says that his conduct was habitual like the clothes he wore. Righteousness and justice were like his robe (meʿil) and turban (ṣanip), symbols of status in his world. We recall that Job has charged the deity with gross negligence in securing justice below.

Job wastes no time returning to the list of body parts: "Eyes I was to the blind; feet to the lame was I" (v. 15). The final pronoun "I" in this verse focuses the attention on Job rather than on those he helped. The pronoun continues in the next verse, this time varied from the short form ʾani to ʾanoki. "A father was I for the needy" continues in the mode of vv. 12-13, while the second half of the verse returns to the earlier judicial imagery: "And the case I didn't know I searched out." Either Job indicates that he investigated cases that were entirely unfamiliar to him and thus assured the person of justice, or the case (rab) stands for the longer phrase "case of someone," hence the person involved in the dispute was not known to Job.

Suddenly, Job shifts the image away from the weak to their predators. He claims to have shattered the fangs of the wicked, rescuing prey from their teeth. Like the judges in his day, Job goes beyond pronouncing guilt or innocence. In short, he enforces the verdict by sheer strength; the cohortative verb ʾašabberah ("I shattered") signifies determination.

The brief recapitulation of expected blessing in vv. 18-20 mixes the images of a well-watered tree and an archer. Both images are widely used in the ancient Near East. But first, Job provides insight into his mind: "I thought, 'I will die in my nest, multiply days like sand'" (v. 18). The images of nest and sand together are unusual, leading some interpreters to postulate a different Hebrew text about a mythical phoenix, attested by Hesiod and Herodotus but nowhere (else) in the ancient Near East. The use of sand to indicate a number beyond counting is well known in the Bible, and it is probable that "nest" simply means "home." Still, the negative picture of dying and the positive one of being surrounded by children is strange.

Readers of Psalm 1 are familiar with the comparison of human life to a tree, and the same theme also occurs in Jeremiah 17:7-8. In both instances, the wicked are said to be like trees with insufficient water while the righteous have adequate moisture. Job has earlier contrasted a tree with mortals to point out that death is final for them. The other image, that of an archer's bow, is charged erotically, both in Ugaritic literature and in the Bible. For Job, the expression "bow in hand" suggests loss of virility, since he laments its failure to materialize. In this weakened condition, Job the warrior is no longer a threat to anyone. Lacking the dew that enables plants to survive the scorching rays of the sun, and with a bow that has no signs of life, Job is completely vulnerable.

Verses 21-25 resume the thought expressed in vv. 7-10. Job thinks his presence at the gate of the city was overwhelming, like that of a king in the midst of his subjects. From his perspective, they listened attentively and eagerly awaited his advice. If this observation continues the thought of vv. 21-25, the missing subject ("*me*" they heard) is the nobility. Otherwise it could be a general reference to all who have come together at the place of judicial decision-making. When he spoke, the verdict was final, and everyone else remained silent in assent. Verse 23 compares Job's presence to life-giving rain, and the next verse likens his smile to light from an unbelievable source. Job thinks he has chosen their path, presumably illuminated by the radiance of his countenance. Job's nostalgia ends on a royal note. He thinks he has dwelt with them like a king among troops, one who comforts mourners. With this comment, he indicts his friends as well as the deity. In need of comfort, Job has encountered only abuse. He will conclude the description of his present misery with this theme of mourning. Thus past and present end on a similar note.

Job's Present Misery (30:1-31)

In chapter 30, Job signals the radical change between past and present with the expression *we'attah* ("But now," vv. 1, 9, 16). Each time it introduces a unit, the first two directed at the mockery he is forced to endure and the third raising the sights to indict the deity. With v. 24, a new unit occurs, this time introduced by the emphatic "surely" (*'ak*), which is then negated because the thought that follows is so blasphemous: "Surely he (Eloah) won't strike out at a ruin if in distress he cries out to him." This final section exposes the degree of Job's present agony.

The silence brought on by Job's kingly bearing in chapter 29 contrasts with the cruel sounds erupting around him in chapter 30. He is now made to endure the arrogance he has inflicted on others, even if unwittingly. What irks him most is the knowledge that such contempt for his diseased body comes from urchins. Job's description of them makes readers wonder if he has spoken truthfully when reporting how attentive he has been to the needs of the poor and orphans. Nothing but contempt for these marginalized mockers finds expression here.

Who are these mockers? Two things about them bother Job. First, they are young, and second, they are "dirt poor." Their social standing is so low, according to v. 1, that Job would not even hire their fathers to tend his sheep dogs. In fact, he says, they scavenge just like dogs. Weak from hunger, they "gnaw dry ground" and eke out subsistence from shrubs in the wilderness. The word *lahmah* in v. 4 either refers to food or to warmth. Job pictures these hungry dregs of society as chewing on a root for nourishment or gathering its wood for charcoal.

Job imagines that the majority of citizens feel the same loathing for these unfortunates that he does, suspecting them of being thieves and therefore banishing them from village life. Driven from society and the livelihood it makes possible, they must find shelter wherever possible—in dangerous ravines, caves, rocks. Job's low estimate of them reaches its most extreme in v. 7, where he accuses them of braying like animals, and in v. 8, where he calls them imbeciles ("children of fools") and nobodies (*beli-šem*), justly (he thinks) whipped out of the land.

Exactly what are these "nobodies" doing? The next unit, vv. 9-15, lists some of their actions, but the combination of specifics and metaphorical affronts creates confusion. How can they keep their distance and spit on him (cf. 17:6)? The two actions cancel each other out. Moreover, these scoundrels who barely survive starvation are said to build siege ramps against Job, as if he were a city and they an attacking army. The language even seems to confuse them with the deity, who is credited with loosening his bowstring and afflicting him. The image conjured up by the Qere *yitrah* ("my tent cord") may suggest the resulting sagging, a sign of weakness and fatigue.

The first "but now" refers to mockery; so does the second one, a form of mockery that has developed into a song of derision. Job blurts out, "I'm their cliché" (v. 9b). As if sensing Job's loathing, they respond in kind. Job thinks they are emboldened to treat him disrespectfully because the deity has also turned against him. The complex images in vv. 12-15 seem to describe military siege, the ramps enabling "offshoots" to destroy Job's road (if that is the meaning of the hapax *pirhah* in v. 12) and advance through a breached wall. Words like "fall" and "ruin" join "terrors" and "sweep away" in pointing to the effect of mockery on Job. Just as mighty wind destroyed his children, a wind takes away his honor. The resulting picture of Job watching while his safety passes like a cloud leaves an unforgettable pall over the entire lament.

The third unit introduced by "but now," vv. 16-23, focuses attention on the deity, the real source of Job's dismay. He is through talking to fellow humans, but what he says about the deity is not pretty. Seized by misery, Job gnaws away, his bones no longer whole, perhaps an echo of the pitiful condition of his mockers in 30:3-4. His clothes have become a burden; the contrast with his previous status of donning righteousness like clothes is noteworthy. In 9:31 he believed the deity would throw him into muck; now he sees it as a reality. The result is that Job has become a cliché, like dust and ashes (v. 19). The expression for mortals has become familiar through long usage. Job sees nothing new in his circumstances, only axioms no one questions. He has attempted prayer but received no answer (v. 20) except a cruel countenance and oppressive hand.

Verse 22 is a parody of an epithet for Baal the rider of clouds, which biblical writers took over for their deity. In Job's version, the god lifts him up and makes him ride the wind, its roar melting him into something that can readily be returned to dust. Just as Job has earlier insisted that he knew his redeemer was alive, now he widens that knowledge to include life's opposite, death. He says, "For I know you'll return me to death, the house appointed for all the living" (v. 23). *Bet 'olam*, the eternal home, was a common expression in the ancient world for the realm of the dead. The operative words for this whole unit are these: "You've turned cruel to me" (v. 21a); the play on the word *śaṭan* ("adversary") in the parallel line speaks volumes (*tiśṭemeni*, "you attack me").

The belief that Eloah can be trusted returns momentarily despite Job's growing suspicion that he has changed horribly. The final unit of chapter 30 opens with an expression of disbelief: "Surely he won't strike out at a ruin if in distress he cries out to him" (v. 24). Job identifies himself with the city in v. 14 and portrays his desperation as worthy of divine action on his behalf. The irony is that his cries for help go unheeded.

A curse in the next verse reinforces Job's goodness, a morality surpassing the deity's, for unlike Eloah Job has grieved for the needy. Like many of the curses that follow, this one lacks the result clause specifying the punishment to befall. In its place, Job describes his own agitation. Expecting good things (cf. 14:19), he has experienced their opposite. Instead of light, gloom has set in for him. A slight change in v. 28 (*ḥammah* to *neḥamah*) would have Job emphasize his lack of comforters. The effect is both physical and psychic; rumbling in his bowels matches his cries in the assembly (cf. v. 20), quite a contrast from his powerful speech in chapter 29. An outcast more detested than society's "nobodies," Job must associate with ostriches and jackals. Imagine the effect of this statement on Job's three friends who have thus far stayed by him. Blackened by the sun's rays, he has become like musical instruments dedicated to mourning. With this allusion to a funeral, the endings of chapters 29 and 30 are linked. Job has moved from consoler to mourner (29:25; 30:31). He has set the stage for directly challenging the deity. He will do that by means of an oath of innocence, which he believes the deity must answer. That is the power of the retributive view; it returns even when Job seems to have struck a devastating blow against it.

An Oath of Innocence (31:1-40)

Chapter 31 consists of a series of curses that Job pronounces on himself. The exact number of self-curses is unclear, although there may be fourteen to symbolize the doubling of a perfect number. Similar declarations of innocence can be found in chapter 125 of the Egyptian "Book of the Dead" and in the Babylonian law code of Hammurabi. The Egyptian oaths were thought to have helped the dead pharaoh pass into the realm of the blessed at death, and the Babylonian oaths declared a person legally innocent before a judicial body. The ritual in which the oath of innocence was pronounced was believed to be magically efficacious, and Job's curses presuppose the same power to bring down the effect of the curse on him should he have committed any of the named offenses.

The curses begin with idolatry, the probable meaning of *betulah* ("virgin") in v. 1, and conclude with proper treatment of tillable land. They go beyond external expression to inner motives, beyond legal requirements about slaves to more stringent demands of primal bonds. They define ethical conduct comprehensively, embracing the whole body; broaden family ties to include the needy and even the despised; and acknowledge a single human family with its origin in the same divine source. In these curses, Job answers Cain's question, "Am I my brother's keeper?" with a resounding "yes." And my sister's keeper too.

In at least two respects, however, the curses do not achieve such lofty heights. Job pronounces a curse on his wife if he has committed adultery ("May my wife grind for another and may others kneel over her," 31:10). In a word, he condemns her to the role of sex object for men (plural). Similarly, the penalty for following his own greed includes a typical futility curse ("May I sow and another reap") but also the uprooting of his children, a peculiar curse, given the death of his offspring in the folktale. In these instances, as in ownership of slaves, Job still is a child of his time.

Surprisingly, four of the curses actually specify a punishment (cf. vv. 8, 10, 22, and 40). The usual form of curses in the ancient world omitted the disaster, perhaps to enhance their psychological effect by making the punishment too horrible even to speak about it. In addition to the two discussed earlier—someone else harvesting Job's crops and killing his offspring; his wife becoming a sex object—these four curses include separating his arm from its socket or breaking it at the elbow as penalty for raising a fist against orphans and the growth of inedible things in place of staples of barley and wheat as punishment for failing to respect the land (letting it lie fallow and not offering its first fruits to the deity). Curses typically correlate the punishment with the offense, sexual sins being punished in kind, and so forth.

The entire oath abounds in verbal links and rhetorical features that give the impression of an ordered cacophony reaching its crescendo with a defiant appeal for the deity to weigh his heart, presumably against a feather symbolizing justice as in the Egyptian concept of a post-mortem judgment. Job does not hesitate to hurl the words "my integrity" (*tummati*) at the deity (v. 6). Perhaps even more brazen is Job's proud confidence, a willingness to wear a signed indictment on his shoulder as proof of his innocence (vv. 35-37). Eager to be heard, he says: "Here's my X (literally, *tau*, the last letter of the Hebrew alphabet); let Shaddai respond, and let my accuser write my indictment" (v. 35). This is not the picture of a broken man; strong of mind and body, Job swears that he would approach his accuser like a prince (*nagid*, v. 37), if only the deity would appear.

Not only does Job's ethical code cover his treatment of other human beings and the good earth; it also extends to worship. He has not made gold his ultimate concern, relying on it for security (v. 24). In this context of piety, he mentions a gesture of the hand "kissing" the mouth as adoration of sun and moon that implies lying to El (vv. 26-28; cf. Prov 30:9 for a similar reference to a crime that denies the deity). A gesture of hand brushing the mouth is known from Mesopotamia and may clarify Job's strange expression.

The offense in v. 1 (breaking a covenant by gazing on a virgin) probably echoes the Canaanite worship of the virgin goddess Anat. Job claims to have cut a covenant with his eyes; this nuance of the verb *karat* derives from bygone days when kings sealed agreements by killing a donkey and walking between its two halves. Tellingly, he concludes this denial that he has committed such a heinous crime by noting, in the form of a rhetorical question, that the deity cannot be duped ("Doesn't he see my ways, count all my steps?" v. 4).

Although Job acknowledges that the same creator made him and his slaves, that awareness does not issue in the abandonment of ownership over other humans. It does, nevertheless, move him to compassionate treatment, if he can be trusted. That care for the well-being of less fortunate individuals extends to the usual three: widows, orphans, and the needy. Most of the references to his dealings with those on the margins are readily transparent, but v. 8 is difficult ("For from my youth he brought me up like a father, from my mother's belly I led her"). Who are the antecedents of the pronouns "he" and "her"? The pronoun "he" probably refers all the way back to v. 15 ("the one who made me"). As for "her," does Job really claim to have guided his mother from infancy? Or should the feminine ending be changed to masculine? It would then refer to the orphan who is mentioned in the previous verse.

The retaliatory desire that existed throughout the ancient world did not prevent Job from recognizing that gloating over others' downfall was wrong (v. 29), nor did fear of the crowd compel him to conceal his transgressions like Adam (vv. 33-34). He has, however, let custom dictate behavior when strangers required hospitality (vv. 31-32).

Perhaps the very existence of these self-curses surprises readers most. Has Job not abandoned the idea of obtaining a fair trial from the divine accuser? That conclusion seems to have been reached in 27:7-23, and even as early as 9:29-31 he had given up on the deity's fairness. He seems unable to forsake his belief that somehow the deity will face him in a trial (13:14-15), arguing the case personally (23:5-7) and not by proxy. Still, Job has come to believe that Eloah has turned vicious, morphing into a true enemy.

Moreover, the effectiveness of Job's curses depended on a predictable world, and Job has insisted that no such universe existed. Everything, he believed, had been turned upside down. How then did Job expect to be declared innocent? Has he returned to his conviction, earlier jettisoned, that the principle of reward and retribution was alive and well? It seems so, if 31:2-3 are to be taken at face value. After lambasting his friends for championing such nonsense, has he gone over to their camp and surrendered his integrity? Has nostalgia (ch. 29) reminded him that by obeying the rules prosperity came his way, and has he now decided to return to the old way of life?

Modern readers need to remember that ancient curses were thought to have been powerful deterrents to criminal activity, else why would pharaohs have had curses against tomb robbers inscribed on their monuments. Even gods were believed to have been subject to the power of a curse. That is why Job adopts the extreme measure of uttering self-curses. He thinks the curses will have no sway over one as innocent as he, and his survival will prove decisively that Eloah has wronged him. For the moment, however, the one who once consoled mourners (29:25) has become like a lyre and flute whose only music is mourning and weeping. For him, even the furrows weep (31:38).

We expect a quick response from the deity, at least to muster a defense against Job's accusations. Precisely how this will take place is unclear. "Will it be a trial, a rational dialogue, a denunciation, a show of threatening force, a frontal attack" (Good, 318)? Meanwhile, we hear the narrator again: "The words of Job are complete" (the verb is cognate with the adjective *tam*, "integrity," that has become the issue Job hopes to settle in the divine presence).

Elihu's Four Speeches (32:1–37:24)

Job's audacious curse has prepared us for the deity's response. Such a speedy resolution will not come, however, and we must listen to four speeches by an insufferable bore that only the narrator interrupts. Even Yahweh waits patiently for him to vent his anger. Nothing that has gone before has prepared us for this brash youth with an impressive family lineage, and his immediate disappearance from the plot after chapter 37 is but one of several things leading interpreters to view the speeches as secondary. Nevertheless they serve an important dramatic function by lowering the emotional temperature brought on by a conflict of wills while also increasing anxiety about whether or not the deity will actually make an appearance.

Who is this intruder? The narrator supplies more information about him than about anyone else, even Job (32:1-5). Before doing so, he has this new character disparage Job's three friends and thus justify his replacing them as Job's instructor. Curiously, he refers to them twice as "these three men" (*'anašim* rather than *re'im*). They stopped answering Job, the narrator says, because he considered himself innocent (or following the Septuagint, Syriac, and Symmachus "he was righteous in their eyes"). The participle *me'anot* may carry a subliminal message of affliction, another meaning of the verb *'anah*, even when denoting an answer. Job certainly perceived their responses as inflicting pain.

We learn the name of this new character, his father's name, his descent, and the clan to which he belonged. His name, Elihu ("He is my El") is familiar from 1 Samuel 1:1, 1 Chronicles 12:21, 26:7, and 27:18. It follows the pattern of names like Elijah ("Yah is my El") and Jeremiah. Berakel, Elihu's father's name, is not attested anywhere else in the Bible but is found in the form Barikilu/i in the business documents of the Murashu house from Babylon. It has the meaning "El has blessed" or "Bless El." The place of origin, Buz, occurs in Jeremiah 25:23 as a locale in Edom along with Dedan and Tema. In Genesis 22:20-21, Buz is Abraham's nephew and a brother of Uz. We recall that Job is said to have lived in Uz. Ram, Elihu's clan, has the same name as an ancestor of David (Ruth 4:19) and an associate of Jerahmel in 1 Chronicles 2:9-10, 25, 27.

This impressive pedigree is nevertheless overshadowed by anger. The first half of v. 2 begins with a verb indicating anger ("His nostrils burned"), then repeats this assertion and names Job as the object of his fury. Why is he so angry? Because, the narrator reports, Job considered himself more righteous than God. Job's three friends, no longer just men but *re'aw*, do not escape Elihu's wrath either. Their offense is that they were unable to find an adequate answer for Job but nevertheless declared him guilty. That is the reading of the Masoretic Text; however, this verse is one of the eighteen scribal alterations (*Tikkune Sopherim*) in the Bible. For an original Elohim the Masoretes have substituted "Job" to remove the disturbing thought that the friends declared Elohim guilty, presumably by default.

As if an explanation for Elihu's late appearance were needed, the narrator explains that he had waited for Job with an arsenal of words out of respect for his elders. Deference did not, it seems, temper his indignation. When he saw that the three men (*'anašim* again) had no answer, his "nose burned" (v. 5). In four short verses, words indicating anger abound, beginning and ending with *wayyiḥar 'ap* ("and he was quite angry"). Altogether the verb *ḥarah* occurs four times, invariably followed by *'ap* ("nose") as the subject of burning. Readers are left with the graphic image of a young man who is as eager to speak as a stallion is to run like the wind. The other theme of this brief introduction is "answer" (vv. 1, 3, 5). Elihu is certain the three have failed to answer Job, and he intends to impart wisdom where they could not.

Elihu's First Speech (32:6b–33:33)

In vv. 6-22 Elihu attempts to justify his entrance into the debate. He explains his reluctance to speak as youthful respect for elders but quickly challenges the traditional association of wisdom with advanced years. True wisdom, he says, comes as a gift of revelation rather than through the accumulation of experience over time. Elihu thinks he has been given special knowledge that simply must be shared, else he will burst like a container of wine in which pressure has built beyond its capacity to resist venting.

The disparity between what Elihu originally thought and his dawning realization is expressed quite simply: "I thought, 'Let days speak, let many years make wisdom known,' however, it's the spirit in a person and Shaddai's breath that impart understanding " (vv. 7-8). That conclusion leads to yet another one that neither wisdom nor justice is the exclusive possession of the aged. Emboldened by this discovery, he determines to share his insight. The additional *'ap-'ani*, "even I," with which Elihu concludes his initial remarks echoes the narrator's use of *'ap* for a burning nose.

Although the narrator has not indicated that others witnessed the debate between Job and his friends, Elihu claims to have waited while the latter searched for words. The verb for searching, *ḥaqar*, is the same one used in chapter 28 to indicate the human search for valuable ore and the divine quest to discover wisdom (vv. 3 and 27). The picture of the three friends digging for words contrasts with an Elihu who is so filled with words that he is about to burst.

Not only did the friends have to dig for an answer, according to Elihu; they also failed miserably, a verdict already given by Job. In short, they failed as an educator, a *mokiaḥ* (v. 12). Lest they take credit for turning the matter over to El and waiting for divine resolution, Elihu hastens to pronounce that way out as a mistake: "Lest you say, 'We have found wisdom; let El answer, not a human'" (v. 13). After chapter 28, the idea of anyone's having found wisdom is patently absurd. Does Elihu recognize the irony underlying his own hubris?

Elihu does not just defy tradition about youthful ignorance and the wisdom of the aged; he also claims novelty in a world that prized the tried and true. Job has not laid out carefully arranged arguments against me, Elihu observes, and I won't quote any of your arguments either. Because the friends have been reduced to silence, Elihu declares his readiness to convey his own insights.

If he has not conveyed his sense of importance thus far, v. 17 leaves no place for thinking otherwise: "I, even I (*'ap-'ani*) will answer with my piece; I, even I, (*'ap-'ani*) will declare my knowledge." To be sure, *'ap-'ani* is idiomatic for "I myself," but in context the doubled use of the expression, combined with the words *ḥelqi* ("my portion") and *deʿi* ("my knowledge"), depict this young speaker as a buffoon. The entire verse is self-congratulatory; it is full of first-person verbs, first-person pronouns, first-person suffixes, and the repetition of *'ap-'ani*, "I myself." Eager to vent his wine, Elihu offers his final justification for speaking: he is incapable of showing partiality. In other words, he is not awed by Job's reputation and will speak freely, knowing that El expects no less ("My maker would whisk me away" if I showed any favoritism).

Thus far, Elihu seems to be addressing Job's three friends, even if speaking of them in the third person ("they") in vv. 15-16. In 33:1-7, he directs his remarks to Job, calling him by name and even using a particle of entreaty, "please" (vv. 1-2). Elsewhere in the book, only the narrator, Yahweh, the adversary, and unnamed intelligent people of 34:34-35 address Job by name. Does this refusal to use common courtesy prove that Elihu will show no favoritism, or is it a sign of disrespect indicative of brash youth? In appealing for a hearing, Elihu asks for full attention, not selective listening ("and listen to *all* my words"). Sensual imagery of the body flows freely here from one whose belly is full ("my mouth," "my lips," "my palate," "my heart"). Claiming to speak clearly, he reinforces his appeal to be heard by asserting special revelation again ("El's spirit made me; Shaddai's breath enlivens me," v. 4). Here is a parody of prophets, who claimed revelation for their oracles, and of any sages who appealed to the divine origin of their thoughts, as in mantic wisdom and apocalyptic (Müller 1972).

First, however, Elihu gives Job an opportunity to speak, an invitation that Job refuses to take up: "If you can, respond; lay out (your case) before me, take a stand" (v. 5). Readers will recall that the narrator has used this verb *yaṣab* (in the *Hitpaʿel* or reflexive stem) when referring to the divine beings and the adversary who presented themselves before the supreme deity, Yahweh. Elihu's high opinion of himself leads to false modesty, the admission that he and Job are equal before El because they were both pinched from clay, an obvious allusion to one of several views of creation in ancient Mesopotamia and in the Bible (Clifford). Fearful that no one can believe Elihu came from such humble origins as that of others, he adds "*gam-ʾani*, even I!" Still, he goes on to say, you need not fear me, for my pressure on you won't be heavy. Is Elihu actually comparing himself with the deity, whom Job has described as burdensome and fearful?

The Argument (32:8-30)

Having finally arrived at his argument, Elihu quotes Job and tries to correct him. Unfortunately, the first citation is erroneous. Job has never said that he is pure or sinless, although he has insisted that his prayer is pure. Zophar had also misquoted his friend: "You say, 'My teaching is pure, and I'm innocent in your sight'" (11:4). Job's actual claim concerns his integrity (*tam*) and his having not sinned to such a degree that he deserved the punishment imposed on him. Elihu is so certain of his information that he insists on having heard Job say exactly what he accuses him of saying. It does not seem to bother Elihu that he attributes a word to Job that occurs nowhere else in the Bible (*ḥap*).

Before turning to a second quotation, Elihu accuses Job of saying that the deity finds pretexts to punish him, becoming a virtual enemy. The general sentiment, though not the exact words, is accurate (cf. 13:24; 19:11). In v. 11, Elihu quotes Job accurately: "He puts my feet in stocks; spies on all my paths" (cf. 13:27). For Job, the verb for divine providence, *šamar* ("to watch over"), has become sinister. Elihu takes umbrage at Job's view of Eloah and simply responds, "In this, you are mistaken!" What Elihu then says has nothing to do with the issue being debated: "For Eloah is greater than a mortal" (v. 12). Job has readily conceded Eloah's power while openly challenging his justice. What Elihu cannot understand is Job's audacity in wishing to enter into a trial with Eloah.

For Elihu, the contested issue concerns revelation. Does El communicate with humans, or does he refuse to answer mortals' cries for help, as Job thinks? Far from remaining silent, El makes the divine will known through visions, dreams, and affliction. That is the brunt of Elihu's first speech. He claims that El speaks in one way and then another, although no one perceives it. A similar use of the numerals one/two occurs in Psalm 62:12 ("Once God has spoken; twice I have heard this").

The similarity of vv. 15-16 with Eliphaz's account of a ghostly visitor in the night (4:12-17) goes beyond subject matter to actual vocabulary (vision of the night, when deep sleep falls on humans). The goal of such frightening dreams, according to Elihu, is to bring about moral rectitude. Similarly, so Elihu argues, El brings affliction on individuals to educate them. Suffering, that is, serves a higher purpose of stimulating good conduct. Perhaps as a pointed barb aimed at Job, Elihu adds that sickness smothers human pride. Ironically, he does not recognize his own self-importance.

Beginning at v. 19, Elihu introduces the idea of the pit awaiting all mortals. He lingers over this scary image long enough to evoke fear in ordinary people, primarily to praise El for providing a means of escaping this threat. How is that achieved? Through an intermediary, a messenger, one in a thousand, who is willing to offer a ransom for the person whose body is wasting away (vv. 23-24). We have seen how often Job has wished for someone to champion his cause against El, always abandoning this hope as unrealistic. His view of this extraordinary figure differed from Elihu's, even if both men employ the same language (*maPak, meliṣ, 'eḥad minni-'alep*). According to Job, the mediator would force El to dispense justice and thus to exonerate the wronged sufferer, whereas Elihu thinks of this messenger as the deity's representative in a search for a convenient means of saving Job's life. Just as slaves were ransomed by a monetary exchange, Job will be bought back by this mediator, "one in a thousand," to use an expression that is found exclusively in wisdom literature.

In Elihu's fertile imagination, the change brought on by the discovery of a ransom is breathtaking. The person whose body has wasted away so that his bones protrude is suddenly transformed into a vibrant youth. He expresses gratitude in prayer, and Eloah looks on his face, shouting like a victorious soldier. The result is that Eloah "returns his just cause," possibly an idiom for pronouncing a verdict of innocence. The changed object of divine forgiveness then confesses his sins and praises the deity for not requiting his sins in kind. Instead of the dark pit, he beholds the light of life. Elihu's enthusiasm is boundless: "Look, El does all this, twice, three times, with a man to rescue him from the pit, to shine with life's radiance" (vv. 29-30). In his excitement, Elihu has raised the numbers of v. 14 by one. There is only one problem. Elihu assumes that Job is guilty of transgressions punishable by divine wrath. For Job to confess his guilt would be a betrayal of his integrity.

Elihu concludes his first speech just as he began it: with an appeal to Job for attentive listening (vv. 31-33). Job is even invited to respond, but he refuses to do so. As reward for silence, he is promised Elihu's wisdom. The verb for "teaching" echoes the earlier term for thousand. Does Elihu think of himself as one in a thousand, Job's rescuer? He certainly claims to desire Job's vindication (v. 32).

Elihu's Second Speech (34:1-37)

In Elihu's second speech, he seems to address bystanders other than Job's three friends and to solicit their judgment. Does he imagine a gathering of elders at the gate who have come to declare Job either innocent or guilty? He flatters these onlookers by calling them wise and even attributes words to them. His attention appears to shift back and forth from them to Job, and his view of Job has become somewhat less compassionate than that articulated in the first speech, where he expresses his own benevolent intention.

Perhaps Elihu's rigid theological claim leaves him no choice but to implicate Job. Because God is both mighty and just, according to Elihu, Job cannot be both innocent and suffering grievously. Divine justice rules out unjust misery, and divine power ensures that events on earth are under control at all times. It follows from this reasoning that anyone who challenges justice must be either a scoundrel or a fool.

Elihu appeals to the astute listeners to render judgment along with him: "Let's choose for ourselves what's right, determine among ourselves what's good" (v. 4). In other words, they are asked to choose what is legal and moral. He reminds them that the ear tests words and the palate tastes food, which is Elihu's way of saying that discrimination is called for in rendering a decision about Job.

Had Elihu followed his own advice, he would have shown more care in the way he presented Job's complaints. Job has not said, "I am innocent" (*ṣadaqti*) but "*If* I am innocent" (9:15; 10:15). He did not say, "El has turned away my case" but "As El lives, who has turned away my case" (27:2). When Job uses the verb *kazab* in 6:28, he denies having lied to his friends, just as he refers to Shaddai's poisoned arrows in 6:4, not to his own arrows. And Job never uses the verb *sakan*, "to benefit," although both Eliphaz and Elihu do (15:3; 22:2, 21; 34:9; 35:3).

What Elihu says next about Job is even less factual than the misquotes. He accuses Job of drinking scorn (*la'ag*) like water (v. 7). In saying this, he has linked Job with the wicked who drink iniquity like water, according to

Eliphaz (15:16). The image that follows is even less apt. Job is said to be making a path to companions who do wrong, when in reality he is stuck on an ash heap. Elihu accuses Job of denying the central tenet of the sages: that it goes well with those who delight in Elohim (v. 9). With this charge, Elihu has finally gotten things right, even if using words that Job did not, and the debate has returned to the question raised by the adversary about disinterested righteousness.

Elihu sidesteps that issue, choosing rather to defend absolute justice. He does so with a strong oath. "Far be it from El to do wickedness or Shaddai to do evil" (v. 10b). His argument, strange to modern readers, depends on the belief that rulers can do no wrong since they act in God's stead. Such an ideal concept of kings was widespread in the ancient Near East, existing alongside rampant abuse of power (Kalugila). In Elihu's mind, only the "ideal" existed, and he goes to great lengths to defend the deity's actions. Having declared his credo in the form of an oath, he repeats it emphatically: "Surely El doesn't do wickedness, Shaddai doesn't distort justice" (v. 12). An individual gets what he deserves, no more and no less, for El sees the path one takes. That simple interpretation of disaster has brought Job nothing but heartache.

Having affirmed divine justice, Elihu hastens to emphasize mortals' absolute dependence on El. He does so by recalling the ancient belief that the creator breathed life into the first man, and after that into every living human. If El were to withdraw that breath, they would return to dust. It follows that El is favorably disposed toward mortals. Furthermore, Elihu says, a reasonable person knows that no one who despises justice would dare rule over others. This principle even applies to earthly rulers, Elihu insists. "Would one say to a king, 'Worthless' or 'Evil' to nobility?" (v. 18), for even they exercise justice impartially.

It now falls to Elihu to explain how the wicked can prosper for a brief time. That may be true, he implies, but they die without warning in the middle of the night, shaken into oblivion and not by any visible hand. Why? Because El sees all mortals' steps, contrary to the belief that the clouds obscure divine vision. No hiding place is dark enough to provide refuge for the wicked (cf. Ps 139:7-12; Amos 9:2-4; Jer 23:24). Moreover, El is not bound by any external rule to mete out justice at a specified time (v. 23), which means that Job was wrong when complaining that the deity does not render justice in a timely manner. The ambiguity of the phrase, "For he has not set upon man again," may permit a different interpretation of v. 23, the issue being one of granting permission to go to El in litigation.

Against Job's insistence that El ignores the cry of the poor, Elihu asserts that the god strikes the wicked precisely because they afflicted the poor

(v. 28). Ironically, their harsh treatment of these defenseless victims elicited cries to heaven that brought prompt action. Like Eliphaz, Elihu faults these sinners for misplaced values (cf. 22:24-26). Even if El hides, who can condemn? With this direct attack on Job, who has complained about being unable to find El, Elihu both condemns Job and urges him to repent. The choice is yours, Elihu suggests; so turn to El and promise not to repeat your offense (vv. 31-32).

Now Elihu quotes smart people who have listened to his words and sided with him against Job. They say, "Job speaks without knowledge; his words are not astute" (v. 35). The wish that follows—that Job be tested to the limit—may continue the remarks of the observers or they may be Elihu's own feeling. What is Job's crime? In Elihu's opinion, he is both a sinner and a rebel, brashly mocking his companions and multiplying words against El. Syntactically, Elihu has hidden his low opinion of Job in the response of unnamed "intelligent people."

Elihu's Third Speech (35:2-16)

Although Job has never actually claimed to be more moral than El, he has implied it when describing the god as remaining idle while rapacity reigns on earth and of favoring the ruthless in society. Elihu has thus rightly grasped the import of Job's attack, if not the exact words. Therefore, when quoting Job as having boasted, "I am more righteous than El," he is halfway correct. Job has come perilously close to such a thought, although in the form of a question: "How can a man be innocent with (ʿim) El?" (9:2b). It was Eliphaz, however, who used the language that Elihu attributes to Job: "Can a man be more righteous than El?" (4:17a) when reporting the word that came to him as a revelation. One might turn Elihu's question around; "Do you think it right" to accuse someone of saying something he has not said?

Elihu's record for accurate reporting takes another hit by what follows in v. 3. "Yet you ask, 'What does it benefit you?' What have I gained by avoiding sin?'" approximates what Eliphaz said in 22:2 when denying that good deeds by humans benefit El. In trying to protect El from charges of failing to reward virtue and punish vice, Eliphaz has cut a vital nerve. Belief in the principle of individual retribution was a central axiom in the ancient world. That belief lay at the heart of Job's complaint, and everything he says presupposes such a worldview, one he thinks has become inoperative in his case. Otherwise, how could he say, "I sinned, what did I do to you, watcher of men?" (7:20).

In vv. 4-8, Elihu offers his corrective to Job's supposed questions. In essence he reminds Job of his insignificance in the vast universe. "Look to the heavens and see; scan the clouds high over you" (v. 5). How can your sin affect El in any way? The same applies to virtue. Your goodness contributes nothing to him. For Elihu, as for Eliphaz whose theology he replicates, the transcendent deity is so far removed from earth below that nothing done by mortals has any impact on him. Both morality and immorality are thus seen as a societal matter alone. In effect, this view of things means that El owes nothing to humans. It follows that no one can demand payment for service rendered to El.

Distance—and sublimity—are not the only reason for the deity's silence in the face of cries for help. Their failure to praise El, indicative of pride, renders petition pointless. With this not-so-subtle barb against Job, Elihu hopes to answer his charge that El pays no attention to the cries of the oppressed (vv. 9-16). In Elihu's mind, those suffering under heavy oppression like Job need to think of Eloah's many comforts ("who gives songs in the night") instead of criticizing him for momentary inaction. Rather than looking to nature for instruction, as the sages have taught, they should realize that their maker teaches them far more than the beasts and birds do. True wisdom, that is, comes from Eloah. With this observation, he has abandoned the fundamental premise of practical wisdom.

Lest Job and his friends miss the larger point, Elihu expresses it in plain language: "Surely it is false that El does not hear, that Shaddai does not observe" (v. 13). The deity's organs for sharpening the intellect, ears and eyes, are always open. What must Job do, then? Recognize that Eloah hears and sees his case even if it looks otherwise. Elihu assures Job that his case is already on the divine docket and that he should wait anxiously for its resolution. The verb form suggests extreme anxiety, whirling in dance or writhing from the pains of giving birth. If Elihu hopes to offer Job any comfort, he quickly dashes it by his final remarks before launching his fourth speech. He reminds Job that Eloah's anger (unlike his own, we should add) has been delayed although Job does not know it. Presumably, Elihu believes that he can see what Job cannot. Now Elihu accuses Job of mouthing emptiness (*hebel*) and piling up ignorance (or "weighing it down"; some manuscripts have the verb *kabad*, "to be heavy," instead of *yakbir*). What an example of the pot calling the kettle black! Elihu's mouth has run nonstop while Job has stood before him mute.

In due time, readers will recognize the irony in Elihu's insistence that Job's case is before El. They will also see that the advice to wait in trepidation can prepare him for the confrontation that will soon occur. Elihu seems to understand his role in the drama as sorting through the earlier speeches and isolating critical issues that will be taken up once more when the divine judge appears. What does he think they are? El's freedom and loftiness; human pride and ignorance. It seems that Elihu is less mistaken about Eloah than he is about Job, at least in this one respect. God does observe and will act.

Elihu's Fourth Speech (36:2–37:24)

Having informed Job that his case is before El and advised him to wait in awe for the god to appear, Elihu then heaps further insult. He does this in two ways, first by saying that El's anger is withheld, when in reality Job reels from its powerful blow, and second by accusing Job of uttering vapid ignorance. It is difficult to conceive of a more effective closure for Elihu than to depict Job, wholly silenced, waiting in fear for the confrontation he has sought. Elihu is not finished, however, for he wants to emphasize the divine use of suffering as a corrective to misconduct and to reflect at length on El's majesty as manifest in a storm.

Therefore Elihu explains why he continues to speak (vv. 2-4). Ironically, he urges Job to wait a little while so Elihu can make known that there are still more words to speak on behalf of Eloah. Job is thus asked to put on hold his anticipation of someone he has risked everything to see. Realizing how much he has asked of Job, he hastens to ascribe to himself qualities that belong to Eloah—truth and wisdom. The reader winces at the thought of anyone, much less someone of Elihu's limited intellect, claiming to have complete knowledge.

As if to shift attention from his own hubris, Elihu quickly returns to the subject of divine discipline (vv. 5-25). Some of what he says now contradicts his earlier statements. For example, El does not despise (*ma'as*), although he has been described as clapping hands, in the sense of jeering, at the wicked (34:26), and he establishes kings permanently, when elsewhere they are said to be overthrown at midnight (34:20). Perhaps Elihu is so intent on stressing the educative value of suffering that he loses track of what he has already said. The heart of his argument occurs in vv. 10-12, where it is said that El uses pain to correct individuals who have taken the wrong turn. Their well-being depends on whether or not they heed the instruction. Listening is not enough; they must also serve (*'bd*), an ironic statement when one recalls that Job is called Yahweh's servant in the prose tale. Only then can they experience the good (*tob*) and pleasantness (*ne'imim*, v. 11). Failure to heed divine *musar* ("instruction") subjects them to crossing over (*'br*) the channel, expiring while still ignorant. The similarity of this warning to the prophetic counsel in Isaiah 1:19-20 can hardly be missed. Nor can Elihu's fine pun on the verbs *'bd* and *'br* ("to serve" and "to cross over").

Elihu recognizes that El's corrective discipline does not always work, for it depends on human choices. The corrupted mind refuses and brings an early death. Job has used the same word, *hanep*, in 27:8 after an imprecatory curse expressing the wish that the godless would be punished rather than an innocent like Job. Elihu gives the noun a cognitive sense by adding the word *leb*, "mind." The ultimate destiny of these rebels who are cut off in their early years is unclear. Elihu uses the word *qedešim*, which is a designation of male prostitutes as well as the ordinary term for holy ones, usually celestial beings. Apparently, Elihu thinks these rebels are in the company of male prostitutes, either before death or afterward in Sheol.

Verses 15-16 seem to add something new to Elihu's theory of educative suffering. They suggest that deliverance comes *in* the affliction, that is, by means of enduring El's harsh discipline, not as a reward for it. Ancient pedagogy is renowned for its cruelty, for teachers freely applied the cane to the backs of students. Elihu's comment is in perfect accord with this view of education: "(El) opens their ears through a thrashing" (v. 15b). The imagery is nearly breathtaking: the person whose ears are opened in this way discovers a feast laid out for him on a table.

It seems that Elihu thinks Job's obsession with a fair trial places him in danger, possibly being lured into offering a bribe to assure a favorable verdict. This entire section, extending from v. 18 to v. 21, is textually ambiguous and stylistically awkward. It reminds one of bits of ethical advice that were used as fillers in otherwise unrelated texts: "Watch out lest . . . do not wish . . . take care, do not." Much of its content is trite, as here. "Do not wish for the night; take care not to choose evil over affliction."

The next section, vv. 22-25, makes the transition from El's corrective discipline to his power as shown in a violent storm. Both themes come together in v. 22. "Look, El is beyond reach in power; who is a teacher (*moreh*) like him?" Remembering Job's contention that El is guilty of wrongdoing, Elihu once again insists that no one can ever say to him, "You have done wrong" (*'awlah*). Instead, everyone who has witnessed divine power should sing the praises of him who gives songs in the night. If that is true, why not wish for the night and its comforts? Elihu appears not to have thought about the inconsistency in his thinking. For him, simple answers, however banal, are preferable to honest questions.

Elihu has spent less time on Job's past than the friends did. His primary interest is Job's present conduct, which he hopes to influence by recalling El's educative discipline and by emphasizing divine majesty. The next section, 36:26–37:13, focuses almost entirely on El's greatness, particularly his splendor as manifest in storms. Against this terrifying display of power, Job's desire to confront El at the court of justice is shown to be ludicrous. That is the brunt of Elihu's description of El's activity in nature.

The introductory comment extols divine mystery, which is then belied by the amount of information provided. A thin line always exists between the desire to protect divine hiddenness and the belief that much can be known about the god. From what follows, it is apparent that Elihu did not really think El was unknowable.

The thunderstorm is a case in point. Elihu views this display of power both positively and negatively. Not only does a storm bring rain that results in a bountiful harvest, but it also sets into motion lightning bolts that strike their targets with unerring accuracy. Elihu therefore sees these dual features of storms as demonstrations of El's judicial role (vv. 31-32). With what ease the god conceals lightning in his palms as if it were a pebble, then commands it to strike its target.

Elihu's view of cosmology was typical of that held by most peoples of the ancient Near East. In it, a cosmic sea existed above the earth, and the waters were held in check by a firmament, sometimes obscured by clouds. Periodically windows were opened, allowing water to flow earthward. The deity rode on the clouds and scattered lightning that covered the roots of the sea above, his voice resounding far and near. Elihu reacts emotionally to this thunder (37:1), so much so that his mind seems fixed on it. The word *qol* ("voice," "thunder") appears five times in the scope of three verses like the constant rumble of thunder in the heat of summer (37:2, 4-5). Ironically, the divine voice has the same effect on the earth as Job's sickness, bringing *rogez*, shuddering (cf. 3:26). The closest comparison Elihu can think of is the roar of a wild animal, most notably that of a lion (*ša'ag*), and the rumbling of an earthquake (*ra'am*, twice). He also uses vocabulary that ordinarily indicates deeds believed to be miracles (*nipla'ot*), great achievements beyond comprehension (v. 5). A participle (*'oseh*, "who does") slips easily into Elihu's discourse to identify the content as hymnic. So does the emphasis on El's surveillance of the earth's edges.

El's majesty is not limited to the phenomena associated with hot weather. He also exercises control over snow and ice. Lest it be overlooked, Elihu calls attention to the weather's impact on humans and animals. The obscure image of stamping the hand of mortals "so they can know El's work" continues the theme of corrective discipline. Perhaps it suggests sealing people inside a shelter like contents of a business document. The wax seal was only to be broken to validate the wording, like the modern reading of a will by an executor. The observation that wild beasts retreat to their lairs to ride out the tempest points to violent summer storms and extreme ice and snow that immobilize some creatures. In this instance, the emphasis seems to be awe rather than punishment.

In Elihu's vivid imagination, El's breathing forms both ice and moisture that fills the clouds. Even the dreaded sirocco, so-called dust devils, which Elihu calls "whirling things," are probably thought to originate in El's mouth and to reflect divine judgment. Nothing lies outside El's control, and all things serve either to punish or to bless (v. 13).

At this point, Elihu addresses Job directly and asks a series of rhetorical questions (37:14-20), a device that the next speaker will use to demonstrate Job's ignorance and weakness even further. Elihu's questions highlight Job's lack of knowledge about nature and his inability to compete with El in mastering the elements. Job is advised to stop and ponder El's mighty accomplishments (*nipla'ot*) and is reminded of a serious gap in his knowledge. The question, "Do you know?" introduces consecutive verses (15-16) that end with a description of El as one who possesses complete knowledge, a claim Elihu has also made for himself. It seems that Job is not alone in being characterized as *tam* ("whole"). The image of Job trying to keep cool when the south wind makes his clothes intolerably hot makes the question, "Can you form the sky along with him (El), hard as a molten mirror?" almost comical. It should be remembered that mirrors in Job's day were made from shiny metal, not glass.

The last two verses of this section take up the issue of litigation. "Tell us what we should say to him; we cannot arrange (our case) from the edge of darkness" (v. 19). The metaphorical use of the word *ḥošek* ("darkness") connotes Job's abysmal ignorance when compared with El's full knowledge. The next rhetorical question pronounces a judgment on Job's insatiable desire to confront El in court. "Should it be told to him that I want to speak, or should anyone say that he wants to be swallowed?" (v. 20). Job has contemplated the possibility of being swallowed by a fierce deity, and the prologue has Yahweh admit to having swallowed him for no reason (2:3). In Elihu's opinion, Job is inviting El to destroy him. The image of the god swallowing mortals places El alongside personified Sheol and Mot, powerful creatures with mouths open to swallow mortals.

Elihu has not yet finished his praise of divine splendor. He therefore contemplates the most powerful force in the universe, the sun that is completely exposed once the wind has driven clouds away. Elihu gives voice to knowledge acquired by previous generations: no one can look directly into the sun without serious damage to the eyes. Golden splendor comes from the north (v. 22a). Thinking about the sun leads Elihu to a similar color of inestimable value, gold, which nicely describes Eloah who comes from the north,

Mt. Saphon, the realm of the gods in Canaanite lore. This domain of the gods is beyond human contact, just as the divine qualities of power and justice are out of mortals' reach. Therefore, Elihu observes, Shaddai, whose righteousness overflows, will not answer (v. 23). Although some interpreters translate the verb *ye'anneh* by "oppress," which is one meaning of *'anah*, the *laken* ("therefore") that follows in Elihu's final remark makes more sense if the verb is understood as "answer."

According to Elihu, Shaddai has no need to respond to Job's self-curse. Nature itself has spoken to confirm other means of revelation such as dreams, visions, and affliction. For this reason, Elihu says, mortals fear Shaddai, whom no intelligent person can see. Like the Israelites who preferred to let Moses endure the danger inherent to seeing Yahweh, Elihu understands the power of fear in the presence of divine splendor. He also believes in Shaddai's hiddenness: "None of the intelligent can see him" (v. 24b). Alternatively, one can read a *lu'* emphatica instead of the negative participle. In that case Elihu asserts that every person who is wise will see Shaddai.

Like the poem about wisdom's inaccessibility in chapter 28, Elihu's speeches conclude by juxtaposing the fear of God and wisdom. While the emphasis in 28:28 includes an element of awe, with Elihu that component achieves prominence because of the wider context, where El's power dominates. At the same time, Elihu's final observation echoes the description of Job in the prologue as a fearer of Elohim. We remember that Israel's sages believed such fear to be both the beginning and first principle of wisdom (Prov 1:7a).

The Divine Speeches and Job's Responses (38:1–42:6)

Beginning with chapter 38, Job finally gets an answer from Yahweh. It takes the form of a dialogue, with both Yahweh and Job speaking twice. The torrent of words this time flows from the deity, while Job is almost reduced to silence. Yahweh's first speech extends from 38:2 to 40:2, and the second one begins at 40:7 and runs through 41:26. By contrast, Job's responses fill only seven verses (40:4-5 and 42:2-6), ironically a symbol of perfection, as if confirming the pervasive theme of his innocence. That is not the view of Job that Yahweh's speeches advance.

The ambiguity that Job seems to have felt when contemplating a response from his afflicter continues in the reactions to the speeches by interpreters. Job vacillated between feelings that the god would clarify matters (23:5-7), or ask questions that would be difficult to answer (9:13-16). That is, Job was uncertain whether Yahweh would come as reliable judge or as brutal attacker. Readers have offered a whole range of responses to the divine speeches. They are said to be a satisfactory answer to Job's questions (1) because Yahweh appears, which is wholly remarkable, (2) because Job is put in his proper place in the universe as a humble servant, and (3) because the universe is shown to be aesthetically pleasing. Others see the speeches as irrelevant, sometimes irrelevance preceded by the adjective "sublime"; irritating; empty; missing the point by stressing power, which was not an issue, and ignoring justice; and a three-hour lecture on natural science.

As if taking his cue from Elihu's description of the storm, Yahweh appears in a whirlwind (*hasse'arah*). Perhaps the real cue comes from Job himself, for in 9:16-17 he exclaimed that even if the deity were to answer, Job would not believe it because the god bruises him in a tempest (*bis'arah*). Lest we forget, it was a mighty wind that destroyed Job's children. Still, in common opinion, the theophany, a technical word for the deity's self-manifestation, was believed to have been accompanied by extraordinary phenomena, usually described as fire, an earthquake, an eerie silence, and a mighty wind. Only special people were privileged to experience a theophany, the most notable of whom were Abraham (Gen 15:17), Moses (Exod 19:6), and Elijah (1 Kgs 19:11-12).

Yahweh's First Speech (38:2–40:2)

Job has expected answers. What he gets are questions. They concern two things, knowledge and action. The questions are rhetorical, requiring no answer. Each one is highly stylized and visually stimulating. The initial question, "Who is this darkening counsel with words devoid of knowledge?" would seem to refer to Elihu, who was the last speaker. The formulaic "Then Yahweh answered *Job* from the whirlwind," the singular demonstrative *zeh,* and the participle (*mahšik*, "the *one* darkening"), however, rule out the friends and Elihu, and Job's admission in 42:3 points to him alone as the target of divine rebuke. Yahweh's silence about Elihu speaks volumes, particularly since he represents Israelite wisdom, unlike Job's three friends who hail from neighboring cultures.

What has Job darkened, according to Yahweh? The word *'esah* has at least two important uses; it designates advice that an astute thinker gives to someone, whether solicited or otherwise, and a plan involving matters as significant as human destiny or cosmic order. The absence of any pronominal suffix to indicate whose counsel has been darkened leaves the matter open. It may refer to any one of the characters in the plot (Job, the friends, Elihu, Yahweh). One thing is certain. Yahweh accuses Job of being ignorant.

Verse 3 echoes Job's own account of his lamented birth, the desire that darkness overtake his birthday, and the declaration that a *geber* has been conceived (3:3). Now Yahweh commands Job to gird his lions like a *geber*. Girding one's loins was preparatory action for strenuous engagement as in battle. Yahweh's additional remark is wholly unexpected: "I will ask questions and you inform me" (38:3b). How can one who lacks knowledge communicate information to another? We detect sarcasm and impatience, hardly the right tone for intellectual debate.

The barrage of questions concerns Job's experience and ability. Have you seen, do you know, were you present, can you control? Together, they inquire about Job's qualifications to enter the ranks of the gods, for the knowledge they solicit and the performances they ask about are properties of deity. They concern the sea, death, snow, ice, the earth's limits, light and darkness, even animals and winged creatures that occupy realms not inhabited by humans. Sarcastic jabs are interspersed with difficult questions, reminders that Job has taken on more than he ever imagined. The defiant "prince" who vowed to approach the deity with head held high is shown to be out of his league and doomed to failure so long as Yahweh sets the parameters of the discussion as might, not right.

The first speech consists of two parts: the first part is cosmic in scope, and the second is located somewhere on the periphery of human habitation. Three images of deity make up the initial line of questioning: (1) master builder; (2) midwife; and (3) commander of armies. Verses 4-7 depict Yahweh as the creator who plans and executes the construction of his cosmic temple. Mesopotamian royal inscriptions frequently describe kings in this fashion. Rulers claim to lay the foundations of temples, determine precise measurements, sink footings, and lay the cornerstone during festive gatherings. Yahweh is described as a craftsman whose building, the earth, elicited songs of praise from celestial beings. A note of sarcasm surfaces twice in the midst of questions: "Tell me, if you know" and "surely you know."

In verses 8-11, Yahweh is pictured as an authoritative presence at the birth of the sea, unfazed by its tendency to burst free and wreak havoc. Even its emergence from the womb is a violent act, a refusal to stay enclosed within two doors symbolic of the labia. Yahweh clothes baby chaos with a dense cloud and places it under strict orders: "You may come this far, no farther; here your proud waves stop" (38:11).

The dominant image in vv. 12-15 is less obvious than the other two but has to do with control over the earth, sea's rival. Job is asked if he has taken the earth by its edges like a sheet and shaken the wicked out as one shakes vermin from bedclothes. Alternatively, has he turned earth over like clay and determined its shape the way a potter forms vessels and a seamstress makes a garment, or has he condemned the wicked to darkness, breaking the arm they have raised against others? In context, the twofold reference to *reša'im*, "wicked," stands out, for the sustained emphasis thus far is cosmic. As we shall see, mortals play an inconsequential role in Yahweh's speeches.

Verses 16-24 inquire about Job's adventuresome spirit. They concern a journey to the vast beyond: the sources of the sea, the gates of death, earth's expanse, the roads traveled by light and darkness, the places where snow and hail are stored, the paths of light and wind. These questions provide no relief for Job, who is once again mocked mercilessly: "You know, for you were born then; the number of your days is many" (38:21). Unable to qualify as primal man, Job definitely cannot claim to be old enough to have witnessed beginnings the way personified wisdom does in Proverbs 8:22-31 when she boasts of being present at the moment of creation.

The overarching image is one of a well-ordered universe, a kind of temple. Gates, bars, doors, roads, and designated paths suggest that the builder has imposed his own design on the finished product. At the same time, these indicators of limits imply resistance to order, even if it is subject to heteronymous authority. Cosmic enemies are real, they admit, but even the most feared personifications (chaos, death, or sea) have limited powers. In this vast expanse, snow and ice (water in hiding) make up the divine arsenal held in store until the day of battle. Far from being able to tell Yahweh all about the expanse of the earth (38:13), Job must recoil from the mocking "if you know all about it." It is similar to the angel's use of such questions in Fourth Ezra when responding to Ezra's pained inquiries about God's conduct and evil's dominance.

According to vv. 25-27, Yahweh's generosity overflows, providing rain for desolate areas where no humans live. The absence of people in these areas is mentioned twice for emphasis. Other creatures live there, as we shall soon learn, and they need food to survive. The image of birth returns in vv. 28-29 with reference to the rain, dew, ice, and frost. "Has the rain a father; or who begot drops of dew? From whose belly does ice come; who birthed heaven's frost?" Yahweh has no apology for female images indicative of divine activity. The sudden shift from meteorological phenomena to constellations continues the quasi-personification; Pleiades, Orion, and Mazzarot are imagined as beings that must be chained and set free at exact times, just as the Bear and her cubs required supervision.

Power and wisdom alternate as central issues in the concluding questions pertaining to the weather (38:33-38). Job is questioned about his knowledge of heaven's statutes and his ability to impose them below, either to order the

clouds to pour forth rain or to command lightning to strike a target he identifies. The visual image is humorous; will lightning respond to your
command with a submissive, "Here I am"? The ancient belief that wisdom
dwelt far away lies behind Yahweh's question, "Who put wisdom in remote
places and gave understanding to Sekwi?" (v. 36). In rabbinic tradition this
unknown word was identified as a cock, perhaps for its uncanny knowledge
about the time of dawn. Before turning from the sky to earth's creatures
outside human habitation, Yahweh asks one additional question: "Who has
sufficient wisdom to number the sky or enough power to tilt heaven's bottles
when the earth below is parched?"

The long section about animals and winged creatures with which
Yahweh concludes the first speech (38:39–39:30) highlights the provision of
good for all of them and the extraordinary power of some. There is no
consistency in this unit, which sometimes links two creatures together and at
other times concentrates on one. The picture is hardly that of idyllic nature;
instead, it is best characterized by blood-red teeth and claws. Predation
begins and ends the section, with the lion searching for prey and the eagle, or
vulture, feasting on carrion.

The first pair are the mighty lion and tiny raven. They are followed by
the mountain goat and doe, the one sure of foot, the other swift of movement. Yahweh asks Job who provides prey for lions and responds when
ravens' young cry to El and wander about while searching for food. The
birthing habits of mountain goats and does claim Yahweh's attention next.
What does Job know about the time of conception, the actual birth of the
young, and the circumstances before they become self-sufficient? Then
Yahweh mentions the wild ass and the huge wild ox, both of whom roam
freely beyond human domestication for personal use. The thought of the
aurochs, or bison, agreeing to be Job's slave, plowing furrows and harvesting
grain, is hilarious.

So far, each new creature has evoked rhetorical questions from Yahweh.
That consistency is broken with the introduction of the ostrich. Stranger still
is the reference to Eloah in the third person as if the section were not part of
a divine speech (but the same thing occurs in 40:9). For these reasons, interpreters often consider this description of the ostrich a later addition. It gives
voice to popular opinion, based on an erroneous deduction, that ostriches do
not care for their young and are stupid, even if swift of movement. The
remark that "she laughs at horse and rider" provides a smooth transition to
the next animal.

It appears that Yahweh cannot conceal his enthusiasm about the
warrior's horse. Did you, Job, endow him with strength or cause him to leap

like a locust? The similarity of movement between horses and locusts did not escape the author of Joel 2:4. Yahweh's emphasis, however, is on the horse's fearlessness, indeed its complete disregard for danger as it eagerly charges into the fray. He lives only for the battle.

With the hawk and the eagle, or vulture, Yahweh concludes his first speech. Whence the hawk's knowledge about flying and migration and the vulture's intelligence to build its nest in an inaccessible place? Did you, Job, teach them these things? The hawk's clear vision from afar enables it to feed its young. The image of little ones lapping up the blood of those slain in battle provides a subtle hint that even the mighty steed may have fallen in battle. The speech ends on this note: "Where the slain are, there is he" (39:30). Human aggression has a positive side effect of feeding one of God's creatures.

Job's First Response (40:3-5)

Curiously, the narrator intrudes to tell readers that Yahweh answered Job (40:1), then has Yahweh ask, "Will a contender with Shaddai correct him, Eloah's instructor (*mokiah*) answer it?" (40:2). Job, who has looked for a *mokiah*, is here identified as one. Perhaps he was right in denying that such a figure exists (9:33) and Elihu was wrong in redefining the arbiter (32:12-22). Just what is the "it" that Job must answer? And where is the avenger? What has happened to the witness?

"Look, I am trifling. What can I answer you? I will lay my hand on my mouth. I have spoken once; I will not answer; twice, I will not again" (40:4-5). Job uses the verb *qalloti*, "to be small, of little worth," the opposite of *kabod*, "heavy," and thus honor. This response is hardly what we expect form one who has so eagerly awaited a chance to lay out a case before the supreme judge. It has been variously interpreted: as the remark of one who has been overwhelmed by power; as the beginning of humble surrender; as admission of guilt; as a concession that he has not taken the god seriously; as recognition of life's swiftness; as a curse (cf. 3:1, *wayqallel*); as the acquisition of universal wisdom; and as pretended humility before a despot. The numerical structuring of his earlier verbal harangue ("once/twice") can suggest that he has already said all that needs to be spoken. He thus refuses to renounce his oath of innocence. He has not changed his mind about the deity, however, despite the display of majestic rhetoric and constant reminders of Job's insignificance in the god's grand scheme of things.

Yahweh's Second Speech (40:6–41:34)

On the assumption that Job's response to Yahweh implies that the rhetoric about divine control over the entire cosmos has left Job firm in his claim of innocence, a second speech by Yahweh makes sense. This time, however, the emphasis falls on two things: justice and pride. The first concerns Yahweh, the second involves Job and his rivals, Behemoth and Leviathan, the one peaceful and at rest, the other violent, fiery, and in turmoil.

The first contested issue, Yahweh's morality as manifest in his rule, leaps to the fore immediately after the repeated demand that Job gird his loins like a *geber* and respond to divine inquiry (cf. 38:3). No question precedes this second demand as it had the first (38:2). Yahweh now asks the question that states "the pivot on which the book turns" (Good, 353). Clearly the most pertinent question of the two speeches, the inquiry was first formulated by the ghostlike visitor in 4:17. At long last Yahweh acknowledges, even if in interrogative form, that the real issue separating Job and the deity concerns justice, not power. The question suggests that Yahweh is stung by the very thought of being considered less moral than Job. "Will you even impugn my justice, deem me guilty so you can be innocent?" (40:8). The form of the two verbs, causative when referring to Yahweh's justice and simple Qal when indicating Job's innocence, is significant. It means that the former is an expressed judgment, the latter an actual quality in hand. Yahweh's answer to his own question comes in the midst of describing the king of all proud beasts. Pausing long enough to ask, "Indeed, who can stand before me? Who opposes me that I must repay?" and to add, "Everything under heaven is mine," or "Under the whole heaven, he is mine" (41:2b-3), Yahweh rejects the principle of retribution and its positive counterpart. Because his power is supreme and his ownership cannot be challenged, no one can demand payment for service rendered. So much for dreams about a moral universe. No such place exists. With this assertion of absolute power, Yahweh has rejected Job's demand for a just order.

Pride, the second issue that dominates this additional speech by Yahweh, comes to expression in 40:11b-12, where Yahweh tells Job to "Look on all the proud and humble them; look on all the proud and debase them; trample the wicked in their place." Job is told to direct his anger elsewhere than on Yahweh (the metaphor reminds one of the narrator's graphic description of Elihu as angry). Now Job is told to scatter the coals of his anger on the proud, who are also called wicked. If you are able to do this, Yahweh assures him, then I will praise you, even I (cf. Elihu's similar use of "even I" in 32:17b but with *ʾap-ʾani* instead of *gam-ʾani*). If Job finds this task of subduing pride in humans beyond his ability, how much more difficult it will be to humble the great Behemoth and Leviathan, the king over all proud beasts (41:26). Yahweh has set before him an impossible task, one beyond the power of his right hand (40:14b). Deliverance (*yešuʿa*), if it comes, will be from someone else, but Yahweh remains quiet about any avenger or redeemer.

What is at stake here, that Yahweh must focus Job's eyes on pride and justice? It is nothing less than wanting to invalidate the order of the cosmos, the divine *mišpaṭ*. The noun has a wide range of meanings including order, custom, justice, and judgment. That is, *mišpaṭ* refers to cosmic structure, social convention, morality, and legal verdict. In short, Yahweh accuses Job of wanting to rearrange the way the world operates. In this, Yahweh is surely correct, for Job desires a moral universe, not the arbitrary one that has brought so much misery to him and his family.

It is precisely this arbitrary world that Yahweh praises, one that has both order and disorder, the one holding its opposite in check. Predators require prey, wild things need freedom, dumb creatures have a right to exist, and the brave should be allowed to court death, if they wish to do so. In Yahweh's world, everything can be itself. The theme that pervades the description of the animals is that of playful laughter (*śaḥaq*, 39:7, 18, 22; 42:20, 29; cf. Prov 8:30-31). Joy and praise, it follows, are the expected attitudes in Yahweh's well-planned universe. From his perspective, Job's desire for a different universe is proof of his ingratitude.

The actions that Yahweh urges Job to perform are ambiguous, like the universe itself. Job is told to clothe himself with honor, a necessary replacement of his low self-esteem that has resulted from the first divine speech, and yet this act would seem to be nullified by his justice in excess, the trampling of the proud and hiding them in the dust. According to 29:14, Job has already donned righteousness and justice as regular garments. Has Yahweh not heard this claim, or does he refuse to believe it? Simple justice is apparently not enough for Yahweh, for whom power alone qualifies someone to join the ranks of the gods.

Whereas 40:7-14 has issued a challenge for Job to stamp out pride, the rest of Yahweh's second speech returns to the bestiary, although now the two animals are a combination of realistic creatures and a vivid imagination. No such creatures exist, even if they resemble the hippopotamus and crocodile in some ways. Herodotus treats these two in succession, and the pharaoh as Horus was allowed to hunt them. In Egyptian iconography, they represent chaos and must be defeated to maintain order. Other biblical references to these personifications of chaos in Isaiah 27:1 and 51:9 and Psalms 74:13-14; 89:11; and 104:25-27 depict creatures that Yahweh has conquered. They bear several names: Rahab, Leviathan, and Tannin. Ugaritic Lotan, a twisting serpent, is identical with Leviathan. In post-biblical apocalyptic, both Behemoth and Leviathan stand for the cosmic dimensions of good and evil (cf. 2 Esd 6:49-52; *2 Bar* 29:4; *1 En* 60:7-9).

The first of these two, called Behemoth, the plural of the word for beasts, has features of a hippopotamus and a water buffalo, but not every descriptive characteristic in the Joban text is accurate. The creature eats grass, lies in the water under lotus trees, opens its mouth fearlessly during a flood, and so forth. More importantly, Behemoth is said to have been made "with you" and to be the "first of El's ways," like personified wisdom (Prov 8:22, with "works" instead of "ways"). The preposition "with" implies temporality, hence "along with" you. An alternative pointing of v. 19b yields "made to dominate his companions" rather than "his maker draws his sword." Notably, Job is not told to conquer it but to look, and El alone can draw his sword against such might (40:19). The reference to the tail of the creature as stiff like a cedar does not match the short tail of a hippo; interpreters usually take this description as indicative of virility, an allusion to its erect penis. Two rhetorical questions conclude this account: "Can he be taken by his eyes? Can one pierce his nose by hooks?" (40:24) and provide a smooth transition to the praise of Leviathan in 40:25–41:26. Unlike Behemoth, Leviathan is named elsewhere in the Bible.

Questions abound in Yahweh's remarks about Leviathan, and the issue of control shifts from the deity to Job. Verses 25-32 emphasize the impossibility of a human exercising authority over this powerful creature. The use of hooks and ropes in capturing crocodiles is echoed in the initial questions, but with Leviathan these efforts will not succeed. The idiocy of such an attempt is shown by several mocking questions: "Will he beg you much or speak gentle words to you? Will he make a pact with you; will you take him for a permanent slave? Can you play with him like a bird; put a leash on him for your girls? Will merchants sell him; will they divide him among traders?" (vv. 27-30). No one will forget the battle once it is engaged, but Yahweh appears to have forgotten that Job's daughters are dead.

In 3:8, Job had wished for professional help in stirring up Leviathan, but Yahweh points out that nobody is fierce enough to rouse him (41:2). With such ease, Yahweh shifts momentarily away from Leviathan to himself. "Indeed, who can stand before me? Who opposes me that I must repay? Everything under heaven is mine" (41:2b-3). Apparently, Yahweh still reels from the impact of Job's moral claim on him, which he resents (40:8). Because he owns the whole world, he is under no obligation to anyone (cf. Ps 51:7-15).

Returning to his description of Leviathan, Yahweh quickly introduces mythical features of fire-breathing sea serpents (41:10-13). Realistic features of crocodiles are interspersed with legendary characteristics that enhance Leviathan's fearsome presence. Poetic imagination soars, and we marvel at the picture of matching scales so closely locked that even air cannot penetrate, and we realize that we have been transported into the realm of fantasy where sea serpents breathe fire and emit smoke from their mouths. With the move to the open sea and eyes of fire, we have left crocodiles behind. The language of this mighty creature churning away at the sea and leaving a white wake behind evoked thoughts of whales in Milton, just as the challenge of capturing Leviathan inspired the author of *Moby Dick*. Yahweh's recollection of Tehom's white hair (41:24) nicely brings together personified Deep and Leviathan. The latter accomplishes one thing Yahweh asked Job to do: "Look on all the proud" (40:11b; 41:26a). Leviathan reigns as king over all proud beasts.

A curious remark in 41:17 reinforces the suspicion that even Yahweh finds pride among humans to be a challenge, and the idea may be a veiled concession in 40:11-14. I refer to the admission that divine beings fear Leviathan's rising and withdraw to safe quarters. The polytheistic background for this observation need not obscure the fact that Yahweh belonged to this group. Does Yahweh also quake before such a creature? Is his boast about controlling Leviathan an idle one?

Finally, why the move out of the ordinary realm of creatures? Behemoth and fire-breathing sea dragons that nevertheless are subject to Yahweh are a convincing argument for divine power and inscrutability, but they also present a challenge to Job to demonstrate his ability to subdue them. "Overcome these representatives of pride and I will praise you as divine." With this comment, Yahweh has reminded Job that he cannot even compete against creatures, however lofty, much less against their creator. Job's demand for justice has been replaced by power, just as he anticipated. How will he respond this time?

Job's Second Response (42:1-6)

The first word of Job's closing remarks alerts readers to difficulties yet to come. The Ketib has *yada'ta*, "you know," and the Qere has *yada'ti*, "I know," defectively written. The difference is huge. In the first reading, Job says, "You know that you can do everything and no scheme of yours can be frustrated," while the second reading attributes this knowledge to Job. Neither interpretation reflects favorably on Yahweh. Divine awareness of something akin to omnipotence ought to have tempered brutality where Job is concerned. A plea of ignorance cannot be used as an excuse for swallowing Job and his family. Alternatively, Job's knowledge that he has challenged one capable of anything may have expanded to include *nipla'ot*, wonders of cosmic proportions, but compassionless strength brings awe, not comfort.

The next verse continues the confusion: "Who is this darkening counsel without knowledge? Therefore, I told what I did not understand, wonders beyond me, and I did not know" (v. 3). Job quotes Yahweh's question from 38:2a, although with considerable poetic license (the Greek and Syriac versions adjust the reading to replicate the Hebrew). Job appears to admit that he did not have adequate grasp of the scope of divine power. In other words, he has understated Yahweh's sovereign rule. Now he knows how uncaring it really is even while the wonders never cease.

Verse 4 also begins with a quotation, although it is not clear exactly who is being quoted. Similar words were spoken by Elihu in 33:31, but also by Job in 13:22 and 21:2-3, so he may be quoting himself. A third possibility is that he tries to summarize Yahweh's fundamental approach to him. "Hear, please, and I will speak; I will ask, and you inform me." Normally, the formula is used elsewhere in the Bible when an inferior addresses a superior, although exceptions exist. The particle of entreaty is extraordinary when used by the deity; but it does occur perhaps to emphasize the unusual nature of the demand (cf. Gen 22:2). Is Job sincere, or does he use sarcasm? Throughout this reply, we cannot tell whether Job is submissive, sarcastic, indignant, or obsequious.

Because Job has listened to Yahweh for some time, he may ask for the same courtesy. "You listen and I will speak; I will ask questions and you teach me." The problem with this interpretation is the absence of any questions by Job. Instead, he speaks about two complementary modes of learning: hearing and seeing. "By ear's hearing, I heard you, and now my eye has seen you" (v. 5). The verbs designate completed action, but tense is uncertain. Hearing and seeing, while complete, may continue in their effect into the present, hence "I hear and see" is also possible. The *waw* creates further ambiguity; some interpreters take it as adversative, thus for them hearing is placed over against seeing as an inferior mode of learning. We recall that Abaddon and Death claimed to have learned about wisdom by rumor (28:22), hearsay being less reliable than Yahweh's knowledge acquired by intensive investigation.

Job's claim to see Yahweh takes us by surprise. After all, the Bible throws a protective veil over the deity because of the danger of looking on holiness. According to words attributed to Yahweh, no one can see God and live (Exod 33:20). That simple statement underscores the danger, and yet the

Bible records exceptions to the rule—Jacob, Moses, Isaiah, Ezekiel, Daniel, and a large group of Israelites on Mt. Sinai. These accounts still emphasize divine hiddenness, even in disclosure. Isaiah draws attention to the strange creatures surrounding the heavenly throne, Ezekiel emphasizes "likeness," and Daniel uses a metaphor of temporality (the Ancient of Days) and describes divine clothing and hair but no more. For his part, Job simply says that he sees Yahweh. That is all, and the language may not be metaphorical.

What is the consequence of knowledge acquired by sound and sight? The answer is what Edwin Good has called the punch line of the book. Unfortunately, its translation is a notorious crux. "Therefore, I despise and reject dust and ashes" (v. 6) is but one of several ways to read this verse (conveniently summarized by Newsom 1996, 629). The initial *'al-ken*, "on account of this," corresponds to *laken* of v. 3b and is best rendered "therefore." In other words, the new discovery as a result of hearing and seeing Yahweh has led to something. But what?

The verb *'em'as* is either from *ma'as*, "to despise," or *masas*, "to melt." If the former, the necessary object can be implicit or it may be found in the final three words, "concerning dust and ashes." Interpreters have provided various objects of loathing: pride, demands for a trial, and miserable condition. Dust and ashes, the expression Abraham applied to himself when interceding for the inhabitants of Sodom and Gomorrah, indicates lowly humanity. In the prologue, Job sits in ashes and his friends scatter dust toward heaven in a ritual of mourning, so dust and ashes may carry this ritualistic connotation.

If one chooses to read Job's first verb as a form of *masas*, it points to his humble state. "I am abased" or, reflexively, "I abase myself" would then reflect his newfound humility, if the words are taken at face value. That is how the LXX translator understood the verb. Some modern interpreters think it has a tinge of contempt and indicates concealed defiance. According to this theory, Job's humility is merely for show. Job finally realizes the scope of divine cruelty and adopts deception as a way of dealing with it. Those who think of Job's humility as authentic often forget that the friends urged him to abase himself, and the epilogue has Yahweh rebuke them for what they have said.

The second verb, *nihamti*, refers to rejecting a pattern of action. Although often translated by "repent," especially when referring to Yahweh's changed intention, the verb does not necessarily imply guilt or wrongdoing. It does consist of the rejection of something and its replacement by something else. Understood this way, it suggests that Job repents of dust and ashes, either his miserable condition or the anticipated ritual of mourning (see Curtis and Patrick).

One way of construing Job's final words is in terms of cognitive dissonance. Job repents of his previous view of the world as established on the principle of reward for virtue and punishment for vice. Job repents of everything associated with such a world, especially guilt and its supposed removal through repentance. In the new universe Job has finally discovered, guilt and innocence have no place. Above all, he rejects a world where suffering is linked to guilt. Repenting of a world where repentance plays no role is hugely ironic.

The Epilogue (42:7-17)

We shall hear nothing more from Job except by indirection. The ever-omniscient narrator reports that Job interceded for his friends and also named his three daughters. From now on, then, the narrator tells the story that began in chapter 1, but this time he brings news of his hero's restoration, Job's lone journey from the ash heap to his house. How is that turn of fortune accomplished? It follows upon his prayer on behalf of his three friends, an intercessory act that is anticipated in the prologue where Job sacrifices on his children's behalf.

Why do the three friends need an intercessor? The narrator tells us that Yahweh's anger (*'ap*) burned against Job's three friends, just like Elihu's, we might add. Yahweh rebukes Eliphaz, informing him that the three have not spoken *nekonah*, "the truth," something established as reliable "to me as my servant Job has." In two verses, 7-8, Job is called "my servant" four times, twice as many as in the first two chapters. Ironically, Job, who has wished for an intercessor to plead his case with the deity, now fulfills that role on behalf of the friends who had completely misjudged him. Moreover, Yahweh requires the three to offer a huge sacrifice—seven bulls and seven rams—to atone for their offense. Job's intercessory prayer is causally connected with his return to favor in Yahweh's eyes. Shockingly, it is said that Yahweh is prevented from doing folly to them; this word for foolishness, *nebala*, is the same word Job had used about his wife's advice to him. Their failure to speak *nekonah* had put them in danger of causing Yahweh to act foolishly. What a departure from the friends' view that human conduct has no effect on deity.

The astonishing thing is that Yahweh says nothing about Job's second response, unless that is where Job has spoken the truth. In 38:2, Yahweh labeled Job's argument as ignorance and as darkening the divine plan. Either Yahweh has heard something in Job's second response that he considers reliable, or Job has pulled the wool over his eyes. The text leaves the matter open. The narrator passes over in silence Job's second response, which requires readers to look for Job's "truthful speech" in his complaints.

Be that as it may, the narrator states that Yahweh changed Job's fortune "when he prayed for his friends." (This is the only instance of the expression *šub šebut* with reference to an individual.) Ritual is alive and well, at least in the epilogue. The sacrifice completed, Yahweh doubled Job's previous possessions, as if in accord with the legal requirement that a thief pay double for what was taken (Exod 22:3, 6). Before giving the specific number of cattle, the narrator attends to something far more important: Job's return to social acceptability. His brothers, sisters, and acquaintances join him at table; eating with another person was an act of hospitality that cemented friendship. By this simple act of fellowship over food, Job's brothers and sisters accomplished what the three friends had failed to do; they comforted and consoled him (*nud* and *naḥam*) "about all the evil Yahweh had brought on him." With this remarkable statement, the narrator has placed full responsibility for Job's calamity on Yahweh, and comfort comes from intimate relationships rather than from theological debate or descriptions of cosmic grandeur. The silence about the adversary of the prologue is surprising, like the forgotten test.

Those eating with Job did more than show up at his doorstep. They each gave him a *qesitah*, an item of monetary exchange, probably silver, and a gold ring, most likely to be worn in the nose or on an earlobe. The word *qesitah* is found elsewhere in the Bible only in Genesis 33:19 and Joshua 24:32; the choice of this word was intended to support a date for the story in patriarchal times,

At this point, the narrator begins to wrap things up for good. He says that Yahweh blessed Job's latter days more than his earlier ones. This seventh use of the verb *barak* in the prose definitely carries the meaning it had when the adversary accused Yahweh of blessing Job by enclosing him within a protective hedge (1:10). Job's blessing includes new sons and daughters (Coogan 1990). Only the three daughters are named, and they are said to be lovelier than any other women in the land. Their suitability as wives is further enhanced by a revolutionary act of generosity on Job's part. He gives each one an inheritance. Normally, girls in ancient Israel could not inherit unless they had no brothers. The names of these daughters of Job have symbolic meanings: dove, cassia (a perfume), and cosmetic box (antinomy was used as mascara). Job's sons are not named. In Ugaritic myth, Baal had seven/eight sons and three daughters, and only the names of the daughters were given. Curiously, Job's wife is not mentioned in the epilogue, although she is presumed to have given birth to ten more children. Nor are servants mentioned as replacements for those lost in the prologue, but Job's renewed wealth would have made the purchase of slaves possible. Given the culture, it is unlikely that the narrator thought Job had given up the practice of owning slaves.

Surrounded by his wife and children, Job ends his days. We are told that he lived long enough to see four generations of progeny. How swiftly time flies in the narrative, as opposed to the poetry, which gives no clues about time's passage. The prose, however, uses seven words to report that Job lived 140 years after this. His life span, double the normal seventy years, exceeded that of people like Abraham, Isaac, and Jacob. The Septuagint inflates the life span to 240, stating that Job was 70 when struck by calamity. Five Hebrew words conclude this masterpiece: "Job died, an old man sated with days" (cf. Gen 25:8). With this language, he has been linked linguistically with Abraham, Isaac, and David.

This happy ending troubles many interpreters. For them, the author suffers from failure of nerve. Having demolished the principle of reward and punishment in the poetry, he now reinstates it, confirming Job's view of divine arbitrariness. Even worse, the epilogue glosses over the loss of life in the prologue, blithely announcing the replacement of the dead by better children, at least where daughters are concerned. Others insist that Job's restored fortune and family have nothing to do with reward for loyal service but simply demonstrate divine freedom. It is clear, however, that Yahweh's anger directed at the three friends and his means of allaying fury rest on the principle of retribution. Moreover, Job's restoration is the result of his intercession following an act of sacrifice. It cannot be denied, in my view, that the prose account is at odds with the poetry.

When we reflect on the whole book and ask about its fundamental problem, the following assessment seems accurate. For the adversary, the problem can be stated succinctly: "Does Job serve God for nothing?" In other words, the disputed issue concerns disinterested righteousness. As might be expected, Job defines the problem as innocent suffering, which implicates the deity as guilty of injustice. Job's three friends think the basic problem is human guilt, and they believe he combines it with rebellion. The remedy, as they see it, is repentance. Elihu thinks the deity sends suffering to educate and discipline humans. Finally, Yahweh reminds mortals of their place in the vast universe and locates the fundamental problem in how a person speaks to (or of) him. Who speaks for the poet? Who knows? Perhaps all of the above.

Postscript: Why Read Job Today?

As I put the finishing touches on this manuscript about an imaginary character of long ago, and the god he trusted but who failed to live up to that trust, I watch in horror while images of victims of Nashville's unprecedented flood flash across the screen of my television. Unlike Job's suffering, and that of his family, what I am seeing is painfully real, with more than 17,000 homes destroyed, numerous businesses ruined, and the loss of much life.

The automobile of an elderly couple on their way to worship at St. George's Episcopal Church was swept away by the strong current crossing the highway, their bodies later found in Richland Creek along which my wife and I regularly walk. Another aged couple drowned in their house, believed to be a sanctuary against the storm. And so it goes, a death here, another there, and devastation in place after place where the serpentine Cumberland river overflowed its banks, reaching a height of more than 56 feet at flood stage and unable to bear more than 14 inches of rain that fell in less than 48 hours.

Days later, I drove outside Music City to a local park and viewed the mountains of trash city workers have hauled to this site, at least for the time being. This disturbing scene represents the hopes and dreams of thousands of residents, all their life savings: appliances, furniture, pictures, virtually everything yanked from the houses that are left standing, reduced to shells. Displaced persons, many too poor to rebuild, ponder their future, made a little less bleak by the amazing outflow of generosity from others.

What am I as a Christian to make of this tragedy, one that takes its place alongside thousands more across the globe? Having been taught that God holds the whole world in his hand and that not a single hair falls from one's head but that the heavenly Father notices, once I have gotten past the masculine gender of such statements, how am I supposed to reconcile belief in providence and nature's fury?

The biblical Job, too, believed in a just God who rewarded loyal service. That conviction, however, was sorely tested, in the end being exposed for what it was, a huge lie. While there is some truth in the view that the instability of evil is the moral order in the world, the good seems no more stable than its rival. The result is an unjust world, one in which accident and randomness are the norm. That is the nature of existence, a realm in which good and evil vie for dominance. And it does no good to speak of paradox, believing that somehow God can balance opposites and that what rational people call injustice is altogether right in God's domain.

What, then, does the Bible contribute to ease the human dilemma, and more specifically, how can Job's test help modern readers? We must remember that Scripture is the testimony of people from a distant land and time to their contemporaries about perceived religious experience. Testimony, as we all know, can be true or false, even a combination of both. The Bible, then, consists of human perceptions of the divine entering lives, and that account is peculiar to a small band of followers of a god they called Yahweh. Its religious views are by nature parochial, even when claiming to be universal.

The author of the book of Job comes close to universal truth when rejecting the truisms being bandied about in the ancient world and attested throughout canonical literature. For Job, God presented a colossal problem, although Job could not decide whether it took the form of absence or animosity. The crucial issue for him came down to his own integrity, the only thing he had left after his life and that of his family were dealt a devastating blow.

Perhaps that is precisely the contribution this book can make to Job's modern companions, most of whom are not paragons of virtue like him but who hold in their breasts both good and evil. Maintaining our integrity in a cruel world is the most important thing while we await relief in the form of death. Even this goal may be off the mark because it is self-centered. Only when integrity is oriented toward helping ease others' burdens will it rise above the world of calculating morality, a quid pro quo that focuses on equivalency.

But how does one maintain integrity when it is impugned on every hand, often by well-intentioned folk? Here, too, the story about Job offers a little guidance. We hold on to our integrity best by questioning everything we have been taught by theologians, whether professional or amateur. We do so because no one fully understands the limits of the intellect, and good people are most prone to think they are exempt from the limitations inherent to mortals.

It may be that even adopting a skeptical stance toward every claim of absolute truth falls short of the essential insight of the biblical book. How so? Job's restoration from his own personal and social hell came not via an intellectual quest, however significant it was, but through sharing a common meal with friends and relatives. Our healing, that is, takes place in fellowship with others whose hearts are linked with ours by bonds of mutual trust.

And what of God? Job's final response to the one from whom he had become estranged through no fault of his own offers no unambiguous clue as to his own reconciliation. Job had been wronged for no reason, which may partially explain his ambiguous last words. Maybe it does not really matter, for like Job's world, ours is replete with the unknown, a mystery that comes, if it comes at all, to the restless heart. Our pain lingers, nevertheless, for loss is real, and we are not, like Job, assuaged by being named "my servant" and commended for speaking the truth to God.

Works Cited

Alonso-Schökel, Luis. 1977. "Toward a Dramatic Reading of the Book of Job." In *Studies in the Book of Job*, ed. Robert Polzin and David Robertson, 45–61. Semeia 7. Missoula: Scholars.

———. 1983. *Job*. Madrid: Cristiandad.

Alter, Robert. 1981. *The Art of Biblical Narrative*. New York: Basic Books.

———. 1985. *The Art of Biblical Poetry*. New York: Basic Books.

Andersen, Francis I. 1976. *Job*. Downers Grove IL: InterVarsity.

Aufrecht, Walter E., ed. 1985. *Studies in the Book of Job*. SRS 16. Waterloo, Ontario: WilfridLaurier University.

Balentine, Samuel E. 1983. *The Hidden God: The Hiding of the Face of God in the Old Testament*. Oxford: Oxford University.

———. 2006. *Job*. Macon GA: Smyth & Helwys.

Baskin, Judith R. 1992. "Rabbinic Interpretations of Job." In *The Voice from the Whirlwind: Interpreting the Book of Job*, ed. Leo G. Perdue and W. Clark Gilpin, 101–10. Nashville: Abingdon.

Bastiaens, Jean Charles. 1992. "The Language of Suffering in Job 16–19 and in the Suffering Servant Passages in Deutero-Isaiah." In *Studies in the Book of Isaiah*, ed. J. Van Ruiten and M. Vervenne, 421–32. BETL 132. Leuven: Leuven University.

Ben Zvi, Ehud, ed. 2006. *Utopia and Dystopia in Prophetic Literature*. Publications of the Finnish Exegetical Society 92. Helsinki: The Finnish Exegetical Society.

Berlin, Adele. 1985. *The Dynamics of Biblical Parallelism*. Bloomington: Indiana University.

Besserman, L. 1979. *The Legend of Job in the Middle Ages*. Cambridge: Harvard University.

Beuken, W. A. M., ed. 1994. *The Book of Job*. BETL 114. Leuven: University Press.

Bloom, Harold, ed. 1988. *The Book of Job*. New York: Chelsea House.

———. 2004. *Where Shall Wisdom Be Found?* New York: Riverhead Books.

Brenner, A. 1981. "God's Answer to Job." *VT* 31: 129–37.

Brown, William. 2002. *Seeing the Psalms: A Theology of Metaphor*. Louisville: Westminster John Knox.

Buber, Martin. 1968. "The Heart Determines [Psalm 73]." In *On the Bible*, 199–210. New York: Schocken.

Carr, David M. 2004. *Writing on the Tablet of the Heart: Origins of Scripture and Literature*. New York: Oxford University.

Charlesworth, James H., ed. 2006. *Resurrection: The Origin and Future of a Biblical Doctrine*. New York & London: T & T Clark.

Cheney, Michael. 1994. *Dust, Wind, and Agony: Character, Speech and Genre in Job*. ConBOT 36. Lund: Almqvist & Wiksell International.

Clifford, Richard J., and John J. Collins, eds. 1992. *Creation in the Biblical Traditions*, CBQMS 24. Washington, DC: Catholic Biblical Association of America.

Clines, David J. A. 1985. "False Naivety in the Prologue to Job." *HAR* 9: 127–36.

———. 1989. *Job 1–20*. Dallas: Word.

———. 1992. "The Arguments of Job's Three Friends." In *Art and Meaning: Rhetoric in Biblical Literature*, ed. Clines, D. M. Gunn, and A. J. Hauser. JSOTSup 19, 199–214. Sheffield: JSOT.

Collins, John J. 1984. *The Apocalyptic Imagination. An Introduction to the Jewish Matrix of Christianity*. New York: Crossroad.

———. 1992. "Early Jewish Apocalypticism." In *ABD* 1, 281–88. New York: Doubleday.

Coogan, Michael D. 1990. "Job's Children." In *Lingering over Words: Studies in Ancient Near Eastern Literature in Honor of William L. Moran*, ed. F. Abusch, J. Huhnergard, and P. Steinkeller. HSS 37, 135–47. Atlanta: Scholars.

———. 2009. "The Social Worlds of the Book of Job." In *Exploring the Longue Duree: Essays in Honor of Lawrence E. Stager*, ed. J. David Schloen, 77–81. Winona Lake IN: Eisenbrauns.

Cooper, Alan. 1982. "Narrative Theory and the Book of Job." *SR* 11: 35–44.

Cotter, David W. 1992. *A Study of Job 4–5 in the Light of Contemporary Literary Theory*. SBLDS 124. Atlanta: Scholars Press.

Cox, Dermot. 1978. *The Triumph of Innocence: Job and the Tradition of the Absurd*. Analecta Gregoriana 212. Rome: Universita Gregoriana.

Crenshaw, James L. 1971. *Prophetic Conflict: Its Effect upon Israelite Religion*. BZAW 124. Berlin: de Gruyter.

———. 1975. *Hymnic Affirmation of Divine Justice: The Doxologies of Amos and Related Texts in the Old Testament*. SBLDS 24. Missoula: Scholars.

———. 1977. "The Human Dilemma and Literature of Dissent." In *Tradition and Theology in the Old Testament*, ed. Douglas A. Knight, 235–38. Philadelphia: Fortress.

———. 1978. *Samson: A Secret Betrayed, a Vow Ignored*. Louisville: Westminster John Knox.

———. 1980. "Impossible Questions, Sayings, and Tasks." In J. Crenshaw, *Urgent Advice and Probing Questions: Collected Writings on Old Testament Wisdom*, 265–78. Macon GA: Mercer. Originally published in *Gnomic Wisdom*, ed. J. D. Crossan, 19–34. Chico CA: Scholars.

———. 1984. *A Whirlpool of Torment: Israelite Traditions of God as an Oppressive Presence.* Philadelphia: Fortress.

———. 1992. "Job, Book of." In *ABD* 3, 858–68. New York: Doubleday.

———. 1993. "Suffering." In *The Oxford Companion to the Bible*, eds. Bruce M. Metzger and Michael D. Coogan, 718–19. Oxford: Oxford University.

———. 1997. "The Primacy of Listening in Ben Sira's Pedagogy." In J. Crenshaw, *Prophets, Sages, & Poets*, 20–28 and 204–207. St. Louis: Chalice. Originally published in *Wisdom, You Are My Sister*, ed. Michael L. Barré. CBQMS 29, 172–87. Washington, DC: The Catholic Biblical Association of America.

———. 1998a. *Education in Ancient Israel: Across the Deadening Silence.* New York: Doubleday.

———. 1998b. "Wisdom and Authority: Sapiential Rhetoric and its Warrants." In J. Crenshaw, *Urgent Advice and Probing Questions: Collected Writings on Old Testament Wisdom*, 326–43. Macon GA: Mercer.

———. 1999. "Flirting with the Language of Prayer (Job 14:13-17)." In J. Crenshaw, *Prophets, Sages & Poets*, 6–13 and 201–203. St. Louis: Chalice. Originally published in *Worship and the Hebrew Bible: Essays in Honor of John T. Willis*, ed. Patrick Graham, Rick Marrs, and Steven McKenzie. JSOT Sup 284, 110–23. Sheffield: JSOT.

———. 2001a. "Job." In *The Oxford Bible Commentary*, ed. John Barton and J. Muddiman, 331–55. Oxford: Oxford University.

———. 2001b. *The Psalms: An Introduction.* Grand Rapids: Eerdmans.

———. 2002. "Some Reflections on the Book of Job." *RevExp* 99: 589–95.

———. 2005a. "A Proverb in the Mouth of a Fool." In *Seeking Out the Wisdom of the Ancients*, eds. Ronald L. Troxel, Kelvin G. Friebel, and Dennis R. Magary, 103–15. Winona Lake: Eisenbrauns.

———. 2005b. *Defending God: Biblical Responses to the Problem of Evil.* New York: Oxford University Press.

———. 2005c. "Introduction and Notes." In *The Renovaré Spiritual Formation Bible*, 1645–1723. San Francisco: HarperSanFrancisco.

———. 2006a. "Deceitful Minds and Theological Dogma: Jer 17:5-11." In *Utopia and Dystopia and Prophetic Literature*. Publications of the Finnish Exegetical Society 92, 105–121. Helsinki: The Finnish Exegetical Society.

———. 2006b. "From the Mundane to the Sublime (Reflections on Qoheleth 11:1-8)." In J. Crenshaw, *Prophets, Sages & Poets*, 61–72 and 217–22. St. Louis: Chalice.

———. 2006c. "Love Is Stronger than Death: Intimations of Life Beyond the Grave." In *Resurrection: The Origin and Future of a Biblical Doctrine*, ed. James H. Charlesworth, 53–78. New York: T & T Clark.

———. 2006d. "Qoheleth's Quantitative Language," In J. Crenshaw, *Prophets, Sages & Poets*, 83–94. St. Louis: Chalice.

———. 2006e. "Qoheleth's Understanding of Intellectual Inquiry." In J. Crenshaw, *Prophets, Sages & Poets*, 29–41 and 207–11. St. Louis: Chalice.

————. 2007. "Qoheleth in Historical Context." *Bib* 88: 285–99.

————. 2009a. "The Book of Sirach." In *NIB* V, 603–867. Nashville: Abingdon.

————. 2009b. "Theodicy." In *NIDB* 5, 551–55. Nashville: Abingdon.

————. 2010. *Old Testament Wisdom. Third Edition.* Louisville: Westminster John Knox.

Curtis, John Briggs. 1979. "On Job's Response to Yahweh." *JBL* 98: 497–511.

Damico, Anthony, and Martin D. Yaffe, eds. 1989. *Thomas Aquinas, The Literal Exposition on Job. A Scriptural Commentary Concerning Providence.* Atlanta: Scholars.

Damon, S. Foster. 1966. *Blake's Job: William Blake's Illustrations of the Book of Job, Introduction and Commentary.* New York: E. P. Dutton.

Day, John. 1993. "How Could Job Be an Edomite?" In *The Book of Job*, ed. W. A. M. Beuken. BETL 114, 391–99. Leuven: University Press.

Day, Peggy L. 1988. *An Adversary in Heaven: Satan in the Hebrew Bible.* HSM 43. Altanta: Scholars.

Dell, Katharine J. 1991. *The Book of Job as Sceptical Literature.* BZAW 197. Berlin: de Gruyter.

Dhorme, Eduard. 1967. *A Commentary on the Book of Job*, E.T. Nashville: Nelson.

Driver, S. R., and Gray G. C. 1977. *A Critical and Exegetical Commentary on the Book of Job.* ICC. Edinburgh: T. & T. Clark.

Duquoc, Christian, and Casiano Floristán, eds. 1983. *Job and the Silence of God.* Concilium New York: Seabury Press.

Ebach, Jürgen. 1995. *Hiobs Post: Gesammelte Aufsätze zum Hiobbuch, zu Themen biblischer Theologie und zur Methodik der Exegese.* Neukirchen-Vluyn: Neukirchener.

Egger-Wenzel, Renate. 1998. *Von der Freiheit Gottes, anders zu sein: Die Zentrale Rolle der Kapitel 9 und 10 für das Ijobbuch.* FzB. Wurzburg: Echter.

Eisen, R. 2004. *The Book of Job in Medieval Jewish Philosophy.* Oxford: Oxford University Press.

Fishbane, Michael. 1971. "Jeremiah IV 23-26 and Job III 3-13: A Recovered Use of the Creation Pattern." *VT* 21: 151–67.

Fohrer, Georg. 1963a. *Das Buch Hiob.* KAT 16. Gutersloh: Gerd Mohn.

————. 1963b. *Studien zum Buche Hiob.* Gutersloh: Gerd Mohn.

Fox, Michael V. 2005. "Job the Pious." *ZAW* 117: 351–66.

Fuchs, Gisela. 1993. *Mythos und Hiobdichtung. Aufnahme und Umdeutung altorientalischer Vorstellungen.* Stuttgart et al.: Kohlhammer.

Geller, Stephen A. 1987. "Where Is Wisdom? A Literary Study of Job 28 in Its Settings." In *Judaic Perspectives on Ancient Israel*, ed. Jacob Neusner, J. Levine, B. A. Frerichs, 155–88. Philadelphia: Fortress.

Girard, René. 1987. *Job: The Victim of His People.* Stanford: Stanford University.

Glatzer, Nahum. 1966. "The Book of Job and Its interpreters." In *Biblical Motifs*, ed. A. Altmann, 197–220. Cambridge: Harvard University.

———, ed. 1969. *The Dimensions of Job*. New York: Schocken.

Good, Edwin M. 1990. *In Turns of Tempest: A Reading of Job with a Translation*. Stanford: Stanford University.

Gordis, Robert. 1965. *The Book of God and Man: A Study of Job*. Chicago: University of Chicago.

———. 1978. *The Book of Job*. New York: Jewish Theological Seminary of America.

Gorea, Maria. 2007. *Job: Ses précurseurs et ses épigones ou comment faire de nouveau avec de l'ancien*. Orient & Méditerranée 1. Paris: De Boccard.

Greenstein, Edward L. 2003. "The Poem on Wisdom in Job 28 in Its Conceptual and Literary Contexts." In *Job 28: Cognition in Context*. Biblical Interpretation Series 64, 253–80. Leiden: Brill.

———. 2007. "'On My Skin and in My Flesh': Personal Experience as a Source of Knowledge in the Book of Job." In *Bringing the Hidden to Light: The Process of Interpretation—Studies in Honor of Stephen A. Geller*, ed. Kathryn F. Kravitz and Diane M. Sharon, 63–77. New York: Jewish Theological Seminary.

Gunn, David. 1978. *The Story of King David: Genre and Interpretation*. Sheffield: JSOT.

Gutíerrez, Gustavo. 1987. *On Job: God-Talk and the Suffering of the Innocent*. Maryknoll NY: Orbis.

Ha, Kyung-Taek. 2005. *Frage und Antwort: Studien zu Hiob 3 im Kontext des Hiobbuches*. HBS 46. Freiburg: Herder.

Habel, Norman C. 1985. *The Book of Job*. OTL. Philadelphia: Westminster.

Hartley, John E. 1988. *The Book of Job*. NICOT. Grand Rapids: Eerdmans.

Hausen, A. 1972. *Hiob in der franziöschen Literatur*. Bern: Herbert Lang.

Hempel, Johannes. 1938. "The Contents of the Literature." In *Record and Revelation: Essays by the Members of the Society for Old Testament Study*, ed. H. Wheeler Robinson, 73. Oxford: Clarendon, 1938.

Hoffman, Yair. 1996. *A Blemished Perfection: The Book of Job in Context*. JSOTSup 213. Sheffield: Academic.

Hurwitz, Avi. 1974. "The Date of the Prose Tale of Job Linguistically Reconsidered." *HTR* 67: 17–34.

Iwanski, Dariusz. 2006. *The Dynamics of Job's Intercession*. AnBib 161. Rome: Pontifical Biblical Institute.

Jacobsen, Thorkild. 1976. *The Treasures of Darkness*. New Haven: Yale University.

Janzen, J. Gerald. 1985. *Job*. Interpretation. Atlanta: John Knox.

———. 2002. "Job's Oath." *RevExp* 99: 581–605.

———. 2009. *At the Scent of Water: The Ground of Hope in the Book of Job*. Grand Rapids, Michigan: Eerdmans.

Jung, C. G. 1970. *Answer to Job*. Meridian Books. World Publishing Company.

Kahn, Jack H. 1975. *Job's Illness. Loss, Grief, and Imagination. A Psychological Interpretation*. Oxford: Pergamon.

Kallen, H. M. 1959. *The Book of Job as a Greek Tragedy.* New York: Hill and Wang.

Kalugila, Leonidas. 1980. *The Wise King.* ConBOT 15. Lund: Gleerup.

Kee, H. C. 1983. "A New Translation and Introduction." In *The Old Testament Pseudepigrapha, Volume 1: Apocalyptic Literature and Testaments,* ed. James H. Charlesworth, 775–828. New Haven: Yale.

Klüger, Rivkah-Schärf. 1967. *Satan in the Old Testament.* Evanstown: Northwestern University.

Koosed, Jennifer L. 2006. *[Per]mutations of Qoheleth: Reading the Body in the Book.* Library of Hebrew Bible/OTS 429. New York: T & T Clark.

Kottsieper, Ingo. 2009. "The Aramaic Tradition: Ahikar." In *Scribes, Sages, and Seers: The Sage in the Eastern Mediterranean World,* ed. Leo G. Perdue. FRLANT 219, 109–24. Göttingen: Vandenhoeck & Ruprecht.

Kubina, Veronika. 1979. *Die Gottesreden im Buche Hiob.* FThS. Freiburg: Herder.

Kugel, James L. 1981. *The Idea of Biblical Poetry. Parallelism and Its History.* New Haven: Yale University.

Laato, Antti, and Johannes C. de Moor, eds. 2003. *Theodicy in the World of the Bible.* Leiden: Brill.

Lichtheim, Miriam. 1973, 1976, 1980. *Ancient Egyptian Literature,* Vols. 1–3. Berkeley: University of California Press.

———. 1992. *Maat in Egyptian Autobiographies and Related Studies.* Göttingen: Vandenhoeck & Ruprecht.

———. 1997. *Moral Values in Ancient Egypt,* OBO 155. Fribourg: University of Fribourg.

Linafelt, Todd. 1996. "The Undecidability of *brk* in the Prologue to Job and Beyond," *BibInt* 4: 154–72.

———, ed. 2000. *Strange Fire: Reading the Bible after the Holocaust.* New York: New York University.

Lindenberger, James M. 1983. *The Aramaic Proverbs of Ahiqar.* Baltimore: Johns Hopkins.

Levêcque, Jean. 1970. *Job et son dieu,* 2 vols. Etude biblique. Paris: Gabalda.

———. 2007. *Job ou le drame de la foi.* Lectio Divîna. Paris: Cerf.

Levenson, Jon D. 1988. *Creation and the Persistence of Evil.* San Francisco: Harper & Row.

Lo, Alison. 2003. *Job 28 as Rhetoric: An Analysis of Job 28 in the Context of Job 22–31.* VTSup 97. Atlanta: SBL.

Lugt, Pieter van der. 1995. *Rhetorical Criticism & the Poetry of the Book of Job.* Leiden: Brill.

Machinist, Peter. 1997. "Job's Daughters and Their Inheritance in the Testament of Job and Its Biblical Congeners." In *The Echoes of Many Texts: Reflections on Jewish and Christian Traditions. Essays in Honor of Lou H. Silberman,* eds. William G. Dever and J. Edward Wright. Brown Judaic Studies 313, 67–80. Atlanta: Scholars Press.

MacLeish, Archibald. 1956. *J.B.* Boston: Houghton Mifflin.

Mettinger, Tryggve N. D. 1992. "The God of Job: Avenger, Tyrant, or Victor?" In *The Voice from the Whirlwind: Interpreting the Book of Job*, ed. Leo G. Perdue and W. Clark Gilpin, 39–49. Nashville: Abingdon.

Mies, Francoise. 2006. *L'Espérance de Job*. BETL 193. Leuven: Peeters.

Miles, Jack. 1995. *God: A Biography*. New York: Knopf.

Miles, Jack, Jr. 1977. "Gagging on Job, or the Comedy of Religious Exhaustion." In *Studies in the Book of Job*, eds. Robert Polzin and David Robertson. Semeia 7, 71–126. Missoula: Society of Biblical Literature.

Miskotte, Kornelius H. 1967. *When the Gods Are Silent*. New York: Harper & Row.

Mitchell, Stephen. 1987. *The Book of Job*. San Francisco: North Point.

Müller, Hans-Peter. 1972. "Mantische Weisheit und Apocalyptik." In *Congress Volume: Uppsala 1971*. VT Sup 22, 268–93. Leiden: Brill.

———. 1978. *Das Hiobproblem*. EF 84. Darmstadt: Wissenschaftliche Buchgesellschaft.

Murphy, Roland E. 1999. *The Book of Job: A Short Reading*. New York: Paulist.

———. 2002. "The Last Truth About God." *RevExp* 99: 581–605.

Nam, Duck-Woo. 2003. *Talking about God. Job 42:7-9 and the Nature of God in the Book of Job*. Studies in Biblical Literature 49. New York: Peter Lang.

Nemo, Philippe. 1998. *Job and the Excess of Evil*. Pittsburg: Duquesne University.

Newsom, Carol A. 1993. "Cultural Politics and the Reading of Job," *BibInt* 1: 119–38.

———. 1994. "The Moral Sense of Nature: Ethics in the Light of God's Speeches to Job." *PSB* 15: 9–27.

———. 1996. "The Book of Job." In *NIB* IV, 319–637. Nashville: Abingdon.

———. 2002. "The Book of Job as Polyphonic Text," *JSOT* 97: 87–108.

———. 2003. *The Book of Job: A Contest of Moral Imaginations*. New York: Oxford University.

Ngwa, Kenneth Numfor. 2005. *The Hermeneutics of the 'Happy' Ending in Job 42:7-17*. BZAW 354. Berlin: de Gruyter.

Nielsen, Eduard. 1993. "Psalm 73: Scandinavian Contributions." In *Understanding Poets and Prophets: Essays in Honour of George Wishart Anderson*, ed. A. G. Auld. JSOTSup 152, 273–83. Sheffield: JSOT.

Oberhänsli-Widmer, Gabrielle. 2003. *Hiob in jüdischer Antike und Moderne: Die Wirkungsgeschichte Hiobs in der jüdischen Literatur*. Neukircken/Vluyn: Neukirchener.

Patrick, Dale. 1976. "The Translation of Job 42:6." *VT* 26: 369–71.

Penchansky, David. 1990. *The Betrayal of God: Ideological Conflict in Job*. Literary Currents in Biblical Interpretation. Louisville: Westminster/John Knox.

Perdue, Leo G. 1991. *Wisdom in Revolt: Metaphorical Theology in the Book of Job*. JSOTSup 112/Bible and Literature Series 29. Sheffield: Almond.

——— and Gilpin W. Clark, eds. 1972. *The Voice from the Whirlwind: Interpreting the Book of Job*. Nashville: Abingdon.

Pope, Marvin H. 1973. *Job*. AB. New York: Doubleday.

Pyeon, Yohan. 2003. *You Have Not Spoken What Is Right About Me: Intertextuality and the Book of Job*. Studies in Biblical Literature 45. New York: Peter Lang.

Ritter-Müller, Petra. 2000. *Kennst du die Welt? Gottes Antwort an Ijob: Eine sprachwissenschaftliche und exegetische Studie zur ersten Gottesrede Ijob 38 und 39*. ATM 5. Münster: LIT.

Rohr, Richard. 1996. *Job and the Mystery of Suffering: Spiritual Reflections*. New York: Crossroads,

Rouillard, P. 1983. "The Figure of Job in the Liturgy: Indignation, Resignation, or Silence?" In *Job and the Silence of God*, eds. C. Duquoc and C. Floristan, 8–12. New York: Conciluim.

Rowley, H. H. 1958. "The Book of Job and Its Meaning," *BJRL* 41: 162–207.

———. 1980. *Job*. NCBC. Grand Rapids: Eerdmans.

Saadiah Ben Joseph Al-Fayyūmī. 1988. *The Book of Theodicy: Translation and Commentary on the Book of Job*. Trans. L. E. Goodman. New Haven: Yale University.

Safire, William. 1992. *The First Dissident: The Book of Job in Today's Politics*. New York: Random House.

Sanders, Paul S., ed. 1968. *Twentieth Century Interpretations of the Book of Job: A Collection of Critical Essays*. Englewood Cliffs: Prentice-Hall.

Sarna, Nahum M. 1957. "Epic Substratum in the Prose of Job." *JBL* 76: 13–25.

Scheindlin, Raymond P. 1998. *The Book of Job: Translation, Introduction, and Notes*. New York: W. W. Norton & Company.

Schmid, Conrad. 2008. "The Authors of Job and Their Historical and Social Setting." In *Scribes, Sages, and Seers*, ed. Leo G. Perdue, 145–53. Göttingen: Vandenhoeck & Ruprecht.

Scholnick, Sylvia Huberman. 1975. "Lawsuit Drama in the Book of Job." Ph.D. Dissertation, Brandeis University.

Schreiner, Susan E. 1994. *Where Shall Wisdom Be Found? Calvin's Exegesis of Job from Medieval and Modern Perspectives*. Chicago: University of Chicago.

Seibert, Eric A. 2009. *Disturbing Divine Behavior: Troubling Old Testament Images of God*. Minneapolis: Fortress.

Simon, Neil. 1975. *God's Favorite*. New York: Samuel French.

Simundson, Daniel J. 1986. *The Message of Job: A Theological Commentary*. Minneapolis: Augsburg.

Sitzler, Dorothea. 1995. *Vorwurf gegen Gott*. SOR 32. Wiesbaden: Harrassowitz.

Spiegel, Shalom. 1991. "Noah, Danel, and Job, Touching on Canaanite Relics in the Legends of the Jews." In *Essential Papers on Israel and the Ancient Near East*, ed. Frederick E. Greenspahn, 193–241. New York: New York University.

Spittler, R. P. 1983. "Translation and Introduction." In *The Old Testament Pseudepigrapha* 1, ed. James H. Charlesworth, 829–68. Garden City NY: Doubleday.

Stone, Michael E. 1990. *Fourth Ezra: A Commentary on the Book of Fourth Ezra*. Minneapolis: Fortress.

Strauss, Hans. 2000. *Hiob: Kapitel 19, 1-42, 17*. BKAT 16/2. Neukerchen-Vluyn: Neukirchener.

Susman, M. 1969. "God the Creator." In *The Dimensions of Job*, ed. Nahum Glatzer. New York: Schocken.

Sutherland, Robert. 2004. *Putting God on Trial: The Biblical Book of Job*. Victoria, B.C.: Trafford.

Syring, Wolf-Dieter. 2004. *Hiob und sein Umwalt: Die Prosatexte des Hiobbuches und ihre Rolle in seiner Redaktions und Rezeptionsgeschichte*. BZAW 336. Berlin: de Gruyter.

Tate, Marvin E. 1971. "The Speeches of Elihu." *RevExp* 68: 487–95.

Taylor, David Bruce. 1990. *Job: A Rational Exposition*. Braunton Devon: Merlin Books.

Terrien, Samuel. 1963. *Job*. Commentaire de l'Ancien Testament. Neuchâtel: Delachaux et Niestlé.

———. 1966. "Quelques remarques sur les affinités de Job avec le Deutéro-Esaïe." In *Volume du Congrès, Genève*. VTSup 15, 295–310. Leiden: Brill.

———. 1978. *The Elusive Presence*. New York: Harper & Row.

———. 1996. *The Iconography of Job through the Centuries: Artists as Biblical Interpreters*. University Park: Pennsylvania State University.

Ticciati, Susannah. 2005. *Job and the Disruption of Identity: Reading Beyond Barth*. London: T. & T. Clark International.

Tilley, Terrence W. 1989. "God and the Silencing of Job." *Modern Theology* 5: 257–70.

Trible, Phyllis. 1978. *God and the Rhetoric of Sexuality*. OBT. Philadelphia: Fortress.

Tsevat, Matitiahu. 1980. *The Meaning of the Book of Job and Other Biblical Studies*. New York: KTAV.

van de Toorn, Karel. 2002. "Sources in Heaven: Revelation as a Scholarly Construct in Second Temple Judaism." In *Kein Land für sich allein*, ed. Ulrich Hübner and Ernst Axel Knauf. OBO 186, 265–77. Freiburg: Universitätsverlag.

van Selms, A. 1985. *Job: A Practical Commentary. Text and Interpretation*. Grand Rapids: Eerdmans.

van Wolde, Ellen. 1997. *Mr. & Mrs. Job*. London: SCM.

———, ed. 2003a. *Job 28: Cognition in Context*. Biblical Interpretation Series 64. Leiden: Brill.

———. 2003b. "Wisdom, Who Can Find It? A Non-Cognitive and Cognitive Study of Job 28:1-11." In *Job 28: Cognition in Context*. Biblical Interpretation Series 64, 1–35. Leiden: Brill.

Vogels, W. 1995. *Job: L'homme qui a bien parlé de Dieu*. Paris: du Cerf.

von Rad, Gerhard. 1983. "The Confessions of Jeremiah." In *Theodicy in the Old Testament*, ed. James L. Crenshaw, 88–99. Philadelphia: Fortress.

Vicchio, Stephen J. 2006a. *Job in the Ancient World*. Eugene OR: Wipf & Stock.

————. 2006b. *Job in the Medieval World.* Eugene OR: Wipf & Stock.

————. 2006c. *Job in the Modern World.* Eugene OR: Wipf & Stock.

Wahl, Harald-Martin. 1993. *Der Gerechte Schopfer.* BZAW 207. Berlin: de Gruyter.

Weinfeld, Moshe. 1988. "Job and its Analysis." In *Text and Context.* JSOTSup 48, 217–26. Sheffield: Almond.

Weiss, Meir. 1983. *The Story of Job's Beginning.* Jerusalem: Magnes.

Westermann, Claus. 1981. *The Structure of the Book of Job: A Form-Critical Analysis.* Philadelphia: Fortress.

Whybray, Roger N. 1998. *Job: A New Biblical Commentary.* Sheffield: Academic.

Wiesel, Eli. 1979. *The Trial of God: A Play in Three Acts.* New York: Schocken.

Wilcox, John T. 1989. *The Bitterness of Job: A Philosophical Reading.* Ann Arbor: University of Michigan.

Wilde, A. de. 1981. *Das Buch Hiob.* OTS 22. Leiden: Brill.

Wilson, Gerald H. 2007. *Job.* NIBC. Peabody MA: Hendrickson.

Wolfers, David. 1995. *Deep Things Out of Darkness: The Book of Job.* Grand Rapids: Eerdmans.

Wright, J. Edward. 2003. *Baruch Ben Neriah: From Biblical Scribe to Apocalyptic Seer.* Columbia: University of South Carolina.

Zhitlowsky, Chaim. 1968. "Job and Faust." In *Two Studies in Yiddish Culture,* ed. Percy Matenko, 75–162. Leiden: Brill.

Zuck, Roy B., ed. 1992. *Sitting with Job: Selected Studies on the Book of Job.* Grand Rapids: Baker.

Zuckermann, Bruce. 1991. *Job the Silent: A Study in Historical Counterpoint.* New York: Oxford University.

152783927 H